KT-494-284

BERLITZ

ITALIAN
for travellers

0 00 44 877

By the staff of Berlitz Guides

How best to use this phrase book

● We suggest that you start with the **Guide to pronunciation** (pp. 6–8), then go on to **Some basic expressions** (pp. 9–15). This gives you not only a minimum vocabulary, but also helps you get used to pronouncing the language. The phonetic transcription throughout the book enables you to pronounce every word correctly.

● Consult the **Contents** pages (3–5) for the section you need. In each chapter you'll find travel facts, hints and useful information. Simple phrases are followed by a list of words applicable to the situation.

● Separate, detailed contents lists are included at the beginning of the extensive **Eating out** and **Shopping guide** sections (Menus, p. 39, Shops and services, p. 97).

● If you want to find out how to say something in Italian, your fastest look-up is via the **Dictionary** section (pp. 164–189). This not only gives you the word, but is also cross-referenced to its use in a phrase on a specific page.

● If you wish to learn more about constructing sentences, check the **Basic grammar** (pp. 159–163).

● Note the **colour margins** are indexed in Italian and English to help both listener and speaker. And, in addition, there is also an **index in Italian** for the use of your listener.

● Throughout the book, this symbol 🖝 suggests phrases your listener can use to answer you. If you still can't understand, hand this phrase book to the Italian-speaker to encourage pointing to an appropriate answer. The English translation for you is just alongside the Italian.

Copyright © 1970, 1986 by Berlitz Guides, a division of Macmillan S.A., Avenue d'Ouchy 61, 1000 Lausanne 6, Switzerland. All rights reserved. No part of this book may be reproduced or transmitted in any form or by any means, electronic or mechanical, including photocopying, recording or by any information storage and retrieval system, without permission in writing from the publisher. Berlitz Trademark Reg. U.S. Patent Office and other countries—Marca Registrada.
Library of Congress Catalog Card No. 85-81373

Second revised edition—6th printing 1988
Printed in Yugoslavia

Contents

Acknowledgments
We are particularly grateful to Francesca Grazzi Rahimi for her
help in the preparation of this book, and to Dr. T.J.A. Bennett who
devised the phonetic transcription.

Guide to pronunciation

An outline of the spelling and sounds of Italian

You'll find the pronunciation of the Italian letters and sounds explained below, as well as the symbols we're using for them in the transcriptions. Note that Italian has some diacritical letters—letters with accent marks—which we don't use in English.

The imitated pronunciation should be read as if it were English except for any special rules set out below. It is based on Standard British pronunciation, though we have tried to take account of General American pronunciation also. Of course, the sounds of any two languages are never exactly the same; but if you follow carefully the indications supplied here, you'll have no difficulty in reading our transcriptions in such a way as to make yourself understood.

Letters written in **bold** should be stressed (pronounced louder).

Consonants

Letter	Approximate pronunciation	Symbol	Example	
b, d, f, k, l, m, n, p, q t, v	as in English			
c	1) before **e** and **i**, like **ch** in chip	ch	**cerco**	**chayr**koa
	2) elsewhere, like **c** in cat	k	**conto**	**koan**toa
ch	like **c** in cat	k	**che**	kay
g	1) before **e** and **i**, like **j** in jet	j	va**ligia**	vah**lee**jah
	2) elsewhere, like **g** in go	g	**grande**	**grahn**day

gh	like g in go	g	ghiaccio	geeahtchoa
gl	like lli in million	ly	gli	lyee
gn	like ni in onion	ñ	bagno	bahñoa
h	always silent		ha	ah
r	trilled like a Scottish r	r	deriva	dehreevah
s	1) generally like s in sit	s	questo	kooaystoa
	2) sometimes like z in zoo	z	viso	veezoa
sc	1) before e and i, like sh in shut	sh	uscita	oosheetah
	2) elsewhere, like sk in skin	sk	scarpa	skahrpah
z/zz	1) generally like ts in hits	ts	grazie	graatseeay
	2) sometimes like ds in roads	dz	romanzo	roamahndzoa

Vowels

a	1) short, like a in car, but shorter	ah	gatto	gahttoa
	2) long, like a in car	aa	casa	kaasah
e	1) can always be pronounced like ay in way, but without moving tongue or lips	ay	sera	sayrah
	2) in correct speech, it is sometimes pronounced like e in get or, when long, more like ai in hair	eh / ai	bello / bene	behlloa / bainay
i	like ee in meet	ee	vini	veenee
o	1) can always be pronounced like oa in goat, but without moving tongue or lips	oa	sole	soalay
	2) in correct speech, it is sometimes pronounced like o in got, or when long, more like aw in law	o / aw	notte / rosa	nottay / rawzah
u	like oo in foot	oo	fumo	foomoa

Two or more vowels

In groups of vowels **a**, **e**, and **o** are strong vowels, and **i** and **u** are weak vowels. When two strong vowels are next to each other, they are pronounced as two separate syllables, e.g., *beato* = baya**h**toa. When a strong and weak vowel are next to each other, the weak one is pronounced more quickly and with less stress (less loudly) than the strong one, e.g., *piede* = pee**ay**day; such sounds are diphthongs and constitute only one syllable. If the weak vowel is stressed, then it is pronounced as a separate syllable, e.g., *due* = **doo**ay. Two weak vowels together are pronounced as a diphthong, and it is generally the second one that is more strongly stressed, e.g., *guida* = goo**ee**dah.

Stressing of words

Generally, the vowel of the next to last syllable is stressed. When a final vowel is stressed, it has an accent written over it *(caffè)*. Normally, when the stress falls on the syllable before the next to last one, it is not indicated by an accent.

Pronunciation of the Italian alphabet

A	ah	H	ahkkah	O	o	V	vee
B	bee	I	ee	P	pee	W	vee **doa**ppeeah
C	chee	J	ee **loong**gah	Q	koo	X	eeks
D	dee	K	**kah**ppah	R	ehrray	Y	ee **gray**kah
E	ay	L	**ehl**lay	S	**ehs**say	Z	**dzay**tah
F	**ehf**fay	M	**ehm**may	T	tee		
G	jee	N	**ehn**nay	U	oo		

Some basic expressions

Yes.	**Sì.**	see
No.	**No.**	no
Please.	**Per favore/**	pair fah**voa**ray/
	Per piacere.	pair peeah**chay**ray
Thank you.	**Grazie.**	**graat**seeay
Thank you very much.	**Molte grazie/**	**moal**tay **graat**seeay/
	Tante grazie.	**tahn**tay **graat**seeay
That's all right/ You're welcome.	**Prego.**	**pray**goa

Greetings *Saluti*

Good morning.	**Buon giorno.**	bwon **joar**noa
Good afternoon.	**Buon giorno.**	bwon **joar**noa
Good evening.	**Buona sera.**	**bwo**nah **say**rah
Good night.	**Buona notte.**	**bwo**nah **not**tay
Good-bye.	**Arrivederci.**	ahrreevay**dair**chee
So long!	**Ciao!**	**chaa**oa
See you later.	**A più tardi.**	ah pee**oo tahr**dee
This is Mr./Mrs./ Miss ...	**Le presento il Signor/la Signora/la Signorina ...**	lay pray**zayn**toa eel seeñoar/lah seeñoarah/ lah seeñoa**ree**nah
How do you do? (Pleased to meet you.)	**Molto lieto(a).** *	**moal**toa lee**ay**toa(ah)
How are you?	**Come sta?**	**koa**may stah
Very well, thanks. And you?	**Molto bene, grazie. E lei?**	**moal**toa **bai**nay **graat**seeay. ay **lai**ee

---

* In the case where there are masculine and feminine forms of a word, we give the masculine first, with the feminine in brackets afterwards; in this example, a woman would say **Molto lieta**.

How's life?	**Come va?**	koamay vah
Fine.	**Bene.**	bainay
I beg your pardon?	**Prego?**	praygoa
Excuse me.	**Mi scusi.**	mee skoozee
Excuse me. (May I get past?)	**Permesso?**	pairmaissoa
Sorry!	**Mi dispiace.**	mee deespeeahchay

Questions *Domande*

Where?	**Dove?**	doavay
How?	**Come?**	koamay
When?	**Quando?**	kwahndoa
What?	**Che cosa/Che?**	kay kawsah/kay
Why?	**Perchè?**	pehrkay
Who?	**Chi?**	kee
Which?	**Quale?**	kwaalay
Where is ...?	**Dov'è/Dove si trova ...?**	doavai/doavay see trawvah
Where are ...?	**Dove sono/ Dove si trovano ...?**	doavay soanoa/doavay see trawvahnoa
Where can I find/ get ...?	**Dove posso trovare ...?**	doavay possoa trovaaray
How far?	**Quanto dista?**	kwahntoa deestah
How long?	**Quanto tempo?**	kwahntoa tehmpoa
How much/How many?	**Quanto/Quanti?**	kwahntoa/kwahntee
How much does this cost?	**Quanto costa questo?**	kwahntoa kostah kooaystoa
When does ... open/ close?	**A che ora apre/ chiude ...?**	ah kay oarah aapray/ keeooday
What do you call this/that in Italian?	**Come si chiama questo/quello in italiano?**	koamay see keeaamah kooaystoa/kooaylloa een eetahleeaanoa
What does this/that mean?	**Che cosa significa questo/quello?**	kay kawsah seeñeefeekah kooaystoa/kooaylloa

Do you speak ...? *Parla ...?*

Do you speak English?	**Parla inglese?**	pahrlah eengglaysay
Is there anyone here who speaks ...?	**C'è qualcuno qui che parla ...?**	chai kwahlkoonoa kooee kay pahrlah
I don't speak (much) Italian.	**Non parlo (bene) l'italiano.**	noan pahrloa (bainay) leetahleeaanoa
Could you speak more slowly?	**Può parlare più lentamente, per favore?**	pwo pahrlaaray peeoo layntahmayntay pair fahvoaray
Could you repeat that?	**Vuol ripetere, per favore?**	vwol reepaitayray pair fahvoaray
Could you spell it?	**Può sillabarlo?**	pwo seellahbaarloa
Please write it down.	**Per favore, me lo scriva.**	pair fahvoaray may loa skreevah
Can you translate this for me?	**Può tradurmi questo?**	pwo trahdoormee kooaystoa
Please point to the word/phrase/ sentence in the book.	**Per favore, mi indichi la parola/ l'espressione/ la frase nel libro.**	pair fahvoaray mee eendeekee lah pahrolah/ laysprehsseeoanay/ lah fraazay nehl leebroa
Just a minute. I'll see if I can find it in this book.	**Un attimo. Guardo se posso trovarla in questo libro.**	oon ahtteemoa. gwahrdoa say possoa troavaarlah een kooaystoa leebroa
It's on page ...	**È a pagina ...**	ai ah paajeenah
I understand.	**Capisco.**	kahpeeskoa
I don't understand.	**Non capisco.**	noan kahpeeskoa
Do you understand?	**Capisce?**	kahpeeshay

Can/May ...? *Posso ...?*

Can I have ...?	**Posso avere ...?**	possoa ahvayray
Can we have ...?	**Possiamo avere ...?**	posseeaamoa ahvayray
Can you show me ...?	**Può mostrarmi ...?**	pwo moastraarmee
I can't.	**Non posso.**	noan possoa
Can you tell me ...?	**Può dirmi ...?**	pwo deermee

Can you help me?	**Può aiutarmi?**	pwo aheeoo**taar**mee
Can I help you?	**Posso aiutarla?**	**poss**oa aheeoo**taar**lah
Can you direct me to ...?	**Può indicarmi la direzione per ...?**	pwo eendee**kahr**mee lah deeraytseeo**an**ay pair

Wanting ... *Vorrei ...*

I'd like ...	**Vorrei ...**	vor**raie**e
We'd like ...	**Vorremmo ...**	vor**rehm**moa
What do you want?	**Che cosa desidera?**	kay **kaw**sah day**zee**dayrah
Give me ...	**Mi dia ...**	mee **dee**ah
Give it to me.	**Me lo dia.**	may loa **dee**ah
Bring me ...	**Mi porti ...**	mee **por**tee
Bring it to me.	**Me lo porti.**	may loa **por**tee
Show me ...	**Mi mostri ...**	mee **moa**stree
Show it to me.	**Me lo mostri.**	may loa **moa**stree
I'm looking for ...	**Cerco ...**	**chayr**koa
I'm hungry.	**Ho fame.**	oa **faa**may
I'm thirsty.	**Ho sete.**	oa **say**tay
I'm tired.	**Sono stanco(a).**	soanoa **stahng**koa(ah)
I'm lost.	**Mi sono perduto(a).**	mee soanoa pehr**doo**toa(ah)
It's important.	**È importante.**	ai eempor**tahn**tay
It's urgent.	**È urgente.**	ai oor**jehn**tay
Hurry up!	**Presto!**	**prehs**toa

It is / There is ... *È/C'è ...*

It is/It's ...	**È ...**	ai
Is it ...?	**È ...?**	ai
It isn't ...	**Non è ...**	noan ai
Here it is. (masc./fem.)	**Eccolo/Eccola.**	**ehk**koaloa/**ehk**koalah
Here they are. (masc./fem.)	**Eccoli/Eccole.**	**ehk**koalee/**ehk**koalay

There it is.	Eccolo/Eccola.	ehkkoaloa/ehkkoalah
There they are.	Eccoli/Eccole.	ehkkoalee/ehkkoalay
There is/There are ...	C'è/Ci sono ...	chai/chee soanoa
Is there/Are there ...?	C'è/Ci sono ...?	chai/chee soanoa
There isn't/aren't ...	Non c'è/Non ci sono ...	noan chai/noan chee soanoa
There isn't/aren't any.	Non ce n'è/Non ce ne sono.	noan chay nai/noan chay nay soanoa

It's ...   È ...

big/small	grande/piccolo*	grahnday/peekkoaloa
quick/slow	rapido/lento	raapeedoa/lehntoa
hot/cold	caldo/freddo	kahldoa/frayddoa
full/empty	pieno/vuoto	peeaynoa/vwawtoa
easy/difficult	facile/difficile	faacheelay/deeffeecheelay
heavy/light	pesante/leggero	paysahntay/laydjairoa
open/shut	aperto/chiuso	ahpehrtoa/keeoosoa
right/wrong	giusto/sbagliato	joostoa/zbahlyaatoa
old/new	vecchio/nuovo	vehkkeeoa/nwawvoa
old/young	anziano/giovane	ahntseeaanoa/joavahnay
beautiful/ugly	bello/brutto	bailloa/broottoa
free (vacant)/ occupied	libero/occupato	leebayroa/okkoopaatoa
good/bad	buono/cattivo	bwawnoa/kahtteevoa
better/worse	migliore/peggiore	meelyoaray/paydjoaray
here/there	qui/là	kooee/lah
early/late	presto/tardi	prehstoa/tahrdee
cheap/expensive	buon mercato/caro	bwawn mayrkahtoa/kaaroa
near/far	vicino/lontano	veecheenoa/lontaanoa
first/last	primo/ultimo	preemoa/oolteemoa

---

*For feminine and plural forms, see grammar section page 160 (adjectives).

Quantities   *Quantità*

a little/a lot	**un po'/molto**	oon po/**moal**toa
few/a few	**pochi/alcuni**	pokee/ahl**koo**nee
much	**molto**	**moal**toa
many	**molti**	**moal**tee
more/less	**più/meno**	pee**oo**/**mai**noa
more than/less than	**più di/meno di**	pee**oo** dee/**mai**noa dee
enough/too	**abbastanza/troppo**	ahbbah**stahnt**sah/**trop**poa
some/any	**del, della, dei, degli, delle**	dayl **dayl**lah daiee **dayl**yee **dayl**lay

Some prepositions ...   *Alcune preposizioni ...*

at	**a***	ah
on	**su**	soo
in	**in**	een
to	**a**	ah
after	**dopo**	**daw**poa
before (time)	**prima di**	**pree**mah dee
before (place)	**davanti a**	dah**vahn**tee ah
for	**per**	pair
from	**da**	dah
with	**con**	kon
without	**senza**	**saynt**sah
through	**per, attraverso**	pair ahttrah**vehr**soa
towards	**verso**	**vehr**soa
until	**fino a**	**fee**noa ah
during	**durante**	doo**rahn**tay
next to	**accanto a**	ahk**kahn**toa ah
near	**vicino a**	vee**chee**noa ah
behind	**dietro**	dee**ay**troa

---

* See also grammar section page 163 (prepositions).

between	**tra, fra**	trah frah
since	**da**	dah
above	**sopra**	soaprah
below	**al di sotto**	ahl dee sottoa
under	**sotto**	sottoa
inside	**dentro**	dayntroa
outside	**fuori**	fwawree
up	**su, in alto**	soo een ahltoa
upstairs	**di sopra**	dee soaprah
down	**giù**	joo
downstairs	**di sotto**	dee sottoa

... and a few more useful words ... e qualche altra parola utile

and	**e**	ay
or	**o**	oa
not	**non**	noan
never	**mai**	mahee
nothing	**nulla/niente**	noollah/neeayntay
something	**qualcosa**	kwahlkawsah
none	**nessuno**	nayssoonoa
very	**molto**	moaltoa
too, also	**anche**	ahngkay
yet	**ancora**	ahngkoarah
but	**ma, però**	mah payro
at once	**subito**	soobeetoa
soon	**presto**	prehstoa
now	**adesso**	ahdehssoa
then	**poi, in seguito**	poaee een saygooeetoa
again	**ancora**	ahngkoarah
perhaps	**forse**	forsay
only	**soltanto**	soltahntoa

Arrival

CONTROLLO DEI PASSAPORTI PASSPORT CONTROL		

Here's my passport.	**Ecco il passaporto.**	ehkkoa eel pahssahportoa
I'll be staying ...	**Resterò ...**	raystayroa
a few days	**qualche giorno**	kwahlkay joarnoa
a week	**una settimana**	oonah saytteemaanah
a month	**un mese**	oon maizay
I don't know yet.	**Non so ancora.**	noan soa ahngkoarah
I'm here on holiday.	**Sono qui in vacanza.**	soanoa kooee een vahkahntsah
I'm here on business.	**Sono qui per affari.**	soanoa kooee pair ahffaaree
I'm just passing through.	**Sono di passaggio.**	soanoa dee pahssadjoa

If things become difficult:

| I'm sorry, I don't understand. | **Mi dispiace, non capisco.** | mee deespeeahchay noan kahpeeskoa |
| Is there anyone here who speaks English? | **C'è qualcuno qui che parla inglese?** | chai kwahlkoonoa kooee kay pahrlah eengglaysay |

DOGANA CUSTOMS		

After collecting your baggage at the airport *(l'aeroporto)* you have a choice: follow the green arrow if you have nothing to declare. Or leave via a doorway marked with a red arrow if you have items to declare (in excess of those allowed).

MERCI DA DICHIARARE GOODS TO DECLARE	**NULLA DA DICHIARARE** NOTHING TO DECLARE

The chart below shows what you can bring in duty-free.*

	Cigarettes		Cigars		Tobacco	Spirits	Wine
Italy 1) 2) 3)	400 300 200	or or or	100 75 50	or or or	500 g. 400 g. 250 g.	¾ l.or 2 l. 1½ l.or 5 l. ¾ l.or 2 l.	
Switzerland	200	or	50	or	250 g.	1 l. and 2 l.	

1) residents of countries outside Europe
2) residents of countries within Europe and entering from an EEC country
3) residents of countries within Europe and entering from another country

I've nothing to declare.	**Non ho nulla da dichiarare.**	noan oa **nool**lah dah deekeeahraaray
I've a carton of cigarettes/bottle of whisky.	**Ho una stecca di sigarette/bottiglia di whisky.**	oa oonah **stayk**kah dee seegah**rayt**tay/ bot**tee**lyah dee "whisky"
Must I pay on this?	**Devo pagare per questo?**	**day**voa pah**gaa**ray pair **kooay**stoa
It's for my personal use.	**È per mio uso personale.**	ai pair **mee**oa **oo**zoa pairsoa**naa**lay

Il passaporto, per favore.	Your passport, please.
Ha qualcosa da dichiarare?	Do you have anything to declare?
Per favore, apra questa borsa.	Please open this bag.
Deve pagare il dazio per questo.	You'll have to pay duty on this.
Ha altri bagagli?	Do you have any more luggage?

---

* All allowances subject to change without notice.

Baggage—Porter *Bagagli—Facchino*

These days porters are only available at airports or the railway stations of large cities. Where no porters are available you'll find luggage trolleys for the use of the passengers.

Porter!	Facchino!	fahkkeenoa
Please take my ...	Per favore, prenda ...	pair fahvoaray prehndah
bag	la mia borsa	lah meeah borsah
luggage	i miei bagagli	ee meeaiee bahgaalyee
suitcase	la mia valigia	lah meeah vahleejah
That's mine.	Quella è mia.	kooayllah ai meeah
Take this luggage ...	Porti questi bagagli ...	portee kooaystee bahgaalyee
to the bus	all'autobus	ahllowtoabooss
to the luggage lockers	alla custodia automatica dei bagagli	ahllah koostawdeeah owtoamaateekah daiee bahgaalyee
How much is that?	Quant'è?	kwahntai
There's one piece missing.	Manca un collo.	mahngkah oon kolloa
Where are the luggage trolleys (carts)?	Dove sono i carrelli portabagagli?	doavay soanoa ee kahrrehllee portahbahgaalyee

Changing money *Cambio*

Where's the currency exchange office?	Dove si trova l'ufficio cambio?	doavay see trawvah looffeechoa kahmbeeoa
Can you change these traveller's cheques (checks)?	Può cambiare questi traveller's cheques?	pwo kahmbeeaaray kooaystee "traveller's cheques"
I want to change some dollars/pounds.	Vorrei cambiare dei dollari/delle sterline.	vorraiee kahmbeeaaray daiee dollahree/dayllay stayrleenay
Can you change this into lire/Swiss francs?	Può cambiare questo in lire/franchi svizzeri?	pwo kahmbeeaaray kooaystoa een leeray/frahngkee sveettsayree
What's the exchange rate?	Qual è il corso del cambio?	kwahl ai eel korsoa dayl kahmbeeoa

BANK—CURRENCY, see page 129

Where is ...? *Dov'è ...?*

Where is the ...?	**Dov'è ...?**	doavai
booking office	**l'ufficio prenotazioni**	looffeechoa praynoatahtseeoanee
car hire	**l'autonoleggio**	lowtoanoalaydjoa
duty-free shop	**il negozio duty-free**	eel naygotseeoa "duty-free"
newsstand	**l'edicola**	laydeekolah
restaurant	**il ristorante**	eel reestoarahntay
shopping area	**la zona dei negozi**	lah dzoanah daiee naygotsee
How do I get to ...?	**Come posso andare a ...?**	koamay possoa ahndaaray ah
Is there a bus into town?	**C'è un autobus per la città?**	chai oon owtoabooss pair lah cheettah
Where can I get a taxi?	**Dove posso prendere un taxi?**	doavay possoa prehndayray oon "taxi"
Where can I hire a car?	**Dove posso noleggiare una macchina?**	doavay possoa noalaydjaaray oonah mahkkeenah

Hotel reservation *Prenotazione d'albergo*

Do you have a hotel guide?	**Ha una guida degli alberghi?**	ah oonah gweedah dailyee ahlbayrgee
Could you reserve a room for me at a hotel/boarding-house?	**Potrebbe prenotarmi una camera in un albergo/una pensione?**	poatrehbbay praynoataarmee oonah kaamayrah een oon ahlbayrgoa/oonah paynseeoanay
in the centre	**in centro**	een chayntroa
near the railway station	**vicino alla stazione**	veecheenoa ahllah stahtseeoanay
a single room	**una camera singola**	oonah kaamayrah seenggoalah
a double room	**una camera doppia**	oonah kaamayrah doappeeah
not too expensive	**non troppo cara**	noan troappoa kaarah
Where is the hotel/boarding house?	**Dov'è l'albergo/la pensione?**	doavai lahlbayrgoa/lah paynseeoanay
Do you have a street map?	**Ha una pianta della città?**	ah oonah peeahntah dayllah cheettah

HOTEL/ACCOMMODATION, see page 22

Car hire (rental)   *Autonoleggio*

To hire a car you must produce a valid driving licence (held for at least one year) and your passport. Some firms set a minimum age at 21, other 25. Holders of major credit cards are normally exempt from deposit payments, otherwise you must pay a substantial (refundable) deposit for a car. Third-party insurance is usually automatically included.

I'd like to hire (rent) a car.	**Vorrei noleggiare una macchina.**	vorraiee noalaydjaaray oonah mahkkeenah
small	**piccola**	peekkoalah
medium-sized	**di media grandezza**	dee maydeeah grahndayttsah
large	**grande**	grahnday
automatic	**automatica**	owtoamahteekah
I'd like it for a day/a week.	**La vorrei per un giorno/una settimana.**	lah vorraiee pair oon joarnoa/oonah saytteemaanah
Are there any week-end arrangements?	**Vi sono condizioni speciali per il week-end?**	vee soanoa koandeetseeoanee spaychaalee pair eel "week-end"
Do you have any special rates?	**Avete tariffe parti-colari?**	ahvaytay tahreeffay pahr-teekoalaaree
What's the charge per day/week?	**Qual è la tariffa giornaliera/setti-manale?**	kwahl ai lah tahreeffah joarnahleeayrah/sayttee-mahnaalay
Is mileage included?	**È compreso il chilometraggio?**	ai koampraysoa eel keelomaytrahdjoa
What's the charge per kilometre?	**Qual è la tariffa al chilometro?**	kwahl ai lah tahreeffah ahl keelawmaytroa
I want to hire the car here and leave it in ...	**Vorrei noleggiare la macchina qui e renderla a ...**	vorraiee noalaydjaaray lah mahkkeenah kooee ay rayndayrlah ah
I want full insurance.	**Voglio l'assicura-zione completa.**	volyoa lahsseekooraht-seeoanay koamplaytah
What's the deposit?	**Quanto è la cauzione?**	kwahntoa ai lah kowtseeoanay
I've a credit card.	**Ho una carta di credito.**	oa oonah kahrtah dee kraydeetoa
Here's my driving licence.	**Ecco la mia patente.**	ehkkoa lah meeah pahtehntay

CAR, see page 75

Taxi *Taxi*

Taxis are clearly marked and available in all the larger towns. If the cab is unmetered, or you have a fair distance to go, ask the fare beforehand. Special rates for night journeys, baggage, etc. should be posted on an official fare chart.

Where can I get a taxi?	**Dove posso trovare un taxi?**	doavay possoa trawvaaray oon "taxi"
Please get me a taxi.	**Per favore, mi trovi un taxi.**	pair fahvoaray mee trawvee oon "taxi"
What's the fare to ...?	**Qual è il prezzo della corsa fino a ...?**	kwahl ai eel prehttsoa dayliah korsah feenoa ah
How far is it to ...?	**Quanto dista ...?**	kwahntoa deestah
Take me to ...	**Mi conduca ...**	mee koandookah
this address	a questo indirizzo	ah kooaystoa eendeereettsoa
the airport	all'aeroporto	ahllahayroportoa
the town centre	in centro città	een chayntroa cheettah
the ... Hotel	all'albergo ...	ahllahlbayrgoa
the railway station	alla stazione	ahllah stahtseeoanay
Turn ... at the next corner.	**Al prossimo angolo giri ...**	ahl prosseemoa ahnggoloa jeeree
left/right	a sinistra/a destra	ah seeneestrah/ah dehstrah
Go straight ahead.	**Vada sempre diritto.**	vahdah sehmpray deereettoa
Please stop here.	**Per favore, si fermi qui.**	pair fahvoaray see fayrmee kooee
I'm in a hurry.	**Ho fretta.**	oa frayttah
Could you drive more slowly?	**Può andare più lentamente?**	pwo ahndaaray peeoo layntahmayntay
Could you help me carry my luggage?	**Può aiutarmi a portare i miei bagagli?**	pwo aheeootaarmee ah portaaray ee meeaiee bahgaaiyee
Could you wait for me?	**Può aspettarmi?**	pwo ahspehttaarmee
I'll be back in 10 minutes.	**Tornerò fra 10 minuti.**	tornayro frah 10 meenootee

TIPPING, see inside back-cover

Hotel—Other accommodation

Early reservation (and confirmation) is essential in most major tourist centres during the high season. Most towns and arrival points have a tourist information office (*azienda di promozione turistica*—ahdzee**ehn**dah dee proamoatsee**oa**nay too**ree**steekah), or *ufficio turistico* (oof**fee**choa too**ree**steekoa), and that's the place to go if you're stuck without a room.

The Italian tourist organization, E.N.I.T., publishes an annual directory of all hotels in Italy with details of minimum and maximum prices and facilities.

albergo/hotel (ahl**bayr**goa/oa**tehl**)	Hotels in Italy are classified as *di lusso* (international luxury class), or *prima, seconda, terza, quarta categoria* (first, second, third, fourth class).
	Note: Especially near railway stations, one often finds *alberghi diurni* (ahl**bayr**gee dee**oor**nee—"daytime hotels"). These have no sleeping accommodation, but provide bathrooms, rest rooms, hairdressers, and other similar services. Most close at midnight.
motel (mo**tehl**)	Increasing in number, improving in service, the Automobile Association of Italy has a list of recommended motels.
locanda (lo**kahn**dah)	A country inn.
pensione (paynsee**oa**nay)	Corresponds to a boarding house; it usually offers *pensione completa* (full board) or *mezza pensione* (half board). Meals are likely to be from a set menu. *Pensioni* are classified first, second or third class.
ostello della gioventù (oa**stehl**loa day**l**lah joavayntoo)	Youth hostel. They are open to holders of membership cards issued by the International Youth Hostel Association.
appartamento ammobiliato (ahppahrtah**maynt**oa ahmmoabeelee**ah**toa)	Furnished flat (apartment). Contact a specialized travel agent if this is the type of arrangement you're looking for.

CAMPING, see page 32

Checking in—Reception *Ufficio ricevimento*

My name is ...	**Mi chiamo ...**	mee keeaamoa
I've a reservation.	**Ho fatto una prenotazione.**	oa fahttoa oonah praynoatahtseeoanay
We've reserved two rooms.	**Abbiamo prenotato due camere.**	ahbbeeaamoa praynoatah-toa dooay kaamayray
Here's the confirmation.	**Ecco la conferma.**	ehkkoa lah konfehrmah
Do you have any vacancies?	**Avete camere libere?**	ahvaytay kaamayray leebayray
I'd like a ... room ...	**Vorrei una camera ...**	vorraiee oonah kaamayrah
single	**singola**	seenggoalah
double	**doppia**	doappeeah
with twin beds	**con due letti**	kon dooay lehttee
with a double bed	**con un letto matrimoniale**	kon oon lehttoa mahtreemoaneeaalay
with a bath	**con bagno**	kon baañoa
with a shower	**con doccia**	kon dotchah
with a balcony	**con balcone**	kon bahlkoanay
with a view	**con vista**	kon veestah
We'd like a room ...	**Vorremmo una camera ...**	vorrehmmoa oonah kaamayrah
in the front	**sul davanti**	sool dahvahntee
at the back	**sul retro**	sool raitroa
facing the sea	**sul mare**	sool maaray
It must be quiet.	**Deve essere tranquilla.**	dayvay ehssayray trahngkooeellah
Is there ...?	**C'è ...?**	chai
air conditioning	**l'aria condizionata**	laareeah kondeetseeonaatah
heating	**il riscaldamento**	eel reeskahldahmayntoa
a radio/television in the room	**la radio/il televisore nella stanza**	lah raadeeoa/eel taylayvee-zoaray nayllah stahntsah
laundry service	**il servizio di lavanderia**	eel sayrveetseeoa dee lahvahndayreeah
room service	**il servizio nella stanza**	eel sayrveetseeoa nayllah stahntsah
hot water	**l'acqua calda**	lahkkwah kahldah
running water	**l'acqua corrente**	lahkkwah korraintay
a private toilet	**il gabinetto privato**	eel gahbeenayttoa preevaatoa

CHECKING OUT, see page 31

| Could you put an extra bed in the room? | Può mettere un altro letto nella camera? | pwo **may**ttehray oon **ah**ltroa **leh**ttoa nay**ll**ah **kaa**mayrah |

How much? *Quanto?*

What's the price ...?	Qual è il prezzo ...?	kwahl ai eel **preh**ttsoa
per night	per una notte	pair **oo**nah **not**tay
per week	per una settimana	pair **oo**nah saytteemaanah
for bed and breakfast	per la camera e la colazione	pair lah **kaa**mayrah ay lah koalahtseeoanay
excluding meals	pasti esclusi	**paa**stee ay**skloo**zee
for full board (A.P.)	per la pensione completa	pair lah paynseeoanay koam**play**tah
for half board (M.A.P.)	per mezza pensione	pair **mehd**zah paynseeoanay
Does that include ...?	Il prezzo comprende ...?	eel **preh**ttsoa koam**pray**nday
breakfast	la colazione	lah koalahtseeoanay
service	il servizio	eel sayr**veet**seeoa
value-added tax (VAT)*	l'I.V.A.	**lee**vah
Is there any reduction for children?	C'è una riduzione per i bambini?	chai **oo**nah reedootseeoanay pair ee bahm**bee**nee
Do you charge for the baby?	Fate pagare per il bambino?	**faa**tay pah**gaa**ray pair eel bahm**bee**noa
That's too expensive.	È troppo caro.	ai **trop**poa **kaa**roa
Haven't you anything cheaper?	Non ha nulla di meno caro?	noan ah **nool**lah dee **mai**noa **kaa**roa

How long *Quanto tempo?*

We'll be staying ...	Resteremo ...	raystay**ray**moa
overnight only	una notte	**oo**nah **not**tay
a few days	qualche giorno	**kwahl**kay **joar**noa
a week (at least)	una settimana (come minimo)	**oo**nah saytteemaanah (**koa**may **mee**neemoa)
I don't know yet.	Non ho ancora deciso.	noan oa ahng**koa**rah day**chee**soa

* Americans note: a type of sales tax in Italy.

NUMBERS, see page 147

Albergo

Decision *Decisione*

May I see the room?	**Posso vedere la camera?**	possoa vay**day**ray lah **kaa**mayrah
That's fine. I'll take it.	**Va bene, la prendo.**	vah bainay lah **prehn**doa
No, I don't like it.	**No, non mi piace.**	noa noan mee pee**ah**chay
It's too ...	**È troppo ...**	ai **trop**poa
cold/hot	**fredda/calda**	**frayd**dah/**kahl**dah
dark/small	**buia/piccola**	**boo**eeah/**peek**koalah
noisy	**rumorosa**	roomoa**roa**zah
I asked for a room with a bath.	**Ho chiesto una camera con bagno.**	oa kee**eh**stoa **oo**nah **kaa**mayrah kon **baa**ñoa
Do you have anything ...?	**Ha qualcosa ...?**	ah kwahl**kaw**sah
better	**migliore**	mee**lyoa**ray
bigger	**più grande**	pee**oo grahn**day
cheaper	**meno caro**	**mai**noa **kaa**roa
quieter	**più tranquillo**	pee**oo** trahngkoo**eel**loa
Do you have a room with a better view?	**Ha una camera con una vista più bella?**	ah **oo**nah **kaa**mayrah kon **oo**nah **vee**stah pee**oo bail**lah

Registration *Registrazione*

Upon arrival at a hotel or boarding house you'll be asked to fill in a registration form (*una scheda*—**oo**nah **skay**dah).

Cognome/Nome	Name/First name
Domicilio/Strada/N°	Home address/Street/Number
Cittadinanza/Professione	Nationality/Profession
Data/Luogo di nascita	Date/Place of birth
Proveniente da .../Diretto a ...	From .../To ...
Numero di passaporto	Passport number
Luogo/Data	Place/Date
Firma	Signature

What does this mean?	**Cosa significa questo?**	**kaw**sah see**ñee**feekah **koo**aystoa

Mi può mostrare il passaporto?	May I see your passport?
Vuol compilare la scheda, per cortesia?	Would you mind filling in this registration form?
Firmi qui, per favore.	Sign here, please.
Quanto tempo si trattiene?	How long will you be staying?

What's my room number?	Qual è il numero della mia stanza?	kwahl ai eel noomayroa dayllah meeah stahntsah
Will you have our luggage sent up?	Può far portare su i nostri bagagli?	pwo faar portaaray soo ee nostree bahgaalyee
Where can I park my car?	Dove posso parcheggiare la macchina?	doavay possoa pahrkaydjaaray lah mahkkeenah
Does the hotel have a garage?	L'albergo ha il garage?	lahlbayrgoa ah eel gahraazh
I'd like to leave this in your safe.	Vorrei depositare questo nella vostra cassaforte.	vorraiee daypozeetaaray kooaystoa nayllah vostrah kahssahfortay

Hotel staff   *Personale d'albergo*

hall porter	il portiere	eel pawrteeayray
maid	la cameriera (nelle camere)	lah kahmayreeayrah (nayllay kaamayray)
manager	il direttore	eel deerehttoaray
page (bellboy)	il fattorino	eel fahttoreenoa
porter	il facchino	eel fahkkeenoa
receptionist	il capo ricevimento	eel kahpoa reechayveemayntoa
switchboard operator	il (la) centralinista	eel (lah) chayntrahleeneestah
waiter	il cameriere	eel kahmayreeayray
waitress	la cameriera	lah kahmayreeayrah

General requirements   *Richieste generali*

The key, please.	La chiave, per favore.	lah keeaavay pair fahvoaray
Will you please wake me at ...?	Potrebbe svegliarmi alle ...?	poatrehbbay zvaylyaarmee ahllay

TELLING THE TIME, see page 153

Is there a bath on this floor?	C'è un bagno a questo piano?	chai oon baañoa ah kooaystoa peeaanoa
What's the voltage?	Qual è il voltaggio?	kwahl ai eel voaltahdjoa
Where's the socket (outlet) for the shaver?	Dov'è la presa per il rasoio?	doavai lah prayzah pair eel rahzoaeeoa
Can we have breakfast in our room?	Possiamo avere la colazione in camera?	posseeaamoa ahvayray lah koalahtseeoanay een kaamayrah
Can you find me a ...?	Può trovarmi ...?	pwo trawvahrmee
babysitter	una babysitter	oonah "babysitter"
secretary	una segretaria	oonah saygraytaareeah
typewriter	una macchina per scrivere	oonah mahkkeenah pair skreevayray
May I have a/an/ some ...?	Posso avere ...?	possoa ahvayray
ashtray	un portacenere	oon portahchaynayray
bath towel	un asciugamano	oon ahshoogahmaanoa
(extra) blanket	una coperta (in più)	oonah kopehrtah (een peeoo)
envelopes	delle buste	dayllay boostay
(more) hangers	degli attaccapanni (in più)	daylyee ahttahkkahpahnnee (een peeoo)
hot-water bottle	una borsa dell'acqua calda	oonah boarsah dehllahk-kwah kahldah
ice cubes	dei cubetti di ghiaccio	daiee koobehttee dee geeahtchoa
needle and thread	un ago e del filo	oon aagoa ay dayl feeloa
(extra) pillow	un guanciale (in più)	oon gwahnchaalay (een peeoo)
reading-lamp	una lampada	oonah lahmpahdah
soap	una saponetta	oonah sahpoanehttah
writing-paper	della carta da lettere	dayllah kahrtah dah lehttayray
Where's the ...?	Dov'è ...?	doavai
bathroom	il bagno	eel baañoa
dining-room	la sala da pranzo	lah saalah dah prahndzoa
emergency exit	l'uscita di sicurezza	loosheetah dee seekoo-rehtsah
hairdresser's	il parrucchiere	eel pahrrookkeeayray
lift (elevator)	l'ascensore	lahshaynsoaray
Where are the toilets?	Dove sono i gabinetti?	doavay soanoa ee gahbee-nehttee

BREAKFAST, see page 38

Telephone—Post (mail)   *Telefono—Posta*

Can you get me Rome 123-45-67?	**Può passarmi Roma 123-45-67?**	pwo pah**ssahr**mee **roa**mah 123-45-67
How much are my telephone charges?	**Quanto devo pagare per la telefonata?**	**kwahn**toa **day**voa pah**gaa**ray pair lah taylayfoa**naa**tah
Do you have stamps?	**Ha dei francobolli?**	ah **dai**ee frahngkoa**boa**llee
Would you please mail this for me?	**Può spedirmi questo, per favore?**	pwo **spay**deer**mee** koo**ay**stoa pair fah**voa**ray
Are there any messages for me?	**Vi sono messaggi per me?**	vee **soa**noa may**ssah**djee pair mai
Is there any mail for me?	**C'è posta per me?**	chai **pos**tah pair mai

Difficulties   *Difficoltà*

The…doesn't work.	**…non funziona.**	…noan foontsee**oa**nah
air conditioner	**il condizionatore d'aria**	eel koandeetseeoanah**toa**ray **daa**reeah
fan	**il ventilatore**	eel vaynteelah**toa**ray
heating	**il riscaldamento**	eel reeskahldah**mayn**toa
light	**la luce**	lah **loo**chay
radio	**la radio**	lah **raa**deeoa
television	**il televisore**	eel taylayveezoaray
The tap (faucet) is dripping.	**Il rubinetto sgocciola.**	eel roobee**neht**toa zgot**choa**lah
There's no hot water.	**Non c'è acqua calda.**	noan chai **ahk**kwah **kahl**dah
The wash-basin is blocked.	**Il lavabo è otturato.**	eel lah**vaa**boa ai ottoo**raa**toa
The window is jammed.	**La finestra è incastrata.**	lah fee**neh**strah ai eengkah**straa**tah
The curtains are stuck.	**Le tende sono bloccate.**	lay **tayn**day **soa**noa blok**kaa**tay
The bulb is burned out.	**La lampadina è bruciata.**	lah lahmpah**dee**nah ai broo**chaa**tah
My room has not been made up.	**La mia camera non è stata rifatta.**	lah **mee**ah **kaa**mayrah noan ai **staa**tah ree**faht**tah

POST OFFICE AND TELEPHONE, see page 132

The ... is broken.	... è rotto(a).	... ai rottoa(ah)
blind	la persiana	lah pairseeaanah
lamp	la lampada	lah lahmpahdah
plug	la spina	lah speenah
shutter	l'imposta	leempoastah
switch	l'interruttore	leentayrroottoaray
Can you get it repaired?	Può ripararlo(la)?	pwo reepahrahrloa(lah)

Laundry—Dry cleaner's   Lavanderia—Lavanderia a secco

I want these clothes ...	Voglio far ... questi abiti.	volyoa faar ... kooaystee aabeetee
cleaned	pulire	pooleeray
ironed	stirare	steeraaray
pressed	stirare a vapore	steeraaray ah vahpoaray
washed	lavare	lahvaaray
When will they be ready?	Quando saranno pronti?	kwahndoa sahrahnnoa proantee
I need them ...	Ne ho bisogno ...	nay oa beezoañoa
tonight	stasera	stahsayrah
tomorrow	domani	doamaanee
before Friday	prima di venerdì	preemah dee vaynayrdee
Can you ... this?	Mi può ... questo?	mee pwo ... kooaystoa
mend	rammendare	rahmmayndaaray
patch	rappezzare	rappehttsaaray
stitch	cucire	koocheeray
Can you sew on this button?	Può attaccare questo bottone?	pwo ahttahkkaaray kooaystoa boattoanay
Can you get this stain out?	Mi può togliere questa macchia?	mee pwo tolyayray kooaystah mahkkeeah
Can this be invisibly mended?	Mi può fare un rammendo invisibile?	mee pwo faaray oon rahm-mayndoa eenveezeebeelay
Is my laundry ready?	È pronta la mia biancheria?	ai prontah lah meeah beeahngkayreeah
This isn't mine.	Questo non è mio.	kooaystoa noan ai meeoa
There's something missing.	Manca un capo.	mahngkah oon kaapoa
There's a hole in this.	C'è un buco in questo.	chai oon bookoa een. kooaystoa

Hairdresser—Barber   *Parrucchiere—Barbiere*

Is there a hairdresser/ beauty salon in the hotel?	C'è il parrucchiere/ l'istituto di bellezza nell'albergo?	chai eel pahrrookkeeayray/ leesteetootoa dee behl-lehttsah nayllahlbayrgoa
Can I make an appointment for Thursday?	Posso avere un appuntamento per giovedì?	possoa ahvayray oon ahppoontahmayntoa pair joavaydee
I'd like it cut and shaped.	Vorrei il taglio e la messa in piega.	vorraiee eel taalyoa ay lah mayssah een peeaygah
I want a haircut, please.	Voglio il taglio dei capelli, per favore.	volyoa eel taalyoa daiee kahpehllee pair fahvoaray
bleach	una decolorazione	oonah daykoaloaraht-seeoanay
blow-dry	l'asciugatura col fono	lashoogahtoorah kol fawno
colour rinse	un cachet	oon kahshay
dye	una tintura	oonah teentoorah
face-pack	la maschera di bellezza	lah mahskayrah dee behllehttsah
manicure	la manicure	lah mahneekoor
permanent wave	la permanente	lah pairmahnayntay
setting lotion	un fissatore	oon feessahtoaray
shampoo and set	shampoo e messa in piega	"shampoo" ay mayssah een peeaygah
with a fringe (bangs)	con la frangia	kon lah frahnjah
I'd like a shampoo for … hair.	Vorrei uno shampoo per capelli …	vorraiee oonoa "shampoo" pair kahpehllee
normal/dry/ greasy (oily)	normali/secchi/ grassi	noarmaalee/saykkee/ grahssee
Do you have a colour chart?	Avete una tabella dei colori?	ahvaytay oonah tahbayllah daiee koaloaree
Don't cut it too short.	Non li tagli troppo corti.	noan lee taalyee troppoa koartee
A little more off the …	Ancora un po'…	ahngkoarah oon po
back	dietro	deeaytroa
neck	sul collo	sool kolloa
sides	ai lati	ahee laatee
top	in cima	een cheemah
I don't want any hairspray.	Non voglio lacca.	noan volyoa lahkkah

DAYS OF THE WEEK, see page 151

I'd like a shave.	**Vorrei che mi radesse.**	vorraiee kay mee rahdayssay
Would you please trim my ...?	**Per favore, vuole spuntarmi ...?**	pair fahvoaray **vwawl**ay spoontahrmee
beard	**la barba**	lah bahrbah
moustache	**i baffi**	ee bahffee
sideboards (sideburns)	**le basette**	lay bahzayttay

Checking out *Partenza*

May I please have my bill?	**Posso avere il conto, per favore?**	possoa ahvayray eel koantoa pair fahvoaray
I'm leaving early in the morning. Please have my bill ready.	**Partirò domani mattina presto. Mi prepari il conto, per favore.**	pahrteeroa doamaanee mahtteenah prehstoa. mee praypaaree eel koantoa pair fahvoaray
We'll be checking out around noon.	**Partiremo verso mezzogiorno.**	pahrteeraymoa vehrsoa mehdzoajoarnoa
I must leave at once.	**Devo partire immediatamente.**	dayvoa pahrteeray eemmaydeeahtahmayntay
Is everything included?	**È tutto incluso?**	ai toottoa eengkloozoa
Can I pay by credit card?	**Posso pagare con la carta di credito?**	possoa pahgaaray kon lah kahrtah dee kraydeetoa
You've made a mistake in this bill, I think.	**Ha fatto un errore nel conto, credo.**	ah fahttoa oon ehrroaray nayl koantoa kraydoa
Can you get us a taxi?	**Può chiamarci un taxi?**	pwo keeahmahrchee oon "taxi"
Would you send someone to bring down our luggage?	**Può mandare qualcuno a portare giù i nostri bagagli?**	pwo mahndaaray kwahlkoonoa ah portaaray joo ee nostree bahgaalyee
Here's the forwarding address	**Ecco il mio prossimo indirizzo.**	ehkkoa eel meeoa prosseemoa eendeereettsoa
You have my home address.	**Avete il mio indirizzo abituale.**	ahvaytay eel meeoa eendeereettsoa ahbeetooaalay
It's been a very enjoyable stay.	**È stato un soggiorno molto piacevole.**	ai staatoa oon soadjoarnoa moaltoa peeahchayvoalay

TIPPING, see inside back-cover

Camping *Campeggio*

In Italy there are many authorized camping sites with excellent facilities. Most camp sites are equipped with water, electricity and toilets. You will find them listed in the telephone directory, under *Campeggio*. The local tourist office has a list of sites, tariffs and facilities available. The Touring Club Italiano also publish a list of campsites and touristic villages. It is on sale in bookshops.

Is there a camp site near here?	C'è un campeggio qui vicino?	chai oon kahmpaydjoa kooee veecheenoa
Can we camp here?	Possiamo campeggiare qui?	posseeaamoa kahmpaydjaaray kooee
Have you room for a tent/caravan (trailer)?	C'è posto per una tenda/una roulotte?	chai poastoa pair oonah taindah/oonah roolot
What's the charge...?	Quanto si paga...?	kwahntoa see paagah
per day	al giorno	ahl joarnoa
per person	per persona	pair payrsoanah
for a car	per una macchina	pair oonah mahkkeenah
for a tent	per una tenda	pair oonah taindah
for a caravan (trailer)	per una roulotte	pair oonah roolot
Is the tourist tax included?	È compresa la tassa di soggiorno?	ai koampraysah lah tahssah dee soadjoarnoa
Is there/Are there (a) ...?	C'è/Ci sono ...?	chai/chee soanoa
drinking water	l'acqua potabile	lahkkwah poataabeelay
electricity	l'elettricità	laylehttreecheetah
playground	il parco giochi	eel pahrkoa joakee
restaurant	il ristorante	eel reestoarahntay
shopping facilities	dei negozi	daiee naygotsee
swimming pool	la piscina	lah peesheenah
Where are the showers/toilets?	Dove sono le docce/ i gabinetti?	doavay soanoa lay dotchay/ ee gahbeenayttee
Where can I get butane gas?	Dove posso trovare del gas butano?	doavay possoa trovaaray dayl gahz bootaanoa
Is there a youth hostel near here?	C'è un ostello della gioventù qui vicino?	chai oon oastehlloa dayl-lah joavayntoo kooee veecheenoa

CAMPING EQUIPMENT, see page 106

Eating out

There are various types of places to eat and drink in Italy. Here are some of them:

Autogrill
(owtoagreel)

large restaurant on a motorway (expressway); usually table and cafeteria service available.

Bar
(bahr)

bar; can be found on virtually every street corner; coffee and drinks served. In most of them you first have to get a ticket from the cashier. Then you go to the counter and order what you want. Only a few bars have tables and chairs. If you want to be served at a table, the charge for your drinks and food will be somewhat higher.

Caffè
(kahffai)

coffee shop; generally food isn't served there except for breakfast. If it offers *panini o toasts* you'll be able to get a snack. Coffee shops always serve alcoholic beverages.

Gelateria
(jaylahtayreeah)

ice-cream parlour; Italian ice-cream is very tasty, rich and creamy, often reminiscent of old-fashioned, homemade ice-cream.

Locanda
(lokahndah)

simple restaurants serving local dishes.

Osteria
(oastayreeah)

inn; wine and simple food are served.

Paninoteca
(pahneenoataykah)

a sort of coffee shop where you can find a great variety of sandwiches *(panini)* served hot or cold.

Pizzeria
(peettsayreeah)

pizza parlour; often other dishes are served, too.

Ristorante
(reestoarahntay)

You'll encounter restaurants classified by stars, forks and knives and endorsed by everyone including travel agencies, automobile associations and gastronomic guilds. Bear in mind that any form of classification is relative. Some restaurants are judged according to their fancy décor while others—linen and chandeliers aside—are rated merely by the quality of their cooking.

Rosticceria (roasteetchayreeah)	originally, it was a shop specializing in grilled meats, chicken and fish. But today *rosticcerie* often have tables where you eat grilled food on the premises.
Sala da tè (saalah dah tai)	serves ice-cream and pastries.
Taverna (tahvehrnah)	a more modest type of *trattoria*.
Tavola calda (taavoalah kahldah)	"hot table"; a cafeteria-style restaurant serving hot dishes at fairly low prices. They're usually crowded but quick; you may have to eat standing up.
Trattoria (trahttoareeah)	a medium-priced restaurant serving meals and drink. The food is simple but can be surprisingly good if you happen to hit upon the right place.

Most restaurants display a menu in the window. Many offer a tourist menu *(menù turistico)*, a fixed-price three- or four-course meal with limited choice, or the speciality of the day *(piatto del giorno)*.

All restaurants, no matter how modest, must now issue a formal bill *(la ricevuta fiscale)* with VAT, or sales tax *(I.V.A.)*. A customer may actually be stopped outside the premises and fined if he cannot produce this receipt. The bill usually includes cover *(il coperto)* and service *(il servizio)* charges as well.

Meal times   *Orari dei pasti*

Breakfast (*la colazione*—lah kolahtseeoanay) at the hotel is normally served from 7 to 10 a.m. (See page 38 for a breakfast menu.)

Lunch (*il pranzo*—eel **prahn**dzoa) is served from 12.30 to 2 p.m.

Dinner (*la cena*—lah **chay**nah) begins at 7 or 8 p.m., but hotels tend to open their dining rooms earlier for the foreign tourists.

TIPPING, see inside back-cover

Note: The names of meals can be confusing. Lunch is sometimes called *colazione* and dinner *pranzo*, especially in towns. If you are invited out, make sure of the time, so you don't turn up at the wrong meal.

Italian cuisine   *Cucina italiana*

To many foreigners, Italian cooking means *spaghetti, macaroni, tagliatelle*... in other words, pasta. In fact, you will be amazed at the rich variety available: tasty hors d'œuvres, long-simmered soups, traditional meat dishes, fresh fish and shellfish, high-quality poultry, an incredible number of cheeses, not to mention the magnificent cakes and ice-cream.

Each region has its own speciality, never lacking in flavour or originality, inspired by sun-drenched fruit and vegetables. Italian cooking is like the country itself: colourful, happy, generous, exuberant.

Cosa desidera?	What would you like?
Le consiglio questo.	I recommend this.
Cosa desidera da bere?	What would you like to drink?
Non abbiamo ...	We haven't got ...
Vuole ...?	Do you want ...?

Hungry?   *Ha fame?*

I'm hungry/I'm thirsty.	**Ho fame/Ho sete.**	oa faamay/oa saytay
Can you recommend a good restaurant?	**Può consigliarmi un buon ristorante?**	pwo koanseelyaarmee oon bwon reestoarahntay
Are there any inexpensive restaurants around here?	**Vi sono dei ristoranti economici qui vicino?**	vee soanoa daiee reestoarahntee aykoanawmeechee kooee veecheenoa

If you want to be sure of getting a table in a well-known restaurant, it may be better to telephone in advance.

I'd like to reserve a table for 4.	Vorrei riservare un tavolo per 4.	vorraiee reesehrvaaray oon taavoala pair 4
We'll come at 8.	Verremo alle 8.	vayrraymoa ahllay 8
Could we have a table ...?	Potremmo avere un tavolo ...?	poatraymmoa ahvayray oon taavoaloa
in the corner	d'angolo	dahnggoaloa
by the window	vicino alla finestra	veecheenoa ahllah feenaystrah
outside	all'aperto	ahllahpehrtoa
on the terrace	sulla terrazza	soollah tayrrahttsah
in a non-smoking area	nel settore per non fumatori	nayl sehttoaray pair noan foomahtoaree

Asking and ordering *Chiedere e ordinare*

Waiter/Waitress!	Cameriere/ Cameriera!	kahmayreeairay/kahmay-reeairah
I'd like something to eat/drink.	Vorrei mangiare/bere qualcosa.	vorraiee mahnjaaray/ bayray kwahlkawsah
May I have the menu, please?	Posso avere il menù?	possoa ahvayray eel maynoo
Do you have a set menu/local dishes?	Avete un menù a prezzo fisso/dei piatti locali?	ahvaytay oon maynoo ah prehttsoa feessoa/daiee peeahttee loakaalee
What do you recommend?	Cosa consiglia?	kawsah konseelyah
I'd like ...	Vorrei ...	vorraiee
Could we have a/ an ..., please?	Potremmo avere ..., per favore?	poatraymmoa ahvayray ... pair fahvoaray
ashtray	un portacenere	oon portahchaynayray
cup	una tazza	oonah tahttsah
extra chair	una sedia in più	oonah saideeah een peeoo
fork	una forchetta	oonah forkehttah
glass	un bicchiere	oon beekkeeairay
knife	un coltello	oon koaltehlloa
napkin (serviette)	un tovagliolo	oon toavahlyawloa
plate	un piatto	oon peeahttoa
spoon	un cucchiaio	oon kookkeeaaeeoa
May I have some ...?	Potrei avere ...?	poatraiee ahvayray
bread	del pane	dayl paanay
butter	del burro	dayl boorroa

NUMBERS, see page 147

lemon	del limone	dayl leemoanay
mustard	della senape	dayllah saynahpay
oil	dell'olio	dayllolyoa
pepper	del pepe	dayl paypay
salt	del sale	dayl saalay
seasoning	del condimento	dayl koandeemayntoa
sugar	dello zucchero	daylloa tsookkayroa
vinegar	dell'aceto	dayllahchaytoa

Some useful expressions for dieters or those with special requirements:

I'm on a diet.	Sono a dieta.	soanoa ah deeaytah
I mustn't eat food containing ...	Non devo mangiare cibi che contengono ...	noan dayvoa mahnjaaray cheebee kay koan- taynggoanoa
flour/fat	farina/grasso	fahreenah/grahssoa
salt/sugar	sale/zucchero	saalay/tsookkayroa
Do you have ... for diabetics?	Avete ... per diabetici?	ahvaytay ... pair deeahbaiteechee
cakes	dei dolci	daiee doalchee
fruit juice	del succo di frutta	dayl sookkoa dee froottah
special menu	un menù speciale	oon maynoo spaychaalay
Do you have vege- tarian dishes?	Avete dei piatti vegetariani?	ahvaytay daiee peeahttée vayjaytahreeaanee
Could I have ... instead of the dessert?	Potrei avere ... invece del dessert?	potraiee ahvayray ... eenvaychay dayl dayssehr
Can I have an artificial sweetener?	Posso avere del dolcificante?	possoa ahvayray dayl doalcheefeekahntay

And ...

I'd like some more.	Ne vorrei ancora.	nai vorraiee ahngkoarah
Can I have more ..., please.	Posso avere ancora un po' di ...?	possoa ahvayray ahngkoarah oon po dee
Just a small portion.	Una piccola porzione.	oonah peekkoalah poartsee- oanay
Nothing more, thanks.	Nient'altro, grazie.	neeayntahltroa graatseeay
Where are the toilets?	Dove sono i gabinetti?	doavay soanoa ee gahbee- nayttee

Breakfast *Colazione*

Italians just have a *cappuccino* and a brioche for breakfast.
Hotels usually propose coffee or tea, bread, butter and jam.
You can ask for fruit juice, an egg and toast, if you like a
more copious breakfast.

I'd like breakfast, please.	**Vorrei fare colazione.**	vorraiee faaray kolah-tseeoanay
I'll have a/an/ some ...	**Desidero ...**	dayzeedayroa
bacon and eggs	**uova e pancetta**	wawvah ay pahnchehttah
boiled egg	**un uovo alla coque**	oon wawvoa ahllah kok
soft/hard	**molle/sodo**	mollay/sodoa
cereal	**dei cereali**	daiee chehrehaalee
eggs	**delle uova**	dayllay wawvah
fried eggs	**delle uova fritte**	dayllay wawvah freettay
scrambled eggs	**delle uova strapazzate**	dayllay wawvah strahpahttsaatay
fruit juice	**un succo di frutta**	oon sookkoa dee froottah
grapefruit	**pompelmo**	pompaylmoa
orange	**arancia**	ahrahnchah
ham and eggs	**uova e prosciutto**	wawvah ay proashoottoa
jam	**della marmellata**	dayllah mahrmayllaatah
marmalade	**della marmellata d'arance**	dayllah mahrmayllaatah dahrahnchay
toast	**del pane tostato**	dayl paanay tostaatoa
May I have some ...?	**Posso avere ...?**	possoa ahvayray
bread	**del pane**	dayl paanay
butter	**del burro**	dayl boorroa
(hot) chocolate	**una cioccolata (calda)**	oonah choakkoalaatah (kahldah)
coffee	**un caffè**	oon kahffai
decaffeinated	**decaffeinato**	daykahffeheenaatoa
black	**nero**	nayroa
with milk	**macchiato**	mahkkeeaatoa
honey	**del miele**	dayl meeaylay
milk	**del latte**	dayl lahttay
cold/hot	**freddo/caldo**	frayddoa/kahldoa
rolls	**dei panini**	daiee pahneenee
tea	**del tè**	dayl tai
with milk	**con latte**	kon lahttay
with lemon	**con limone**	kon leemoanay
(hot) water	**dell'acqua (calda)**	dayllahkkwah (kahldah)

What's on the menu? *Che c'è sul menù?*

Under the headings below you'll find alphabetical lists of dishes that might be offered on an Italian menu with their English equivalent. You can simply show the book to the waiter. If you want some cheese, for instance, let *him* point to what's available on the appropriate list. Use pages 36 and 37 for ordering in general.

	page	
Starters (Appetizers)	41	**Antipasti**
Pizza	42	**Pizza**
Omelets	42	**Frittate**
Soups	43	**Minestre, zuppe**
Pasta	44	**Pasta**
Sauces	44	**Salse**
Rice	45	**Riso**
Fish and seafood	46	**Pesce e frutti di mare**
Meat	48	**Carne**
Game and poultry	50	**Cacciagione e pollame**
Vegetables and salads	52	**Verdure e insalate**
Spices and herbs	53	**Spezie e odori**
Cheese	53	**Formaggio**
Fruit	54	**Frutta**
Dessert	55	**Dolce**
Drinks	56	**Bevande**
Wine	56	**Vino**
Nonalcoholic drinks	60	**Bevande analcoliche**
Snacks—Picnic	63	**Spuntini—Picnic**

Note: Italian cooking remains essentially regional. Each of the nation's 18 regions has its own specialities. There are, of course, many well-known dishes that are common to all Italy. But here again the terminology may vary from place to place. (There are at least half a dozen names for octopus or squid!) So in the lists that follow, be prepared for regional variations.

Reading the menu *Per leggere il menù*

Menù a prezzo fisso	Set menu
Piatto del giorno	Dish of the day
Lo chef consiglia ...	The chef recommends ...
Specialità della casa	Specialities of the house
Specialità locali	Local specialities
Contorno a scelta	Choice of vegetables
I nostri piatti di carne sono serviti con contorno	Our meat dishes are accompanied by vegetables
Su ordinazione	Made to order
Supplemento	Extra charge
Verdure di stagione	Vegetables in season
Attesa: 15 minuti	Waiting time: 15 minutes
Pane, grissini e coperto L. ...	Bread, *grissini* and cover L. ...
A scelta	Choice
Piatti freddi	Cold dishes

antipasti	ahnteepahstee	hors d'œuvres
bevande	bayvahnday	drinks
cacciagione	kahtchahjoanay	game
carne	kahrnay	meat
carne ai ferri	kahrnay ahee fehrree	grilled meat
crostacei	kroastahchayee	shellfish
dessert	dayssehr	dessert
formaggi	foarmahdjee	cheese
frutta	froottah	fruit
frutti di mare	froottee dee maaray	seafood
gelati	jaylaatee	ice-cream
insalate	eensahlaatay	salads
minestre	meenehstray	soups
pastasciutta	pahstahshoottah	pasta
pesci	payshee	fish
pollame	poallaamay	poultry
primi piatti	preemee peeahttee	first course
riso	reezoa	rice
secondi piatti	saykoandee peeahttee	second (main) course
verdure	vehrdooray	vegetables
vini	veenee	wines

Appetizers *Antipasti*

I'd like an appetizer.	**Vorrei un antipasto.**	vorraiee oon ahnteepahstoa
acciughe	ahtchoogay	anchovies
affettati misti	ahffayttaatee meestee	cold cuts of pork
antipasto assortito	ahnteepahtoa ahssoar-teetoa	assorted appetizer
carciofi	kahrchofee	artichokes
caviale	kahveeaalay	caviar
coppa	koappah	cured pork shoulder
frutti di mare	froottee dee maaray	mixed seafood
gamberetti	gahmbayrayttee	shrimps
mortadella	moartahdehllah	Bologna sausage
olive	oleevay	olives
ostriche	ostreekay	oysters
prosciutto	proashoottoa	ham
cotto	kottoa	cooked ham
crudo di Parma	kroodoa dee pahrmah	cured ham from Parma
salame	sahlaamay	salami
salmone affumicato	sahlmoanay affoomeekaatoa	smoked salmon
sardine all'olio	sahrdeenay ahllolyoa	sardines in oil
sottaceti	soattahchaytee	pickled vegetables
tonno	tonnoa	tunny in oil

bagna cauda
(baañah kahoodah)
raw vegetables accompagnied by a hot sauce made from anchovies, garlic, oil, butter and sometimes truffles (Northern Italy)

carciofini sottolio
(kahrchofeenee soattolyoa)
artichoke hearts in olive oil

insalata di frutti di mare
(eensahlaatah dee froottee dee maaray)
prawns and squid with lemon, pickles and olives

insalata di pollo
(eensahlaatah dee poalloa)
chicken salad with green salad, lemon, cream

insalata russa
(eensahlaatah roossah)
diced boiled vegetables in mayonnaise

mozzarella con pomodori
(motsahrayllah kon poamoadawree)
mozzarella cheese with tomatoes, basilic, pepper and olive oil

Ristorante

prosciutto crudo con melone
(proa**shoot**toa **kroo**doa kon may**loa**nay)

sliced melon with cured ham from Parma

Pizza

Pizza (plural *pizze*) is surely one of Italy's best-known culinary exports. And the variety of toppings is endless, from simple cheese and tomato to assorted seafood. A *calzone* has basically the same ingredients, but the pastry forms a sort of sealed sandwich, with the filling inside.

Here are the best known variations on the theme:

capricciosa
(kahpreet**choa**sah)

the cook's speciality

margherita
(mahrgay**ree**tah)

named after Italy's first queen, the *pizza* ingredients, tomato, cheese and basil, reflect the national colours

napoletana
(nahpoalay**taa**nah)

the classic *pizza* with anchovies, ham, capers, tomatoes, cheese and oregano

quattro stagioni
(**kwaht**troa stah**joa**nee)

''four seasons'' – containing a variety of vegetables: tomatoes, artichoke, mushrooms, olives, plus cheese, ham and bacon

siciliana
(seechee**lee**aaanee)

with black olives, capers and cheese

Omelets   *Frittate*

I'd like an omelet.	**Vorrei una frittata.**	vorr**ai**ee **oo**nah free**ttaa**tah
frittata	free**ttaa**tah	omelet
di asparagi	dee ahspaa**rah**jee	asparagus
di carciofi	dee kahr**choa**fee	artichokes
di cipolle	dee chee**poal**lay	onions
di spinaci	dee spee**naa**chee	spinach
di zucchine	dee tsook**kee**nay	dried baby marrow (zucchini)
frittata campagnola	free**ttaa**tah kahmpah-**ñoa**lah	an omelet with onion, grated cheese, milk and cream
frittata primaverile	free**ttaa**tah preemah-vay**ree**lay	omelet with vegetables

Soups   *Minestre, zuppe*

In Italy, soup goes by many names, as the following list shows. Some of them are sufficient for a main course. An Italian meal always includes a soup or a dish of *pastasciutta*.

brodo	brawdoa	bouillon, broth, soup
di manzo	dee mahndzoa	meat broth
di pollo	dee poalloa	chicken broth
busecca	boozaykkah	thick tripe, vegetable and bean soup
cacciucco	kahtchookkoa	spicy seafood stew (chowder)
crema di legumi	krehmah dee laygoomee	vegetable cream soup
crema di pomodori	krehmah dee poamoadawree	tomato cream soup
minestra	meenehstrah	soup
in brodo	een brawdoa	bouillon with noodles or rice
di funghi	dee foonggee	cream of mushroom
minestrone	meenehstroanay	a thick vegetable soup (sometimes with noodles) sprinkled with parmesan cheese
passato di verdura	pahssaatoa dee vehrdoorah	mashed vegetable soup, generally with croutons
pasta e fagioli	pahstah ay fahjoalee	noodles and beans
pastina in brodo	pahsteenah een brawdoa	broth with little noodles
zuppa	tsooppah	soup
alla cacciatora	ahllah kahtchahtoarah	meat with mushrooms
alla marinara	ahllah mahreenaarah	spicy fish stew (chowder)
alla pavese	ahllah pahvayzay	consommé with poached egg, croutons and grated cheese
alla veneta	ahllah vaynaytah	vegetables with white wine and noodles
di datteri di mare	dee dahttayree dee maaray	sea dates (kind of mussel)
di frutti di mare	dee froottee dee maaray	seafood
di pesce	dee payshay	spicy fish stew (chowder)
di vongole	dee vonggoalay	clams and white wine

Pasta

Pasta (or *pastasciutta*), the generic name for a wide range of noodles and noodle-related dishes, constitutes the traditional Italian first course. In addition to the well-known *spaghetti*, pasta comes in a bewildering variety of sizes and shapes—ribbons, strings, tubes, shells or stars—known under as many different appellations. It can be served on its own, in broth, with butter or tomato sauce, stuffed with meat, cheese or vegetables, and is often accompanied by a highly flavoured sauce such as those described below.

agnolotti (ahñoalottee)	a round pasta parcel with a filling of chopped meat, vegetables and cheese
cannelloni (kahnnayllawnee)	tubular dough stuffed with meat, cheese or vegetables, covered with a white sauce and baked
cappelletti (kahppayllayttee)	small ravioli filled with meat, herbs, ham, cheese and eggs
fettuccine (fayttootcheenay)	narrow flat noodles
lasagne (lahzaañay)	thin layers of white or green *(lasagne verdi)* dough alternating with tomato sauce and sausage meat, white sauce and grated cheese; baked in the oven
rigatoni (reegahtawnee)	large macaroni, similar to *cannelloni* but smaller and ridged
tagliatelle (tahlyahtehllay)	flat noodles
tortellini (toartehlleenee)	rings of dough filled with seasoned minced meat and served in broth or with a sauce

Sauces *Salse*

It's the sauce that makes spaghetti and macaroni so delicious—Italian cooks are masters of the art.

aglio, olio, peperoncino (ahlyoa olyoa paypayroancheenoa)	garlic, olive oil, sweet peppers, anchovies and parmesan

al burro (ahl **boor**roa)	with butter and grated parmesan
al sugo (ahl **soog**oa)	with tomato sauce and grated parmesan
amatriciana (ahmahtree**chaa**nah)	tomatoes, red peppers, bacon, onions, garlic and white wine
bolognese (boaloa**ñay**zay)	tomatoes, minced meat, onions and herbs
carbonara (kahrboa**naa**rah)	smoked ham, cheese, eggs and olive oil
carrettiera (kahrraytteeayrah)	tuna, mushrooms, tomato purée, freshly ground pepper
marinara (mahree**naa**rah)	tomatoes, olives, garlic, clams and mussels
pesto (**pay**stoa)	basil leaves, garlic, cheese, and sometimes pine kernels and marjoram
pommarola (poammah**raw**lah)	tomatoes, garlic, basil
puttanesca (poottah**nay**skah)	capers, black olives, parsley, garlic, olive oil, black pepper
ragù (rah**goo**)	like *bolognese*
con le vongole (kon lay **voan**goalay)	clams, garlic, parsley, pepper, olive oil, sometimes tomatoes

Rice   *Riso*

In Northern Italy, a rice dish is often offered as a first course to replace pasta. Cooked on its own or together with vegetables, meat, herbs, fish and/or seafood, rice may also be served with a sauce.

risi e bisi	reesee ay **bee**see	rice with peas and bacon
riso in bianco	**ree**soa een bee**ahng**koa	boiled rice with butter and grated parmesan
risotto	ree**sot**toa	rice casserole
con fegatini	kon faygah**tee**nee	with chicken livers
con funghi	kon **foong**gee	with mushrooms
alla milanese	**ahl**lah meelah**nai**say	marrow, white wine, saffron and parmesan

Fish and seafood *Pesci e frutti di mare*

Don't miss the opportunity to sample some of the wide variety of fresh fish and seafood in coastal areas. Some inland regions offer special preparations of fish from their rivers, lakes and streams. Fish is most commonly baked or poached until just done, then dressed with a delicate sauce.

I'd like some fish.	**Vorrei del pesce.**	vorraiee dayl payshay
What kind of seafood do you have?	**Che genere di frutti di mare avete?**	kay jehnayray dee froottee dee maaray ahvaytay
acciughe	ahtchoogay	anchovies
aguglie	ahgoolyay	garfish
anguilla	ahnggooeellah	eel
aragosta	ahrahgoastah	lobster
aringa	ahreenggah	herring
arselle	ahrsehllay	scallops
baccalà	bahkkahlah	dried salt cod
bianchetti	beeahngkayttee	whitebait
branzino	brahndzeenoa	(sea) bass
calamaretti	kahlahmahrayttee	baby squid
calamari	kahlahmaaree	squid
carpa	kahrpah	carp
cozze	koatsay	mussels
dentice	dehnteechay	type of sea bream
eperlano	aypayrlaanoa	smelt
gamberetti	gahmbayrayttee	shrimps
gamberi	gahmbayree	crayfish
granchi	grahngkee	crabs
gronghi	groanggee	conger eel
lamprede	lahmprayday	lampreys
luccio	lootchoa	pike
lumache di mare	loomaakay dee maaray	sea snails
merlano	mayrlaanoa	whiting
merluzzo	mayrloottsoa	cod
nasello	nahsehlloa	coal-fish
orata	oaraatah	type of sea bream
ostriche	ostreekay	oysters
pesce persico	payshay pehrseekoa	perch
pesce spada	payshay spaadah	swordfish
polpo	poalpoa	octopus
razza	rahttsah	ray
ricci	reetchee	sea urchins
rombo	roamboa	turbot
salmone	sahlmoanay	salmon

sardine	sahrdeenay	sardines
scampi	skahmpee	prawns
scorfano	skoarfahnoa	sea-scorpion, sculpin
sgombro	zgoambroa	mackerel
seppia	sayppeeah	cuttlefish
sogliola	sawlyoalah	sole
spigola	speegoalah	sea bass
storione	stoareeoanay	sturgeon
tonno	toannoa	tunny (tuna)
triglie	treelyay	red mullet
trota	trawtah	trout
vongole	vonggoalay	clams

baked	**al forno**	ahl fornoa
boiled	**lesso**	layssoa
(deep) fried	**(ben) fritto**	(bain) freettoa
grilled	**alla griglia**	ahllah greelyah
marinated	**marinato**	mahreenaatoa
poached	**affogato**	ahffoagaatoa
smoked	**affumicato**	ahffoomeekaatoa
steamed	**cotto a vapore**	kottoa ah vahpoaray
stewed	**in umido**	een oomeedoa

Fish specialities *Specialità di pesce*

anguilla alla veneziana
(ahnggooeellah ahllah vaynaytseeaanah)
eel cooked in sauce made from tunny (tuna) and lemon

baccalà alla vicentina
(bahkkahlah ahllah veechaynteenah)
cod cooked in milk with onion, garlic, parsley, anchovies and cinnamon

fritto misto
(freettoa meestoa)
a fry of various small fish and shellfish

pesci in carpione
(payshee een kahrpeeoanay)
boiled fish, cooked in vinegar, served cold with lemon

pesci al cartoccio
(payshee ahl kahrtotchoa)
baked in a parchment envelope with onions, parsley and herbs

sgombri in umido
(zgoambree een oomeedoa)
stewed mackerel in white wine with green peas

stoccafisso
(stoakkahfeessoa)
dried cod cooked with tomatoes, olives and artichoke

sogliole alla mugnaia
(sawlyolay ahllah mooñaaeeah)

sole sautéed in butter, garnished with parsley and lemon

triglie alla livornese
(treelyay ahllah leevoarnaysay)

baked red mullet

Meat *Carne*

I'd like some …	Vorrei …	vorraiee
beef	**del manzo**	dayl **mahn**dzoa
lamb	**dell'agnello**	dayllahñehlloa
mutton	**del montone**	dayl moantoanay
pork	**del maiale**	dayl maaeeaalay
veal	**del vitello**	dayl vee**tehl**loa
animelle di vitello	ahnee**mehl**lay dee veetehlloa	sweetbreads
arrosto	ahr**roas**toa	roast
bistecca	bees**tayk**kah	steak
di filetto	dee fee**leht**toa	rib steak
braciola	brah**choa**lah	chop
cervello	chayr**vehl**loa	brains
cosciotto	koa**shawt**toa	leg
costola	**kos**toalah	rib
costoletta	koastoa**layt**tah	cutlet
fegato	**fay**gahtoa	liver
fesa	**fay**sah	round cut from rump
filetto	fee**layt**toa	fillet
lingua	**leeng**gwah	tongue
lombata/lombo	loam**baa**tah/**loam**boa	loin
medaglioni	maydah**lyoa**nee	round fillet
midollo	mee**doal**loa	marrow
nodini	noa**dee**nee	veal chops
pancetta affumicata	pahn**cheht**tah ahffoo-mee**kaa**tah	bacon
polpette	poal**payt**tay	meatballs
polpettone	poalpayt**toa**nay	meat loaf of seasoned beef or veal
porcellino da latte/ porchetta	poarchay**lleen**oa dah **lahttay**/poar**kayt**tah	suck(l)ing pig
prosciutto	proa**shoot**toa	ham
rognoni	roa**ñoa**nee	kidneys
rosbif	**ros**beef	roast beef
salsicce	sahl**seet**chay	sausages
salumi	sah**loo**mee	assorted pork products

scaloppina	skahloappeenah	escalope
spalla	spahllah	shoulder
tripe	treeppay	tripe

Meat dishes *Piatti di carne*

abbacchio
(ahbbahkkeeoa)
roast lamb, often served in a casserole with anchovies

bistecca alla fiorentina
(beestaykkah ahllah feeoaraynteenah)
a grilled steak flavoured with pepper, lemon juice and parsley

cima alla genovese
(cheemah ahllah jaynoavaysay)
rolled veal stuffed with eggs, sausage and mushrooms

costata al prosciutto
(koastaatah ahl proashoottoa)
a chop filled with ham, cheese and truffles; breaded and fried until golden brown

costoletta alla milanese
(koastoalayttah ahllah meelahnaysay)
breaded veal cutlet, flavoured with cheese

fegato alla veneziana
(faygahtoa ahllah vaynaytseeaanah)
thin slices of calf's liver fried with onions

involtini
(eenvoalteenee)
thin slices of meat (beef, veal or pork) rolled and stuffed

ossi buchi
(ossee bookee)
veal or beef knuckle braised and served in a highly flavoured sauce

piccata al marsala
(peekkaatah ahl mahrsaalah)
thin veal escalope braised in marsala sauce

saltimbocca alla romana
(sahlteemboakkah ahllah roamaanah)
veal escalope braised in marsala wine with ham and sage

scaloppina alla Valdostana
(skahloappeenah ahllah vahldoastaanah)
veal escalope filled with cheese and ham

spezzatino
(spaytsahteenoa)
meat or poultry stew

spiedino
(speeaydeenoa)
pieces of meat grilled or roasted on a skewer

stracotto
(strahkottoa)

meat stew slowly cooked for several hours

trippe alla fiorentina
(treeppay ahllah feeoraynteenah)

tripe and beef braised in a tomato sauce, served with cheese

vitello tonnato
(veetaylloa toannaatoa)

cold veal with tuna fish sauce

zampone
(tsahmpoanay)

pig's trotter filled with seasoned pork, boiled and served in slices

How do you like your meat?   *Come vuole la carne?*

baked	**al forno**	ahl fornoa
barbecued	**alla graticola/alla griglia**	ahllah grahteekoalah/ ahllah greelyah
boiled	**lesso**	layssoa
braised	**brasato**	brahsaatoa
broiled	**allo spiedo**	ahlloa speeehdoa
casseroled	**in casseruola**	een kassayrwolah
fried	**fritto**	freettoa
grilled	**ai ferri**	ahee fehrree
roast(ed)	**arrosto**	ahrroastoa
spit-roasted	**allo spiedo**	ahlloa speeehdoa
stewed	**in umido**	een oomeedoa
stuffed	**farcito**	fahrcheetoa
underdone (rare)	**al sangue**	ahl sahnggooay
medium	**a puntino**	ah poonteenoa
well-done	**ben cotto**	bain kottoa

Game and poultry   *Cacciagione e pollame*

Many small fowl not regarded as game birds in America or Britain are served as first or main courses in Italy. They're usually grilled or roasted. Among small fowl considered as gourmet dishes are lark, plover, thrush and ortolan.

I'd like some game.	**Vorrei della cacciagione.**	vorraiee dayllah kahtchahjoanay
What poultry dishes do you serve?	**Che piatti di pollame servite?**	kay peeahttee dee poallaamay sayrveetay

allodola	ahllodoalah	lark
anatra	aanahtrah	duck
beccaccia	baykkahtchah	woodcock
beccaccino	baykkahtcheenoa	snipe
camoscio	kahmoshoa	chamois
cappone	kahppoanay	capon
capretto	kahprayttoa	kid goat
capriolo	kahpreeoloa	roebuck
cervo	chehrvoa	deer
cinghiale	cheenggeeaalay	wild boar
coniglio	koaneelyoa	rabbit
fagiano	fahjaanoa	pheasant
faraona	fahrahoanah	guinea fowl
gallina	gahlleenah	stewing fowl
gallo cedrone	gahlloa chehdroanay	grouse
lepre	laipray	hare
oca	okah	goose
ortolano	oartoalaanoa	ortolan
pernice	payrneechay	partridge
piccione	peetchoanay	pigeon
piviere	peeveeehray	plover
pollo	poalloa	chicken
pollo novello	poalloa noavehlloa	spring chicken
quaglia	kwahlyah	quail
selvaggina	saylvahdjeenah	venison
tacchino	tahkkeenoa	turkey
tordo	toardoa	thrush

capretto ripieno al forno
(kahprayttoa reepeeaynoa ahl fornoa)

stuffed kid, oven-roasted

galletto amburghese
(gahllayttoa ahmboorgaysay)

young tender chicken, oven-roasted

palombacce allo spiedo
(pahloambahtchay ahlloa speeehdoa)

wood pigeon, spit-roasted

polenta e coniglio
(poalehntah ay koaneelyoa)

rabbit stew served with a mush made from maize flour (cornmeal mush)

polenta e uccelli
(poalehntah ay ootchehllee)

various small birds roasted on a spit and served with polenta (see immediately above)

pollo alla diavola
(poalloa ahllah deeaavoalah)

highly spiced and grilled chicken

Vegetables—Salads   *Verdure—Insalate*

What kind of vegetables have you got?	**Che genere di verdure avete?**	kay jehnayray dee vehrdooray ahvaytay
I'd like a (mixed) salad.	**Vorrei un'insalata (mista).**	vorraiee ooneensahlaatah (meestah)

asparagi	ahspaarahjee	asparagus
barbabietola	bahrbahbeeehtoalah	beetroot
broccoli	brokkolee	broccoli
carciofi	kahrchofee	artichokes
carote	kahrawtay	carrots
cavolfiore	kahvoalfeeoaray	cauliflower
cavolo	kaavoaloa	cabbage
cavolini di Bruxelles	kahvoaleenee dee broossayl	brussels sprouts
ceci	chaychee	chick-peas
cetriolini	chaytreeoaleenee	gherkins
cetriolo	chaytreeoloa	cucumber
cicoria	cheekoreeah	endive (Am. chicory)
cipolle	cheepollay	onions
fagioli	fahjoalee	haricot beans
fagiolini	fahjoaleenee	French (green) beans
fave	faavay	broad beans
finocchio	feenokkeeoa	fennel
funghi	foonggee	mushrooms
indivia	eendeeveeah	chicory (Am. endive)
insalata (verde)	eensahlaatah (vayrday)	(green) salad
lattuga	lahttoogah	lettuce
lenticchie	laynteekkeeay	lentils
melanzane	maylahntsaanay	aubergine (eggplant)
patate	pahtaatay	potatoes
peperoni	paypayroanee	sweet peppers
piselli	peesehllee	peas
pomodoro	poamoadawroa	tomato
porcini	poarcheenee	boletus mushrooms
porro	porroa	leeks
radicchio	rahdeekkeeoa	a kind of bitter, red and white lettuce
ravanelli	rahvahnehllee	radishes
sedano	sehdahnoa	celery
spinaci	speenaachee	spinach
tartufi	tahrtoofee	truffles
verdura mista	vehrdoorah meestah	mixed vegetables
verza	vehrdzah	green cabbage
zucca	tsookkah	pumpkin, gourd
zucchini	tsookkeenee	zucchini

Spices and herbs *Spezie e odori*

aglio	ahlyoa	garlic
basilico	bahzeeleekoa	basil
cannella	kahnnehllah	cinnamon
capperi	kahppehree	capers
chiodi di garofano	keeodee dee gahrofahnoa	cloves
cipollina	cheepoalleenah	chive
cumino	koomeenoa	cumin
lauro	lahooroa	bay
maggiorana	madjoaraanah	marjoram
menta	mayntah	mint
noce moscata	noachay moaskaatah	nutmeg
origano	oareegahnoa	origan
prezzemolo	prehttsaymoaloa	parsley
rosmarino	roazmahreenoa	rosemary
salvia	sahlveeah	sage
scalogno	skahloañoa	shallot
timo	teemoa	thyme
zafferano	dzahffehraanoa	saffron
zenzero	dzehndzehroa	ginger

Cheese *Formaggio*

Italy produces a great variety of cheese, many of them little known outside the locality in which they're made.

Bel Paese (behl pahayzay)	smooth cheese with delicate taste
caciocavallo (kahchoakahvahlloa)	firm, slightly sweet cheese from cow's or sheep's milk
gorgonzola (goargoandzoiah)	most famous of the Italian blue-veined cheese, rich with a tangy flavour
mozzarella (motsahrehllah)	soft, unripened cheese with a bland, slightly sweet flavour, made from buffalo's milk in southern Italy, elsewhere with cow's milk
parmigiano (-reggiano) (pahrmeejaanoa-raydjaanoa)	parmesan (also called *grana*), a hard cheese generally grated for use in hot dishes and pasta but also eaten alone
pecorino (paykoareenoa)	a hard cheese made from sheep's milk
ricotta (reekottah)	soft cow's or sheep's milk cheese

Fruit *Frutta*

Do you have fresh fruit?	**Avete della frutta fresca?**	ahvaytay dayllah froottah frayskah
I'd like a fresh fruit cocktail.	**Vorrei una macedonia di frutta.**	vorraiee oonah mahchaydoneeah dee froottah

albicocca	ahlbeekokkah	apricot
ananas	ahnahnahss	pineapple
anguria	ahnggooreeah	watermelon
arachide	ahrahkeeday	peanuts
arancia	ahrahnchah	orange
banana	bahnaanah	banana
caco	kaakoa	persimmon
castagna	kahstaañah	chestnut
cedro	chaydroa	lime
ciliege	cheeleeayjay	cherries
cocomero	koakoamayroa	watermelon
cotogna	koatoañah	quince
datteri	dahttayree	dates
fico	feekoa	fig
fragole	fraagoalay	strawberries
lamponi	lahmpoanee	raspberries
limone	leemoanay	lemon
mandarino	mahndahreenoa	tangerine
mandorle	mahndoarlay	almonds
mela	maylah	apple
melone	mayloanay	melon
mirtilli	meerteellee	blueberries
more	moray	blackberries
nocciole	noatcholay	hazelnuts
noce di cocco	noachay dee kokkoa	coconut
noci	noachee	walnuts
pera	payrah	pear
pesca	pehskah	peach
pinoli	peenolee	pine kernels
pompelmo	poampaylmoa	grapefruit
prugna	prooñah	plum
prugna secca	prooñah saykkah	prune
ribes	reebays	redcurrants
ribes nero	reebays nayroa	blackcurrants
susina	soozeenah	plum
uva	oovah	grapes
bianca/nera	beeahngkah/nayrah	white/black
uva passa	oovah pahssah	raisins
uva spina	oovah speenah	gooseberries

Dessert *Dolce*

You'll find a profusion of cakes and tarts to round off the meal. Among the more interesting is the *zuppa inglese*—not a soup at all but a kind of trifle (see below). *Granita* is a partially frozen dessert made with coffee or fruit juice. Or try some of the delicious ice-cream for which Italy is renown.

I'd like a dessert, please.	**Vorrei un dessert, per favore.**	vorraiee oon dayssehr pair fahvoaray
What do you recommend?	**Cosa consiglia?**	kawsah koanseelyah
Something light, please.	**Qualcosa di leggero, per favore.**	kwahlkawsah dee laydjairoa pair fahvoaray
I'd like a slice of cake.	**Vorrei una fetta di torta.**	vorraiee oonah fehttah dee toartah
with/without (whipped) cream	**con/senza panna (montata)**	kon/sayntsah pahnnah (moantaatah)
budino	boodeenoa	pudding
crema	kraimah	custard
crostata di mele	kroastaatah dee maylay	apple pie
dolce	doalchay	cake
gelato	jaylaatoa	ice-cream
alla fragola	ahllah fraagoalah	strawberry
al limone	ahl leemoanay	lemon
alla vaniglia	ahllah vahneelyah	vanilla
misto	meestoa	mixed
tartufi di cioccolata	tahrtoofee dee choakkoalaatah	chocolate truffles
torta	toartah	cake
di cioccolata	dee choakkoalaatah	chocolate cake
di frutta	dee froottah	fruit cake
cassata (kassaatah)		ice cream with candied fruit (Am. spumoni)
cassata siciliana (kassaatah seecheeleeaanah)		sponge cake garnished with sweet cream cheese, chocolate and candied fruit
zabaglione (dzahbahlyoanay)		a mixture of eggyolks, sugar and Marsala wine; served warm
zuppa inglese (dzooppah eengglaysay)		sponge cake steeped in rum with candied fruit and custard or whipped cream

Drinks *Bevande*

Aperitifs *Aperitivi*

The average Italian is just as fond of his favourite *aperitivo* (ahpehree**tee**voa) as we are of our cocktail or highball. Often bittersweet, some aperitifs have a wine and brandy base with herbs and bitters while others may have a vegetable base. Here are some aperitifs you may want to try:

Americano (ahmayree**kaa**noa)	despite its name, one of the most popular Italian aperitifs; a vermouth to which bitters, brandy and lemon peel are added	
Aperol (ahpayroal)	a non-alcoholic bitters	
Campari (kahm**paa**ree)	reddish-brown bitters, flavoured with orange peel and herbs, it has a quinine taste	
Cynar (cheenaar)	produced from artichoke	
Martini (mahr**tee**nee)	a brand-name vermouth not to be confused with a martini cocktail	
neat (straight)	**liscio**	**lee**shoa
on the rocks	**con ghiaccio**	kon gee**ah**tchoa
with (seltzer) water	**con acqua (di seltz)**	kon **ah**kkwah (dee sehltz)

> **SALUTE!/CIN-CIN!**
> (sah**loo**tay/cheen cheen)
> YOUR HEALTH!/CHEERS!

Wine *Vino*

Italy is one of the most important wine producers in Europe. Vineyards are found all over the Italian peninsula and islands.

Some of the country's most reputed wines (like *Barbaresco, Barbera* and *Barolo*) come from the Piedmont in north-western Italy. But most other regions have noted wine, too. This is your opportunity to sample local wine, some of which is of surprisingly good quality.

Chianti is doubtless Italy's best-known wine outside of its borders. The best of it is produced between Florence and Siena. The term *Chianti classico* on the label indicates that the production of this wine has been carefully supervised. A *Chianti* of superior quality carries the term *riserva* on the label.

Some restaurants list their wines in a corner of the menu while others have them marked up on the wall. As much of the nation's wine doesn't travel well, don't expect a *trattoria* to offer more than a few types of wine. Most of the wine must be drunk young so don't look too hard for vintage labels. In smaller places you might get *vino aperto* (open wine) or *vino della casa* (house wine) at a moderate price, served in one-quarter, one-half or one-litre carafes.

May I have the wine list, please.	**Per favore, mi porti la lista dei vini.**	pair fahvoaray mee portee lah leestah daiee veenee
I'd like a bottle of white/red wine.	**Vorrei una bottiglia di vino bianco/ rosso.**	vorraiee oonah botteelyah dee veenoa beeahngkoa/ roassoa
half a bottle	**mezza bottiglia**	mehdzah botteelyah
a carafe	**una caraffa**	oonah kahrahffah
half a litre	**mezzo litro**	mehdzoa leetroa
a glass	**un bicchiere**	oon beekkeeairay
A bottle of champagne, please.	**Una bottiglia di champagne, per favore.**	oonah botteelyah dee shampahñ pair fahvoaray
Where does this wine come from?	**Da dove viene questo vino?**	dah doavay veeaynay kooaystoa veenoa

red	**rosso**	roassoa
white	**bianco**	beeahngkoa
rosé	**rosatello**	rawzahtehlloa
dry	**secco**	sehkkoa
full-bodied	**pieno**	peeaynoa
light	**leggero**	laydjairoa
sparkling	**spumante**	spoomahntay
sweet	**dolce**	doalchay

The following chart will help you to choose your wine if you want to do some serious wine-tasting.

Type of wine	Examples	Accompanies
sweet white wine	*Orvieto* from Umbria (the export variety is usually dry), *Aleatico* and *Vino Santo* from Tuscany and the famed *Marsala* from Sicily.	desserts, especially custard, pudding, cake
dry white wine	*Frascati* from Latium or *Verdicchio dei Castelli di Jesi* from the Adriatic Marches; local white wine generally falls into this category	fish, seafood, cold or boiled meat, fowl (the unconventional Romans enjoy drinking *Frascati* with a heavy meal)
rosé	*Lagrein* from Trentino-Alto Adige	goes with almost anything but especially cold dishes, eggs, pork and lamb
light-bodied red wine	*Bardolino* and *Valpolicella* from the Lake of Garda; local red wine, including Italian-Swiss *Merlot,* usually fits this category	roast chicken, turkey, veal, lamb, steaks, ham, liver, quail, pheasant, soft-textured cheeses, stews and pasta
full-bodied red wine	*Barolo, Barbera* and *Barbaresco* from Piedmont	duck, goose, kidneys, most game, tangy cheese like *gorgon-zola*—in short, any strong-flavoured dishes
sparkling white wine	*Asti spumante* (Italians like to refer to it as champagne but it's slightly sweet)	goes nicely with dessert and pastry; if it's dry, you might try *spumante* as an aperitif or with shellfish, nuts or dried fruit

Beer *Birra*

Beer is always available and growing in popularity. Italian brands are weaker than northern European beers.

I'd like a beer, please.	**Vorrei una birra, per favore.**	vorraiee oonah beerrah pair fahvoaray
Do you have ... beer?	**Avete della birra ...?**	ahvaytay dayllah beerrah
bottled	**in bottiglia**	een botteelyah
draught	**alla spina**	ahllah speenah
foreign	**straniera**	strahneeayrah
light/dark	**bionda/scura**	beeoandah/skoorah

Other alcoholic drinks *Altre bevande alcoliche*

Coffee shops and bars usually have a good stock of foreign and domestic liquor—even some of your favourite brands.

aperitif	**un aperitivo**	oon ahpayreeteevoa
brandy	**un brandy**	oon ''brandy''
cognac	**un cognac**	oon ''cognac''
gin and tonic	**un gin e tonico**	oon ''gin'' ay toneekoa
liqueur	**un liquore**	oon lookwoaray
port	**un porto**	oon portoa
rum	**un rum**	oon room
vermouth	**un vermouth**	oon vehrmoot
vodka	**una vodka**	oonah vodkah
whisky (and soda)	**un whisky (e soda)**	oon ''whisky'' (ay sodah)

glass	**un bicchiere**	oon beekkeeairay
bottle	**una bottiglia**	oonah botteelyah
double (a double shot)	**doppio**	doappeeoa
neat (straight)	**liscio**	leeshoa
on the rocks	**con ghiaccio**	kon geeahtchoa

You'll certainly want to take the occasion to sip an after-dinner drink. If you'd like something which approaches French cognac try *Vecchia Romagna*. If you feel a digestive is called for ask for an *amaro* (bitter), or a glass of *Fernet-Branca* should fit the bill.

| I'd like to try a glass of ..., please. | **Vorrei assaggiare un bicchiere di ...** | vorraiee ahssahdjaaray oon beekkeeairay dee |
| Are there any local specialities? | **Avete specialità locali?** | ahvaytay spaychahleetah loakaalee |

Nonalcoholic drinks   *Bevande analcoliche*

The Italian *caffè espresso* has a rich aroma and is excellent everywhere. Served in demi-tasses, it's stronger than what we're used to at home. However, if you'd like to try a more concentrated cup of espresso coffee, ask for a *ristretto* (ree**strayt**toa). As against this, a *caffè lungo* (kahf**fay loong**goa) is a slightly weaker cup of espresso coffee.

For breakfast don't miss the opportunity to drink a *cappuccino* (kahppoot**chee**noa), a delicious mixture of coffee and hot milk, dusted with cocoa. In summer, iced tea and coffee are popular.

I'd like a/an ...	**Vorrei ...**	vorraiee
chocolate	**un cioccolato**	oon choakkoalaatoa
coffee	**un caffè**	oon kahffai
with cream	**con panna**	kon **pahn**nah
iced coffee	**un caffè freddo**	oon kahffay frayddoa
fruit juice	**un succo di frutta**	oon **sook**koa dee **froot**tah
grapefruit	**di pompelmo**	dee poampaylmoa
lemon	**di limone**	dee lee**moa**nay
orange	**d'arancia**	dahrahnchah
herb tea	**una tisana**	oonah teezaanah
lemonade	**una limonata**	oonah leemoanaatah
milk	**del latte**	dayl **laht**tay
milkshake	**un frullato di latte**	oon froollaatoa dee **laht**tay
mineral water	**dell'acqua minerale**	dayl**lahk**kwah meenay-raalay
fizzy (carbonated)	**gasata**	gahzaatah
still	**naturale**	nahtooraalay
orangeade	**un'aranciata**	oonahrahnchaatah
tea	**un tè**	oon tai
with milk/lemon	**con latte/limone**	kon **laht**tay/leemoanay
iced tea	**un tè freddo**	oon tai frayddoa
tomato juice	**un succo di pomodoro**	oon **sook**koa dee poamoadawroa
tonic water	**dell'acqua tonica**	dayl**lahk**kwah toneekah

Complaints *Reclami*

There is a plate/glass missing.	**Manca un piatto/un bicchiere.**	mahngkah oon peeahttoa/oon beekkeeairay
I have no knive/fork/spoon.	**Non ho il coltello/la forchetta/il cucchiaio.**	noan oa eel koltehlloa/lah forkehttah/eel kookkeeaaeeoa
That's not what I ordered.	**Non è ciò che avevo ordinato.**	noan ai cho kay ahvayvoa oardeenaatoa
I asked for ...	**Avevo chiesto ...**	ahvayvoa keeehstoa
There must be some mistake.	**Ci deve essere un errore.**	chee dayvay ehssayray oon ehrroaray
May I change this?	**Posso cambiare questo?**	possoa kahmbeeaaray kooaystoa
I asked for a small portion (for the child).	**Avevo chiesto una piccola porzione (per il bambino).**	ahvayvoa keeehstoa oonah peekkoalah poartseeoanay (pair eel bahmbeenoa)
The meat is ...	**La carne è ...**	lah kahrnay ai
overdone	**troppo cotta**	troppoa kottah
underdone	**poco cotta**	pokoa kottah
too rare	**troppo al sangue**	troppoa ahl sahnggooay
too tough	**troppo dura**	troppoa doorah
This is too ...	**Questo è troppo ...**	kooaystoa ai troppoa
bitter/salty	**amaro/salato**	ahmaaroa/sahlaatoa
sweet	**dolce**	doalchay
I don't like it.	**Non mi piace.**	noan mee peeahchay
The food is cold.	**Il cibo è freddo.**	eel cheeboa ai frayddoa
This isn't fresh.	**Questo non è fresco.**	kooaystoa noan ai frayskoa
What's taking you so long?	**Perchè impiegate tanto tempo?**	pehrkai eempeeaygaatay tahntoa tehmpoa
Have you forgotten our drinks?	**Ha dimenticato le nostre bevande?**	ah deemaynteekaatoa lay nostray bayvahnday
The wine tastes of cork.	**Il vino sa di tappo.**	eel veenoa sah dee tahppoa
This isn't clean.	**Questo non è pulito.**	kooaystoa noan ai pooleetoa
Would you ask the head waiter to come over?	**Vuole chiedere al capo cameriere di venire qui?**	vwolay keeaydayray ahl kaapoa kahmayreeehray dee vayneeray kooee

The bill (check)   *Il conto*

Though the bill usually includes the service charge *(il servizio)*, it is customary to leave a tip *(la mancia)* for the waiter. Note that you will occasionally also find one or both of the following items added to your bill: *coperto* (cover charge), *supplemento* (surcharge).

I'd like to pay.	**Vorrei pagare.**	vorraiee pahgaaray
We'd like to pay separately.	**Vorremmo pagare separatamente.**	vorrehmmoa pahgaaray saypahrahtahmayntay
I think you've made a mistake in this bill.	**Penso che abbiate fatto un errore nel conto.**	pehnsoa kay ahbbeeaatay fahttoa oon ayrroaray nayl koantoa
What is this amount for?	**Per che cos'è questo importo?**	pair kay kozai kooaystoa eemportoa
Is service included?	**È compreso il servizio?**	ai koampraysoa eel sayrveetseeoa
Is the cover charge included?	**È compreso il coperto?**	ai koampraysoa eel kopairtoa
Is everything included?	**È tutto compreso?**	ai toottoa koampraysoa
Do you accept traveller's cheques?	**Accettate i traveller's cheques?**	ahtchayttaatay ee "traveller's cheques"
Can I pay with this credit card?	**Posso pagare con questa carta di credito?**	possoa pahgaaray kon kooaystah kahrtah dee kraydeetoa
Thank you, this is for you.	**Grazie, questo è per lei.**	graatseeay kooaystoa ai pair lehee
Keep the change.	**Tenga il resto.**	taynggah eel rehstoa
That was a delicious meal.	**È stato un pasto delizioso.**	ai staatoa oon paastoa dayleetseeoasoa
We enjoyed it, thank you.	**Ci è piaciuto, grazie.**	chee ai peeahchootoa graatseeay

> **SERVIZIO COMPRESO**
> SERVICE INCLUDED

TIPPING, see inside back-cover

Snacks—Picnic *Spuntini—Picnic*

Bars and snack bars stay open from early morning till late at night. Most have a selection of sandwiches *(panini imbottiti)* and pastries *(pasticcini),* inexpensive if you eat at the counter. There are, of course, *pizzerie* for a sit-down pizza or, if you're in a hurry, places selling pizza by the slice. In a *paninoteca,* you can find all sorts of *panini* to eat on the spot or to bring away. The same in a *rosticceria,* plus a great variety of food ready to eat at home or in a picnic.

I'll have one of those, please.	**Per favore, vorrei uno di quelli.**	pair fahvoaray vorraiee oonoa dee kooayllee
Give me two of these and one of those.	**Mi dia due di questi e uno di quelli.**	mee deeah dooay dee kooaystee ay oonoa dee kooayllee
to the left/right above/below	**a sinistra/a destra sopra/sotto**	ah seeneestrah/a dehstrah soaprah/soattoa
It's to take away.	**È da portare via.**	ai dah poartaaray veeah
How much is that?	**Quant'è?**	kwahntai
I'd like a/some …	**Vorrei …**	vorraiee
chicken	**un pollo**	oon poalloa
half a roasted chicken	**metà pollo arrosto**	maytah poalloa ahrroastoa
chips	**delle patatine fritte**	dayllay pahtahteenay freettay
(slice of) pizza	**una (fetta di) pizza**	oonah (fayttah dee) peettzah
sandwich	**un panino imbottito**	oon pahneenoa eembotteetoa
cheese	**al formaggio**	ahl foarmadjoa
ham	**al prosciutto cotto**	ahl proashoottoa kottoa
Parma ham	**al prosciutto crudo**	ahl proashoottoa kroodoa
salami	**al salame**	ahl sahlaamay

Here's a basic list of food and drink that might come in useful when shopping for a picnic.

Please give me a/an/ some …	**Per favore, mi dia …**	pair fahvoaray mee deeah
apples	**delle mele**	dayllay maylay
bananas	**delle banane**	dayllay bahnaanay

biscuits (Br.)	dei biscotti	daiee beeskoattee
beer	della birra	dayllah beerrah
bread	del pane	dayl paanay
butter	del burro	dayl boorroa
cake	una torta	oonah toartah
cheese	del formaggio	dayl foarmahdjoa
chips (Am.)	delle patatine fritte	dayllay pahtahteenay freettay
chocolate bar	una stecca di cioccolato	oonah staykkah dee chokkoalaatoa
coffee	del caffè	dayl kahffai
instant	solubile	soaloobeelay
cold cuts	degli affettati	daylyee ahffehttaatee
cookies	dei biscotti	daiee beeskoattee
crackers	dei cracker	daiee "cracker"
crisps	delle patatine fritte	dayllay pahtahteenay freettay
eggs	delle uova	dayllay wawvah
frankfurters	dei Würstel	daiee "würstel"
gherkins (pickles)	dei cetriolini	daiee chaytreeoaleenee
grapes	dell'uva	daylloovah
ham	del prosciutto	dayl proashoottoa
ice-cream	del gelato	dayl jaylaatoa
lemon	un limone	oon leemoanay
milk	del latte	dayl lahttay
mustard	della senape	dayllah saynahpay
(olive) oil	dell'olio (d'oliva)	dayllolyoa (doleevah)
oranges	delle arance	dayllay ahrahnchay
pastries	dei pasticcini	daiee pahsteetcheenee
peaches	delle pesche	dayllay payskay
peppers	dei peperoni	daiee paypayroanee.
pickles	dei sottaceti	daiee soattahchaytee
plums	delle prugne	dayllay prooñay
rolls	dei panini	daiee pahneenee
salad	dell'insalata	daylleensahlaatah
salami	del salame	dayl sahlaamay
salt	del sale	dayl saalay
sausages	delle salsicce	dayllay sahlseetchay
soft drink	una bibita	oonah beebeetah
sugar	dello zucchero	daylloa tsookkayroa
tea	del tè	dayl tai
tomatoes	dei pomodori	daiee poamoadawree
vinegar	dell'aceto	dayllahchaytoa
(mineral) water	dell'acqua (minerale)	dayllahkkwah (meenay-raalay)
wine	del vino	dayl veenoa
yoghurt	uno yogurt	oonoa eeoagoort

Travelling around

Plane *Aereo*

Is there a flight to Naples?	**C'è un volo per Napoli?**	chai oon voaloa pair naapoalee
Is it a direct flight?	**È un volo diretto?**	ai oon voaloa deerayttoa
When's the next flight to Palermo?	**A che ora è il prossimo volo per Palermo?**	ah kay oarah ai eel prosseemoa voaloa pair pahlehrmoa
Do I have to change planes?	**Devo cambiare aereo?**	dayvoa kahmbeeaaray ahairayoa
Is there a connection to Venice?	**C'è una coincidenza per Venezia?**	chai oonah koeenchee-dehntsah pair vaynaytseeah
I'd like a ticket to Milan.	**Vorrei un biglietto per Milano.**	vorraiee oon beelyayttoa pair meelaanoa
single (one-way)	**andata**	ahndaatah
return (roundtrip)	**andata e ritorno**	ahndaatah ay reetornoa
What time do we take off?	**A che ora si parte?**	ah kay oarah see pahrtay
What time should I check in?	**A che ora devo presentarmi?**	ah kay oarah dayvoa prayzehntaarmee
Is there a bus to the airport?	**C'è un autobus per l'aeroporto?**	chai oon owtoabooss pair lahayroportoa
What's the flight number?	**Qual è il numero del volo?**	kwahl ai eel noomayroa dayl voaloa
What time do we arrive?	**A che ora arriveremo?**	ah kay oarah ahrreevay-raymoa
I'd like to ... my reservation on flight no ...	**Vorrei ... la mia prenotazione sul volo ...**	vorraiee ... lah meeah praynoatahtseeoanay sool voaloa
cancel	**annullare**	ahnnoollaaray
change	**cambiare**	kahmbeeaaray
confirm	**confermare**	koanfayrmaaray

ARRIVO ARRIVAL	**PARTENZA** DEPARTURE

Train *Treno*

Italian trains *try* to run on time as advertised. If you haven't booked, it's wise to arrive at the station at least 20 minutes before departure to be sure of a seat: Italy's trains are often very crowded.

The following list describes the various types of trains:

TEE (teh-eh-eh)	Trans Europ Express; a luxury, international service with first class only; additional fare and reservation required
Rapido (R) (raapeedoa)	Long-distance express train stopping at major cities only; first and second class
Intercity (IC) ("intercity")	Inter-city express with very few stops; a luxury, international service with first and second class
Espresso (EXP)/ Direttissimo (aysprehssoa/ deerehtteesseemoa)	Long-distance train, stopping at main stations
Diretto (D) (deerehttoa)	Slower than the *Espresso,* it makes a number of local stops
Locale (L) (loakaalay)	A local train which stops at almost every station
Accelerato (A) (ahtchaylayraatoa)	Same as a *Locale*
Littorina (leettoareenah)	Small diesel used on short runs

Here are some more useful terms which you may need.

Carrozza ristorante (kahrrottsah reestorahntay)	Dining-car
Vagone letto (vahgoanay lehttoa)	Sleeping-car with individual compartments and washing facilities
Carrozza cuccette (kahrrottsah kootchehttay)	A berth with blankets and pillows
Bagagliaio (bahgahlyaaeeoa)	Guard's van (baggage car): normally only registered luggage permitted

To the railway station   *Per andare alla stazione*

Where's the railway station?	**Dove si trova la stazione (ferroviaria)?**	doavay see trawvah lah stahtseeooanay (fehrroveeaareeah)
Taxi, please!	**Taxi, per favore!**	"taxi" pair fahvoaray
Take me to the railway station.	**Mi porti alla stazione.**	mee portee ahllah stahtseeoanay
What's the fare?	**Quant'è?**	kwahntai

ENTRATA	ENTRANCE
USCITA	EXIT
AI BINARI	TO THE PLATFORMS
INFORMAZIONI	INFORMATION

Where's the ...?   *Dov'è ...?*

Where is/are the ...?	**Dov'è ...?**	doavai
bar	**il bar**	eel "bar"
booking office	**l'ufficio prenotazioni**	looffeechoa praynoatahtseeoanee
currency-exchange office	**l'ufficio cambio**	looffeechoa kahmbeeoa
left-luggage office (baggage check)	**il deposito bagagli**	eel daypawzeetoa bahgaalyee
lost property (lost-and-found) office	**l'ufficio oggetti smarriti**	looffeechoa odjehttee smahrreetee
luggage lockers	**la custodia automatica dei bagagli**	lah koostawdeeah owtoamaateekah daiee bahgaalyee
newsstand	**l'edicola**	laydeekoalah
platform 7	**il binario 7**	eel beenaareeoa 7
reservations office	**l'ufficio prenotazioni**	looffeechoa praynoatahtseeoanee
restaurant	**il ristorante**	eel reestorahntay
snack bar	**lo "snack bar"**	loa "snack bar"
ticket office	**la biglietteria**	lah beelyayttayreeah
waiting room	**la sala d'aspetto**	lah saalah dahspehttoa
Where are the toilets?	**Dove sono i gabinetti?**	doavay soanoa ee gahbeenayttee

TAXI, see page 21

Inquiries *Informazioni*

When is the ... train to Rome?	Quando parte ... treno per Roma?	kwahndoa pahrtay ... traynoa pair roamah
first/last	il primo/l'ultimo	eel preemoa/loolteemoa
next	il prossimo	eel prosseemoa
What time does the train for Milan leave?	A che ora parte il treno per Milano?	ah kay oarah pahrtay eel traynoa pair meelaanoa
What's the fare to Ancona?	Quanto costa il biglietto per Ancona?	kwahntoa kostah eel bee-lyayttoa pair ahngkoanah
Is it a through train?	È un treno diretto?	ai oon traynoa deerehttoa
Is there a connection to ...?	C'è una coincidenza per ...?	chai oonah koaeenchee-dayntsah pair
Do I have to change trains?	Devo cambiare treno?	dayvoa kahmbeeaaray traynoa
How long will the train stop at ...?	Quanto tempo si fermerà il treno a ...?	kwahntoa tehmpoa see fayrmayrah eel traynoa ah
Is there sufficient time to change?	C'è il tempo per cambiare?	chai eel tehmpoa pair kahmbeeaaray
Will the train leave on time?	Partirà in orario il treno?	pahrteerah een oaraareeoa eel traynoa
What time does the train arrive at Florence?	A che ora arriverà a Firenze il treno?	ah kay oarah ahrreevayrah ah feerehntsay eel traynoa
Is there a dining-car/ sleeping-car on the train?	C'è una carrozza ristorante/un vagone letto sul treno?	chai oonah kahrrottsah reestoarahntay/oon vahgoa-nay lehttoa sool traynoa
Does the train stop at Lugano?	Il treno si fermerà a Lugano?	eel traynoa see fayrmayrah ah loogaanoa
What platform does the train for Verona leave from?	Da che binario parte il treno per Verona?	dah kay beenaareeoa pahrtay eel traynoa pair vayroanah
What platform does the train from Bari arrive at?	A che binario arriva il treno proveniente da Bari?	ah kay beenaareeoa ahrreevah eel traynoa pro-vayneeehntay dah baaree
I'd like to buy a timetable.	Vorrei comprare un orario ferroviario.	vorraiee koampraaray oon oaraareeoa fehrro-veeaareeoa

È un treno diretto.	It's a through train.
Deve cambiare a ...	You have to change at ...
Cambi a ... e prenda un treno locale.	Change at ... and get a local train.
Il binario 7 è ...	Platform 7 is ...
laggiù/su dalle scale a sinistra/a destra	over there/upstairs on the left/on the right
C'è un treno per ... alle ...	There's a train to ... at ...
Il suo treno partirà dal binario 8.	Your train will leave from platform 8.
Ci sarà un ritardo di ... minuti.	There'll be a delay of ... minutes.
Prima classe in testa/ nel mezzo/in coda.	First class at the front/ in the middle/at the end.

Tickets *Biglietti*

I want a ticket to Rome.	Desidero un biglietto per Roma.	dayzeedayroa oon bee-lyayttoa pair roamah
single (one-way)	andata	ahndaatah
return (roundtrip)	andata e ritorno	ahndaatah ay reetornoa
first/second class	prima/seconda classe	preemah/saykoandah klahssay
half price	metà tariffa	maytah tahreeffah

Reservation *Prenotazione*

I want to book a ...	Vorrei prenotare ...	vorraie praynoataaray
seat (by the window)	un posto (vicino al finestrino)	oon postoa (veecheenoa ahl feenaystreenoa)
berth	una cuccetta	oonah kootchehttah
upper	superiore	soopayreeoaray
middle	nel mezzo	nayl mehdzoa
lower	inferiore	eenfayreeoaray
berth in the sleeping car	un posto nel vagone letto	oon postoa nayl vahgoanay lehttoa

All aboard   *In vettura!*

Is this the right platform for the train to Bellinzona?	È il binario giusto per il treno che va a Bellinzona?	ai eel beenaareeo joostoa pair eel traynoa kay vah ah behlleendzoanah
Is this the right train to Genoa?	È il treno giusto per Genova?	ai eel traynoa joostoa pair jainoavah
Excuse me. May I get by?	Mi scusi. Posso passare?	mee skoozee. possoa pahssaaray
Is this seat taken?	È occupato questo posto?	ai oakkoopaatoa kooaystoa postoa

| FUMATORI SMOKER | NON FUMATORI NONSMOKER |

I think that's my seat.	Penso che questo sia il mio posto.	paynsoa kay kooaystoa seeah eel meeoa postoa
Would you let me know before we get to Milan?	Può avvisarmi prima di arrivare a Milano?	pwo ahvveezaarmee preemah dee ahrreevaaray ah meelaanoa
What station is this?	Che stazione è?	kay stahtseeoanay ai
How long does the train stop here?	Quanto tempo si ferma qui il treno?	kwahntoa tehmpoa see fayrmah kooee eel traynoa
When do we get to Pisa?	Quando arriveremo a Pisa?	kwahndoa ahrreevay-raymoa ah peezah

Sleeping   *Nel vagone letto*

Are there any free compartments in the sleeping-car?	Ci sono degli scompartimenti liberi nel vagone letto?	chee soanoa dailyee skoampahrteemayntee leebayree nail vahgoanay lehttoa
Where's the sleeping-car?	Dov'è il vagone letto?	doavai eel vahgoanay lehttoa
Where's my berth?	Dov'è la mia cuccetta?	doavai lah meeah kootchehttah
I'd like a lower berth.	Vorrei la cuccetta inferiore.	vorraiee lah kootchehttah eenfayreeoaray

Would you make up our berths?	Può preparare le nostre cuccette?	pwo praypahraaray lay nostray kootchehttay
Would you call me at 7 o'clock?	Può svegliarmi alle 7?	pwo svaylyahrmee ahllay 7
Would you bring me some coffee in the morning?	Può portarmi un caffè domani mattina?	pwo portahrmee oon kahffai doamaanee mahtteenah

Eating *Nella carrozza ristorante*

You can get snacks and drinks in the buffet-car and in the dining-car when it isn't being used for main meals. On some trains an attendant comes around with snacks, tea, coffee and soft drinks.

| Where's the dining-car? | Dov'è la carrozza ristorante? | doavai lah kahrrottsah reestorahntay |

Baggage and porters *Bagagli e facchini*

Porter!	Facchino!	fahkkeenoa
Can you help me with my luggage?	Può prendere il mio bagaglio?	pwo prehndayray eel meeoa bahgaalyoa
Where are the luggage trolleys (carts)?	Dove sono i carrelli portabagagli?	doavay soanoa ee kahrrehl-lee portahbahgaalyee
Where are the luggage lockers?	Dove sono le custodie automatiche dei bagagli?	doavay soanoa lay koostawdeeay owtoamaa-teekay daiee bahgaalyee
Where's the left-luggage office (baggage check)?	Dov'è il deposito bagagli?	doavai eel daypawzeetoa bahgaalyee
I'd like to leave my luggage, please.	Vorrei depositare i miei bagagli, per favore.	vorraiee daypozeetaaray ee meeaiee bahgaalyee pair fahvoaray
I'd like to register (check) my luggage.	Vorrei far registrare i miei bagagli.	vorraiee fahr rayjeestraa-ray ee meeaiee bahgaalyee

REGISTRAZIONE BAGAGLI
REGISTERING (CHECKING) BAGGAGE

PORTERS, see also page 18

Coach (long-distance bus)   *Pullman/Corriera*

You'll find information on destinations and timetables at the coach terminals, usually situated near railway stations. Many travel agencies offer coach tours.

When's the next coach to ...?	**A che ora parte il prossimo pullman per ...?**	ah kay oarah **pahr**tay eel **prosseemoa pool**mahn pair
Does this coach stop at ...?	**Questa corriera si ferma a ...?**	kooaystah korreeayrah see **fayr**mah ah
How long does the journey (trip) take?	**Quanto tempo dura il percorso?**	**kwahn**toa **tehm**poa doorah eel payrkoarsoa

Note: Most of the phrases on the previous pages can be used or adapted for travelling on local transport.

Bus—Tram (streetcar)   *Autobus—Tram*

Many cities have introduced an automatic system of fare-paying: either you insert the exact change into a ticket dispenser at the bus or tram stop or you punch your ticket in the machine.

If you're planning to get around a lot in one city by bus, tram, or *metropolitana* (see next page), enquire about a booklet of tickets or special runabout tickets, such as *biglietto giornaliero* (one-day ticket).

I'd like a booklet of tickets.	**Vorrei un blocchetto di biglietti.**	vorraiee oon blok**kehtt**oa dee beely**ayt**tee
Where can I get a bus to the Vatican?	**Dove posso prendere l'autobus per il Vaticano?**	doavay possoa **prehn**dayray **low**toabooss pair eel vahteek**aan**oa
What bus do I take for the Colosseum?	**Quale autobus devo prendere per andare al Colosseo?**	**kwaa**lay **ow**toabooss day-voa **prehn**dayray pair ahn-**daar**ay ahl koaloass**aioa**
Where's the bus stop?	**Dove si trova la fermata dell'autobus?**	doavay see **traw**vah lah fehr**maat**ah day**llowt**oabooss

When is the ... bus to the Lido?	A che ora parte ... autobus per il Lido?	ah kay oarah pahrtay ... owtoabooss pair eel leedoa
first/last	il primo/l'ultimo	eel preemoa/loolteemoa
next	il prossimo	eel prosseemoa
How much is the fare to ...?	Quanto costa il biglietto per ...?	kwahntoa kostah eel beelyayttoa pair
Do I have to change buses?	Devo cambiare autobus?	dayvoa kahmbeeaaray owtoabooss
How many bus stops are there to ...?	Quante fermate ci sono fino a ...?	kwahntay fayrmaatay chee soanoa feenoa ah
Will you tell me when to get off?	Può dirmi quando devo scendere?	pwo deermee kwahndoa dayvoa shayndayray
I want to get off at Piazza di Spagna.	Voglio scendere a Piazza di Spagna.	volyoa shayndayray ah peeahtsah dee spahñah

| FERMATA D'AUTOBUS | REGULAR BUS STOP |
| FERMATA A RICHIESTA | STOPS ON REQUEST |

Underground (subway) *Metropolitana*

The *metropolitana* in Rome and Milan corresponds to the
London underground or the New York subway. In both
cities, the fare is always the same, irrespective of the distance you travel. Big maps in every *Metro* station make the
system easy to use.

Where's the nearest underground station?	Dove si trova la più vicina stazione della metropolitana?	doavay see trawvah lah peeoo veecheenah stahtseeoanay dayllah maytroapoaleetaanah
Does this train go to ...?	Questo treno va a ...?	kooaystoa traynoa vah ah
Where do I change for ...?	Dove cambio per andare a ...?	doavay kahmbeeoa pair ahndaaray ah
Is the next sta-tion ...?	La prossima stazione è ...?	lah prosseemah stahtseeoanay ai
Which line should I take for ...?	Che linea devo prendere per ...?	kay leenayah dayvoa prehndayray pair

74

TRAVELLING AROUND

Boat service *Battello*

When does the next boat for … leave?	A che ora parte il prossimo battello per …?	ah kay oarah pahrtay eel prosseemoa bahttehlloa pair
Where's the embarkation point?	Dove ci si imbarca?	doavay chee see eembahrkah
How long does the crossing take?	Quanto tempo dura la traversata?	kwahntoa tehmpoa doorah lah trahvayrsaatah
At which ports do we stop?	A che porti si ferma?	ah kay portee see fayrmah
I'd like to take a cruise.	Vorrei fare una crociera.	vorraiee faaray oonah kroachayrah
boat	il battello/la nave	eel bahttehlloa/lah naavay
cabin	la cabina	lah kahbeenah
single/double	a un letto/a due letti	ah oon lehttoa/ah dooay lehttee
deck	il ponte	eel poantay
ferry	il traghetto	eel trahgehttoa
hydrofoil	l'aliscafo	lahleeskaafoa
life belt/boat	la cintura/il canotto di salvataggio	lah cheentoorah/eel kahnottoa dee sahlvahtahdjoa
ship	la nave	lah naavay

Bicycle hire *Noleggio biciclette*

In many cities of Italy there is the possibility to hire a bicycle. Ask any tourist office for the address of a rental firm.

| I'd like to hire a bicycle. | Vorrei noleggiare una bicicletta. | vorraiee noalaydjaaray oonah beecheeklehttah |

Other means of transport *Altri mezzi di trasporto*

cable car	la funivia	lah fooneeveeah
helicopter	l'elicottero	layleekottayroa
moped	il motorino	eel moatoareenoa
motorbike/scooter	la moto/la motoretta	lah motoa/lah motoarehttah

Or perhaps you prefer:

| to hitchhike | fare l'autostop | faaray lowtoastop |
| to walk | camminare | kahmmeenaaray |

Escursioni

Car *Macchina*

In general roads are good in Italy and Switzerland. Motorways (expressways) are subject to tolls *(il pedaggio)* in Italy. If you use the motorways in Switzerland you must purchase a sticker (valid for one year) to be displayed on the windscreen.

A red reflector warning triangle must be carried for use in case of a breakdown, and seat-belts *(le cinture di sicurezza)* are obligatory in Switzerland.

Where's the nearest filling station?	**Dov'è la stazione di rifornimento più vicina?**	doavai lah stahtseeoanay dee reeforneemayntoa peeoo veecheenah
Full tank, please.	**Il pieno, per favore.**	eel peeainoa pair fahvoaray
Give me ... litres of petrol (gasoline).	**Mi dia ... litri di benzina.**	mee deeah ... leetree dee bayndzeenah
super (premium)/ regular/unleaded/ diesel	**super/normale/ senza piombo/ gasolio**	soopayr/noarmaalay/ sayntsah peeoamboa/ gahzolyoa
Please check the ...	**Per favore, controlli ...**	pair fahvoaray koantroallee
battery brake fluid oil/water	**la batteria l'olio dei freni l'olio/l'acqua**	lah bahttayreeah lolyoa daiee fraynee lolyoa/lahkkwah
Would you check the tyre pressure?	**Può controllare la pressione delle gomme?**	pwo koantroallaaray lah praysseeoanay dayllay goammay
1.6 front, 1.8 rear.	**1,6 davanti, 1,8 dietro.**	oonoa ay sehee dahvahntee oonoa ay ottoa deeehtroa
Please check the spare tyre, too.	**Per favore, controlli anche la ruota di scorta.**	pair fahvoaray koantroallee ahngkay lah rwawtah dee skortah
Can you mend this puncture (fix this flat)?	**Può riparare questa foratura?**	pwo reepahraaray kooaystah forahtoorah
Would you please change the ...?	**Potrebbe cambiare ...**	poatrehbbay kahmbeeaaray
bulb fan belt	**la lampadina la cinghia del ventilatore**	lah lahmpahdeenah lah cheenggeeah dayl vaynteelahtoaray

CAR HIRE, see page 20

spark(ing) plugs	le candele	lay kahndaylay
tyre	la gomma	lah goammah
wipers	i tergicristalli	ee tayrjeekreestahllee
Would you clean the windscreen (windshield)?	Mi pulisca il parabrezza, per favore.	mee pooleeskah eel pahrahbraydzah pair fahvoaray

Asking the way *Per chiedere la strada*

Can you tell me the way to ...?	Può dirmi qual è la strada per ...?	pwo deermee kwahl ai lah straadah pair
How do I get to ...?	Come si va a ...?	koamay see vah ah
Are we on the right road for ...?	Siamo sulla strada giusta per ...?	seeaamoa soollah straadah joostah pair
How far is the next village?	Quanto dista il prossimo villaggio?	kwahntoa deestah eel prosseemoa veellahdjoa
How far is it to ... from here?	Quanto dista ... da qui?	kwahntoa deestah ... dah kooee
Is there a motorway (expressway)?	C'è un'autostrada?	chai oonowtoastraadah
Is there a road with little traffic?	C'è una strada con poco traffico?	chai oonah straadah kon pokoa trahffeekoa
How long does it take by car/on foot?	Quanto tempo ci vuole in macchina/a piedi?	kwahntoa tehmpoa chee vwolay een mahkkeenah/ah peeaydee
Can I drive to the centre of town?	Si può andare in macchina nel centro città?	see pwo ahndaaray een mahkkeenah nayl chayntroa cheettah
Can you tell me, where ... is?	Può dirmi dove si trova ...?	pwo deermee doavay see trawvah
How can I find this place?	Come posso trovare questo posto?	koamay possoa trovaaray kooaystoa poastoa
Where can I find this address?	Dove posso trovare questo indirizzo?	doavay possoa trovaaray kooaystoa eendeereettsoa
Where's this?	Dov'è questo?	doavai kooaystoa
Can you show me on the map where I am?	Può indicarmi sulla carta dove mi trovo?	pwo eendeekaarmee soollah kahrtah doavay mee trawvoa

Lei è sulla strada sbagliata.	You're on the wrong road.
Vada diritto.	Go straight ahead.
È laggiù a ...	It's down there on the ...
sinistra/destra	left/right
di fronte/dietro ...	opposite/behind ...
accanto a/dopo ...	next to/after ...
nord/sud	north/south
est/ovest	east/west
Vada fino al primo/ secondo incrocio.	Go to the first/second crossroad (intersection).
Al semaforo, giri a sinistra.	Turn left at the traffic lights.
Giri a destra al prossimo angolo.	Turn right at the next corner.
Prenda la strada per ...	Take the road for ...
Segua la direzione per Stresa.	Follow the sign for "Stresa".
Deve tornare indietro ...	You have to go back to ...

Parking *Parcheggio*

In town centres, most street parking is limited. The blue zones require the *disco di sosta* or parking disc (obtainable from petrol stations), which you set to show when you arrived and when you must leave.

Where can I park?	Dove posso parcheggiare?	doavay possoa pahrkaydjaaray
Is there a car park nearby?	C'è un parcheggio qui vicino?	chai oon pahrkaydjoa kooee veecheenoa
May I park here?	Posso parcheggiare qui?	possoa pahrkaydjaaray kooee
How long can I park here?	Quanto tempo posso restare qui?	kwahntoa tehmpoa possoa raystaaray kooee
What's the charge per hour?	Quanto si paga all'ora?	kwahntoa see paagah ahlloarah
Do you have some change for the parking meter?	Ha della moneta per il parchimetro?	ah dayllah moanaytah pair eel pahrkeemaytroa

Breakdown—Road assistance   *Guasti—Assistenza stradale*

Where's the nearest garage?	**Dov'è il garage più vicino?**	doavai eel gahraazh peeoo veecheenoa
Excuse me. My car has broken down.	**Mi scusi. Ho un guasto all'automobile.**	mee skoozee. oa oon gwaastoa ahllowtoamawbeelay
May I use your phone?	**Posso usare il suo telefono?**	possoa oozaaray eel sooa taylayfoanoa
I've had a breakdown at ...	**Ho avuto un guasto a ...**	oa ahvootoa oon gwaastoa ah
Can you send a mechanic?	**Può mandare un meccanico?**	pwo mahndaaray oon maykkaaneekoa
My car won't start.	**La mia macchina non parte.**	lah meeah mahkkeenah noan pahrtay
The battery is dead.	**La batteria è scarica.**	lah bahttayreeah ai skaareekah
I've run out of petrol (gasoline).	**Sono rimasto(a) senza benzina.**	soanoa reemahstoa(ah) sayntsah bayndzeenah
I have a flat tyre.	**Ho una gomma sgonfia.**	oa oonah goammah sgoanfeeah
The engine is overheating.	**Il motore è surriscaldato.**	eel moatoaray ai soorreeskahldaatoa
There is something wrong with ...	**Qualcosa non va con ...**	kwahlkawsah noan vah kon
brakes	**i freni**	ee fraynee
carburettor	**il carburatore**	eel kahrboorahtoaray
exhaust pipe	**il tubo di scappamento**	eel tooboa dee skahppahmayntoa
radiator	**il radiatore**	eel rahdeeahtoaray
wheel	**la ruota**	lah rwawtah
Can you send a breakdown van (tow truck)?	**Può mandare un carro attrezzi?**	pwo mahndaaray oon kahrroa attrehttsee
How long will you be?	**Quanto tempo impiegherete?**	kwahntoa tehmpoa eempeeaygayraytay

Accident—Police   *Incidenti—Polizia*

Please call the police.	**Per favore, chiami la polizia.**	pair fahvoaray keeaamee lah poaleetseeah

There's been an accident.	C'è stato un incidente.	chai staatoa oon eencheedayntay
Where's the nearest telephone?	Dov'è il telefono più vicino?	doavai eel taylayfoanoa peeoo veecheenoa
Call a doctor/an ambulance quickly.	Chiami un medico/un'ambulanza, presto.	keeaamee oon maideekoa/oonahmboolahntsah prehstoa
There are people injured.	Ci sono dei feriti.	chee soanoa daiee fayreetee
What's your name and address?	Qual è il suo nome e indirizzo?	kwahl ai eel soooa noamay ay eendeereetsoa
What's your insurance company?	Qual è la sua assicurazione?	kwahl ai lah sooah ahsseekoorahtseeoanay

Road signs *Segnali stradali*

ACCENDERE I FARI IN GALLERIA	Switch on headlights before entering tunnel
ACCOSTARE A DESTRA (SINISTRA)	Keep right (left)
ALT	Stop
AREA DI SERVIZIO	Service area
CADUTA MASSI	Falling rocks
CARABINIERI	Police
CIRCONVALLAZIONE	Ring road (belt highway)
CORSIA D'EMERGENZA	Emergency parking zone
CURVE PER 5 KM.	Bends (curves) for 5 km.
DEVIAZIONE	Diversion/detour
DIVIETO DI SOSTA	No parking
DIVIETO DI SORPASSO	No overtaking (passing)
LAVORI IN CORSO	Road works ahead (men working)
PASSAGGIO A LIVELLO	Level (railroad) crossing
PERICOLO	Danger
POLIZIA STRADALE	Highway police
RALLENTARE	Reduce speed
SENSO UNICO	One way
SOCCORSO A.C.I.	A.C.I. emergency road service
STRADA DISSESTATA	Poor road surface
TRANSITO CON CATENE	Chains required
VICOLO CIECO	Dead end
VIETATO L'ACCESSO	No entry
VIGILI URBANI	City police
ZONA PEDONALE	Pedestrian zone

Sightseeing

Where's the tourist office?	Dov'è l'ufficio turistico?	doavai looffeechoa tooreesteekoa
What are the main points of interest?	Quali sono i principali punti di interesse?	kwaalee soanoa ee preencheepaalee poontee dee eentayrayssay
We're here for ...	Siamo qui per ...	seeaamoa kooee pair
only a few hours	alcune ore soltanto	ahlkoonay oaray soltahntoa
a day	un giorno	oon joarnoa
a week	una settimana	oonah saytteemaanah
Can you recommend a sightseeing tour/an excursion?	Può consigliare un giro turistico/una gita?	pwo konseelyaaray oon jeeroa tooreesteekoa/ oonah jeetah
What's the point of departure?	Da dove si parte?	dah doavay see pahrtay
Will the bus pick us up at the hotel?	Il pullman passerà a prenderci all'hotel?	eel poolmahn pahssayrah ah prehndehrchee ahllotehl
How much does the tour cost?	Quanto costa il giro?	kwahntoa koastah eel jeeroa
What time does the tour start?	A che ora inizia il giro?	ah kay oarah eeneetseeah eel jeeroa
Is lunch included?	Il pranzo è compreso?	eel prahndzoa ai koampraysoa
What time do we get back?	A che ora si ritorna?	ah kay oarah see reetoarnah
Do we have free time in ...?	Avremo del tempo libero a ...?	ahvraymoa dayl tehmpoa leebayroa ah
Is there an English-speaking guide?	C'è una guida che parla inglese?	chai oonah gooeedah kay pahrlah eengglaysay
I'd like to hire a private guide for ...	Vorrei avere una guida privata per ...	vorraiee ahvayray oonah gooeedah preevaatah pair
half a day	mezza giornata	mehddzah joarnaatah
a full day	una giornata intera	oonah joarnaatah eentayrah

Where is/Where are the ...?	Dove si trova/Dove si trovano ...?	doavay see trawvah/ doavay see trawvahnoa
abbey	l'abbazia	lahbbahtseeah
art gallery	la galleria d'arte	lah gahllayreeah dahrtay
artists' quarter	il quartiere degli artisti	eel kwahrteeayray daylyee ahrteestee
botanical gardens	i giardini botanici	ee jahrdeenee botaa- neechee
building	l'edificio	laydeefeechoa
business district	il quartiere degli affari	eel kwahrteeayray daylyee ahffaaree
castle	il castello	eel kahstehlloa
catacombs	le catacombe	lay kahtahkombay
cathedral	la cattedrale	lah kahttaydraalay
cave	la grotta	lah grottah
cemetery	il cimitero	eel cheemeetairoa
city centre	il centro città	eel chayntroa cheettah
chapel	la cappella	lah kahppehllah
church	la chiesa	lah keeayzah
concert hall	la sala dei concerti	lah saalah daiee kon- chehrtee
convent	il convento	eel konvayntoa
court house	il palazzo di giustizia	eel pahlahttsoa dee joosteetseeah
downtown area	il centro (città)	eel chayntroa (cheettah)
exhibition	l'esposizione	layspozeetseeoanay
factory	la fabbrica	lah fahbbreekah
fair	la fiera	lah feeayrah
flea market	il mercato delle pulci	eel mehrkaatoa dayllay poolchee
fortress	la fortezza	lah fortehttsah
fountain	la fontana	lah foantaanah
gardens	i giardini	ee jahrdeenee
harbour	il porto	eel portoa
lake	il lago	eel laagoa
library	la biblioteca	lah beebleeotaikah
market	il mercato	eel mayrkaatoa
memorial	il memoriale	eel maymoareeaalay
monastery	il monastero	eel moanahstairoa
monument	il monumento	eel moanoomayntoa
museum	il museo	eel moozaioa
old town	la città vecchia	lah cheettah vehkkeeah
opera house	il teatro dell'opera	eel tayaatroa dayllopayrah
palace	il palazzo	eel pahlahttsoa
park	il parco	eel pahrkoa
parliament building	il Parlamento	eel pahrlahmayntoa

planetarium	il planetario	eel plahnaytaareeoa
royal palace	il palazzo reale	eel pahlahttsoa rayaalay
ruins	le rovine	lay roveenay
shopping area	la zona dei negozi	lah dzonah daiee naygotsee
square	la piazza	lah peeahtsah
stadium	lo stadio	loa staadeeoa
statue	la statua	lah staatooah
stock exchange	la borsa valori	lah borsah vahloaree
theatre	il teatro	eel tayaatroa
tomb	la tomba	lah toambah
tower	la torre	lah toarray
town hall	il municipio	eel mooneecheepeeoa
university	l'università	looneevayrseetah
zoo	lo zoo	loa dzoo

Admission *All'entrata*

Is ... open on Sundays?	È aperto la domenica il ...?	ai ahpehrtoa lah doamayneekah eel
When does it open?	Quando apre?	kwahndoa aapray
When does it close?	Quando chiude?	kwahndoa keeooday
How much is the entrance fee?	Quanto costa l'entrata?	kwahntoa kostah layntraatah
Is there any reduction for ...?	C'è una riduzione per ...?	chai oonah reedootseeoanay pair
children	i bambini	ee bahmbeenee
disabled	gli andicappati	lyee ahndeekahppaatee
groups	i gruppi	ee grooppee
pensioners	i pensionati	ee paynseeoanaatee
students	gli studenti	lyee stoodayntee
Have you a guide-book (in English)?	Avete una guida turistica (in inglese)?	ahvaytay oonah gooeedah tooreesteekah (een eeengglaysay)
Can I buy a catalogue?	Posso comprare un catalogo?	possoa koampraaray oon kahtaaloagoa
Is it all right to take pictures?	È permesso fare delle fotografie?	ai pehrmayssoa faaray dayllay foatoagrahfeeay

---

| **ENTRATA LIBERA** | ADMISSION FREE |
| **VIETATO FOTOGRAFARE** | NO CAMERAS ALLOWED |

Who—What—When? *Chi—Cosa—Quando?*

What's that building?	**Che cos'è quest'edificio?**	kay kosai kooaystaydee-feechoa
Who was the ...?	**Chi è stato ...?**	kee ai staatoa
architect	**l'architetto**	lahrkeetehttoa
artist	**l'artista**	lahrteestah
painter	**il pittore**	eel peettoaray
sculptor	**lo scultore**	loa skooltoaray
Who built it?	**Chi lo costruì?**	kee loa koastrooee
Who painted that picture?	**Chi dipinse questo quadro?**	kee deepeensay kooaystoa kwaadroa
When did he live?	**Quando è vissuto?**	kwahndoa ai veessootoa
When was it built?	**Quando fu costruito?**	kwahndoa foo koastrooeetoa
Where's the house where ... lived?	**Dove si trova la casa in cui visse ...?**	doavay see trawvah lah kaasah een kooee veessay
We're interested in ...	**Ci interessiamo di ...**	chee eentayraysseeaamoa dee
antiques	**antichità**	ahnteekeetah
archaeology	**archeologia**	ahrkayoaloajeeah
art	**arte**	ahrtay
botany	**botanica**	botaaneekah
ceramics	**ceramiche**	chayraameekay
coins	**monete**	monaitay
fine arts	**belle arti**	behllay ahrtee
furniture	**mobilio**	mobeelyoa
geology	**geologia**	jayoaloajeeah
handicrafts	**artigianato**	ahrteejahnaatoa
history	**storia**	storeeah
medicine	**medicina**	maydeecheenah
music	**musica**	moozeekah
natural history	**storia naturale**	storeeah nahtooraalay
ornithology	**ornitologia**	oarneetoaloajeeah
painting	**pittura**	peettoorah
pottery	**terrecotte**	tehrraykottay
prehistory	**preistoria**	prayeestoreeah
religion	**religione**	rayleejoanay
sculpture	**scultura**	skooltoorah
zoology	**zoologia**	dzoaoaloajeeah
Where's the ... department?	**Dov'è il reparto di/del ...?**	doavai eel raypahrtoa dee/dayl

It's ...	È ...	ai
amazing	**sorprendente**	soarprayn**dehn**tay
awful	**orribile**	orree**bee**lay
beautiful	**bello**	**behl**loa
excellent	**eccellente**	ehtchehl**layn**tay
gloomy	**malinconico**	mahleengkaw**nee**koa
impressive	**impressionante**	eemprayssee**oanahn**tay
interesting	**interessante**	eentayrays**sahn**tay
magnificent	**magnifico**	mah**ñee**feekoa
nice	**bello**	**behl**loa
overwhelming	**sbalorditivo**	sbahloardee**tee**voa
strange	**strano**	**straa**noa
superb	**superbo**	soo**pehr**boa
terrifying	**terrificante**	tayrreefee**kahn**tay
tremendous	**fantastico**	fahn**tahs**teekoa
ugly	**brutto**	**broot**toa

Religious services   *Funzioni religiose*

Most churches and cathedrals are open to the public, except, of course, during mass.

If you are interested in taking pictures, you should obtain permission first. Shorts and backless dresses are definitely out when visiting churches.

Is there a/an ... near here?	**C'è una ... qui vicino?**	chai **oo**nah ... **koo**ee vee**chee**noa
Catholic church	**chiesa cattolica**	kee**ay**zah kaht**toa**leekah
Protestant church	**chiesa protestante**	kee**ay**zah proatay**stahn**tay
synagogue	**sinagoga**	seenah**gaw**gah
mosque	**moschea**	moa**skai**ah
At what time is ...?	**A che ora è ...?**	ah kay **oa**rah ai
mass	**la messa**	lah **mays**sah
the service	**la funzione**	lah foontsee**oa**nay
Where can I find a ... who speaks English?	**Dove posso trovare un ... che parla inglese?**	**doa**vay **pos**soa troa**vaa**ray oon ... kay **pahr**lah eeng**glay**say
priest/minister	**prete/pastore**	**prai**tay/pahs**toa**ray
rabbi	**rabbino**	rahb**bee**noa
I'd like to visit the church.	**Vorrei visitare la chiesa.**	vor**rai**ee veezee**taa**ray lah kee**ay**zah

In the countryside *In campagna*

Is there a scenic route to ...?	C'è una strada panoramica per ...?	chai oonah straadah pahnoaraameekah pair
How far is it to ...?	Quanto dista ...?	kwahntoa deestah
Can we walk?	Possiamo andare a piedi?	posseeaamoa ahndaaray ah peeaydee
How high is that mountain?	Quanto è alta quella montagna?	kwahntoa ai ahltah kooayllah moantaañah
What's the name of that ...?	Come si chiama questo ...?	koamay see keeaamah kooaystoa
animal/bird	animale/uccello	ahneemaalay/ootchehlloa
flower/tree	fiore/albero	feeoaray/ahlbayroa

Landmarks *Punti di riferimento*

bridge	il ponte	eel poantay
cliff	la scogliera	lah skoalyayrah
farm	la fattoria	lah fahttoareeah
field	il campo	eel kahmpoa
footpath	il sentiero	eel saynteeayroa
forest	la foresta	lah fawrehstah
garden	il giardino	eel jahrdeenoa
hamlet	il gruppo di casolari	eel grooppoa dee kahsoalaaree
hill	la collina	lah koalleenah
house	la casa	lah kaasah
lake	il lago	eel laagoa
meadow	il prato	eel praatoa
mountain	la montagna	lah moantaañah
(mountain) pass	il passo	eel pahssoa
peak	il picco	eel peekkoa
pond	lo stagno	loa staañoa
river	il fiume	eel feeoomay
road	la strada	lah straadah
sea	il mare	eel maaray
spring	la sorgente	lah soarjayntay
valley	la valle	lah vahllay
village	il villaggio/il paese	eel veellahdjoa/eel pahayzay
vineyard	la vigna	lah veeñah
wall	il muro	eel mooroa
waterfall	la cascata	lah kahskaatah
well	il pozzo	eel poatsoa
wood	il bosco	eel boaskoa

ASKING THE WAY, see page 76

Relaxing

Cinema (movies) — Theatre   *Cinema — Teatro*

You can find out what's playing from newspapers and bill-boards. In Rome and in the main towns in Italy look for the weekly entertainment guides available at major newsstands, at the tourist office and the hotel reception.

What's showing at the cinema tonight?	**Cosa danno al cinema questa sera?**	kawsah dahnnoa ahl cheenaymah kooaystah sayrah
What's playing at the ... theatre?	**Che spettacolo c'è al teatro ...?**	kay spayttaakoaloa chai ahl tayaatroa
What sort of play is it?	**Che genere di commedia è?**	kay jainayray dee koammaideeah ai
Who's it by?	**Di chi è?**	dee kee ai
Can you recommend (a) ...?	**Può consigliarmi ...?**	pwo konseelyaarmee
good film	**un buon film**	oon bwawn "film"
comedy	**una commedia**	oonah koammaideeah
musical	**una commedia musicale**	oonah koammaideeah moozeekaalay
Where's that new film by ... being shown?	**In che cinema danno il nuovo film di ...?**	een kay cheenaymah dahnnoa eel nwovoa "film" dee
Who's in it?	**Chi sono gli attori?**	kee soanoa lyee ahttoaree
Who's playing the lead?	**Chi interpreta il ruolo principale?**	kee eentehrprehtah eel rwoloa preencheepaalay
Who's the director?	**Chi è il regista?**	kee ai eel rayjeestah
At what theatre is that new play by ... being performed?	**In quale teatro viene rappresentata la nuova commedia di ...?**	een kwaalay tayaatroa veeaynay rahppraysayntaatah lah nwovah koammaideeah dee
Is there a sound-and-light show on somewhere?	**C'è uno spettacolo suoni e luci da qualche parte?**	chai oonoa spayttaakoaloa swonee ay loochee dah kwahlkay paartay

What time does it begin?	**A che ora incomincia?**	ah kay oarah eengkoameenchah
Are there any seats for tonight?	**Ci sono posti per questa sera?**	chee soanoa postee pair kooaystah sayrah
How much are the seats?	**Quanto costano i posti?**	kwahntoa kostahnoa ee postee
I want to reserve 2 seats for the show on Friday evening.	**Desidero prenotare 2 posti per lo spettacolo di venerdì sera.**	dayzeedayroa praynoataaray 2 postee pair loa spayttaakoaloa dee vaynayrdee sayrah
Can I have a ticket for the matinée on Tuesday?	**Posso avere un biglietto per lo spettacolo del pomeriggio di martedì?**	possoa ahvayray oon beelyayttoa pair loa spayttaakoaloa dayl poamayreedjoa dee mahrtaydee?
I want a seat in the stalls (orchestra).	**Desidero una poltrona.**	dayzeedayroa oonah poaltroanah
Not too far back.	**Non troppo indietro.**	noan troppoa eendeeaytroa
Somewhere in the middle.	**A metà circa.**	ah maytah cheerkah
How much are the seats in the circle (mezzanine)?	**Quanto costano i posti in galleria?**	kwahntoa kostahnoa ee postee een gahllayreeah
May I please have a programme?	**Per favore, posso avere un programma?**	pair fahvoaray possoa ahvayray oon prograhmmah
Where's the cloakroom?	**Dov'è il guardaroba?**	doavai eel gwahrdahrobah

Sono spiacente, è tutto esaurito.	I'm sorry, we're sold out.
Vi sono solo alcuni posti in galleria.	There are only a few seats left in the circle (mezzanine).
Posso vedere il suo biglietto?	May I see your ticket?*
Questo è il suo posto.	This is your seat.

---

* It's customary to tip usherettes *(la maschera)* in most Italian theatres.

DAYS OF THE WEEK, see page 151

Opera—Ballet—Concert *Opera—Balletto—Concerto*

Can you recommend a ...?	Può consigliarmi ...?	pwo konseelyahrmee
ballet	un balletto	oon bahllehttoa
concert	un concerto	oon koancehrtoa
opera	un'opera	oonopayrah
operetta	un'operetta	oonopayrayttah
Where's the opera house/the concert hall?	Dov'è il teatro dell'opera/la sala dei concerti?	doavai eel tayaatroa dayllopayrah/lah saalah daiee koancehrtee
What's on at the opera tonight?	Cosa danno all'Opera questa sera?	kawsah dahnnoa ahllopayrah kooaystah sayrah
Who's singing/dancing?	Chi canta/balla?	kee kahntah/bahllah
What orchestra is playing?	Che orchestra suona?	kay oarkaystrah swonah
What are they playing?	Cosa suonano?	kawsah swonahnoa
Who's the conductor/soloist?	Chi è il maestro/il solista?	kee ai eel mahehstroa/eel soleestah

Nightclub *Night-club*

Can you recommend a good nightclub?	Può consigliarmi un buon night-club?	pwo konseelyahrmee oon bwon "night-club"
Is there a floor show?	C'è il varietà?	chai eel vahreeaytah
What time does the floor show start?	A che ora inizia il varietà?	ah kay oarah eeneetseeah eel vahreeaytah
Is evening dress necessary?	È necessario l'abito da sera?	ai naychayssaareeoa laabeetoa dah sayrah

Discos *Discoteche*

Where can we go dancing?	Dove possiamo andare a ballare?	doavay posseeaamoa ahndaaray ah bahllaaray
Is there a discotheque in town?	C'è una discoteca in città?	chai oonah deeskoataykah een cheettah
Would you like to dance?	Vuole ballare?	vwolay bahllaaray

Sports *Sport*

Football (soccer), tennis, boxing, wrestling and bicycle, car and horse racing are among popular spectator sports. If you like sailing, fishing, horseback riding, golf, tennis, hiking, cycling, swimming, golf or trap shooting, you'll find plenty of opportunity to satisfy your recreational bent.

Is there a football (soccer) match anywhere this Saturday?	C'è una partita di calcio da qualche parte, sabato?	chai oonah pahrteetah dee kahlchoa dah kwahlkay pahrtay saabahtoa
Which teams are playing?	Che squadre giocano?	kay skwaadray joakahnoa
Can you get me a ticket?	Mi può procurare un biglietto?	mee pwo proakooraaray oon beelyayttoa

basketball	la pallacanestro	lah pahllahkahnehstroa
boxing	il pugilato	eel poojeelaatoa
car racing	la corsa automobilistica	lah koarsah owtoamoabeeleesteeka
cycling	il ciclismo	eel cheekleezmoa
football (soccer)	il calcio	eel kahlchoa
horse racing	la corsa di cavalli	lah koarsah dee kahvahllee
skiing	lo sci	loa shee
swimming	il nuoto	eel nwotoa
tennis	il tennis	eel "tennis"
volleyball	la pallavolo	lah pahllahvoaloa

I'd like to see a boxing match.	Vorrei vedere un incontro di pugilato.	vorraiee vaydayray oon eengkoantroa dee poojeelaatoa
What's the admission charge?	Quanto costa l'entrata?	kwahntoa kostah layntraatah
Where's the nearest golf course?	Dove si trova il campo da golf più vicino?	doavay see trawvah eel kahmpoa dah golf peeoo veecheenoa
Where are the tennis courts?	Dove sono i campi da tennis?	doavay soanoa ee kahmpee dah "tennis"
What's the charge per ...?	Qual è il prezzo per ...?	kwahl ai eel prehttsoa pair
day/round/hour	un giorno/una partita/un'ora	oon joarnoa/oonah pahrteetah/oonoarah

Can I hire (rent) rackets?	**Posso noleggiare le racchette?**	possoa noalaydjaaray lay rahkkehttay
Where is the race course (track)?	**Dov'è l'ippodromo?**	doavai leeppoadrawmoa
Is there any good fishing around here?	**Ci sono buone possibilità di pesca in questa zona?**	chee soanoa bwawnay posseebeeleetah dee payskah een kooaystah dzoanah
Do I need a permit?	**È necessario il permesso?**	ai naychayssaareeoa eel payrmayssoa
Where can I get one?	**Dove posso procurarmene uno?**	doavay possoa proakoorahrmaynay oonoa
Can one swim in the lake/river?	**Si può nuotare nel lago/fiume?**	see pwo nwawtaaray nayl laagoa/feeoomay
Is there a swimming pool here?	**C'è una piscina qui?**	chai oonah peesheenah kooee
Is it open-air or indoor?	**È una piscina all'aperto o coperta?**	ai oonah peesheenah ahllahpehrtoa oa koapehrtah
Is it heated?	**È riscaldata?**	ai reeskahldaatah
What's the temperature of the water?	**Qual è la temperatura dell'acqua?**	kwahl ai lah taympayrahtoorah dayllahkkwah
Is there a sandy beach?	**C'è una spiaggia di sabbia?**	chai oonah speeahdjah dee sahbbeeah

On the beach   *In spiaggia*

Is it safe for swimming?	**Si può nuotare senza pericolo?**	see pwo nwawtaaray sayntsah payreekoaloa
Is there a lifeguard?	**C'è un bagnino?**	chai oon bahñeenoa
There are some big waves.	**Ci sono cavalloni.**	chee soanoa kahvahlloanee
Is it safe for children?	**È sicuro per i bambini?**	ai seekooroa pair ee bahmbeenee
Are there any dangerous currents?	**Vi sono correnti pericolose?**	vee soanoa koarrayntee payreekoaloasay
What time is high tide/low tide?	**A che ora è l'alta marea/la bassa marea?**	ah kay oarah ai lahltah mahrayah/lah bahssah mahrayah

I want to hire a/an/ some ...	**Vorrei noleggiare ...**	vorraiee noalaydjaaray
bathing hut (cabana)	**una cabina**	oonah kahbeenah
deck-chair	**una sedia a sdraio**	oonah saydeeah ah sdraaeeoa
motorboat	**una barca a motore**	oonah bahrkah ah motoaray
rowing-boat	**una barca a remi**	oonah bahrkah ah raymee
sailboard	**una tavola a vela**	oonah taavolah ah vailah
sailing-boat	**una barca a vela**	oonah bahrkah ah vailah
sunshade (umbrella)	**un ombrellone**	oon oambraylloanay
surfboard	**un sandolino**	oon sahndoaleenoa
water-skis	**degli sci nautici**	daylyee shee nowteechee

SPIAGGIA PRIVATA	PRIVATE BEACH
DIVIETO DI BALNEAZIONE	NO SWIMMING

Winter sports   *Sport invernali*

Is there a skating rink near here?	**C'è una pista di pattinaggio qui vicino?**	chai oonah peestah dee pahtteenadjoa kooee veecheenoa
I'd like to ski.	**Vorrei sciare.**	vorraiee sheeaaray
downhill/cross-country skiing	**sci di pista/sci di fondo**	shee dee peestah/shee dee foandoa
Are there any ski runs for ...?	**Vi sono delle piste per ...?**	vee soanoa dayllay peestay pair
beginners	**principianti**	preencheepeeahntee
average skiers	**sciatori medi**	sheeahtoaree maydee
good skiers	**buoni sciatori**	bwawnee sheeahtoaree
Can I take skiing lesson there?	**Posso prendere delle lezioni di sci?**	possoa prehndayray dayllay laytseeoanee dee shee
Are there ski lifts?	**Ci sono delle sciovie?**	chee soanoa dayllay sheeoveeai
I want to hire a/ some ...	**Vorrei noleggiare ...**	vorraiee noalaydjaaray
poles	**dei bastoni**	daiee bahstoanee
skates	**dei pattini**	daiee pahtteenee
ski boots	**degli scarponi da sci**	daylyee skahrpoanee dah shee
skiing equipment	**una tenuta da sci**	oonah taynootah dah shee
skis	**degli sci**	daylyee shee

Making friends

Introductions *Presentazioni*

May I introduce ...?	**Posso presentarle ...?**	possoa prayzayntaarlay
John, this is ...	**Giovanni, ti presento ...**	jovahnnee tee prayzayntoa
My name is ...	**Mi chiamo ...**	mee keeaamoa
Pleased to meet you.	**Piacere.**	peeahchayray
What's your name?	**Come si chiama?**	koamay see keeaamah
How are you?	**Come sta?**	koamay stah
Fine, thanks. And you?	**Bene, grazie. E lei?**	bainay graatseeay. ay laiee

Follow-up *Per rompere il ghiaccio*

How long have you been here?	**Da quanto tempo è qui?**	dah kwahntoa tehmpoa ai kooee
We've been here a week.	**Siamo qui da una settimana.**	seeaamoa kooee dah oonah saytteemaanah
Is this your first visit?	**È la prima volta che viene?**	ai lah preemah voltah kay veeaynay
No, we came here last year.	**No, siamo già venuti l'anno scorso.**	noa seeaamoa jah vaynootee lahnnoa skoarsoa
Are you enjoying your stay?	**Le piace il suo soggiorno?**	lay peeaachay eel sooo soadjoarnoa
Yes, I like it very much.	**Sì, mi piace molto.**	see mee peeaachay moaltoa
I like the landscape a lot.	**Mi piace molto il paesaggio.**	mee peeaachay moaltoa eel pahayzahdjoa
Do you travel a lot?	**Viaggia molto?**	veeahdjah moaltoa
Where do you come from?	**Da dove viene?**	dah doavay veeaynay
I'm from ...	**Sono di ...**	soanoa dee
What nationality are you?	**Di che nazionalità è?**	dee kai nahtseeoanahleetah ai

COUNTRIES, see page 146

I'm ...	Sono ...	soanoa
American	americano(a)	ahmayreekaanoa(ah)
British	britannico(a)	breetahnneekoa(ah)
Canadian	canadese	kahnahdaysay
English	inglese	eengglaysay
Irish	irlandese	eerlahndaysay
Scottish	scozzese	skotsaysay
Where are you staying?	Dove soggiorna?	doavay soadjoarnah
Are you on your own?	È solo(a)?	ai soaloa(ah)
I'm with my ...	Sono con ...	soanoa kon
wife	mia moglie	meeah moalyay
husband	mio marito	meeoa mahreetoa
family	la mia famiglia	lah meeah fahmeelyah
parents	i miei genitori	ee meeaiee jayneetoaree
boyfriend	il mio ragazzo	eel meeoa rahgahttsoa
girlfriend	la mia ragazza	lah meeah rahgahttsah

grandfather/ grandmother	il nonno/la nonna	eel nonnoa/la nonnah
father/mother	il padre/la madre	eel paadray/lah maadray
son/daughter	il figlio/la figlia	eel feelyoa/lah feelyah
brother/sister	il fratello/la sorella	eel frahtehlloa/lah sorehllah
uncle/aunt	lo zio/la zia	loa dzeeoa/lah dzeeah
nephew/niece	il nipote/la nipote	eel neepoatay/lah neepoatay
cousin	il cugino/la cugina	eel koojeenoa/lah koojeenah

Are you married/ single?	È sposato(a)/scapolo (nubile)?	ai spozaatoa(ah)/skaapoa-loa (noobeelay)
Do you have children?	Ha dei bambini?	ah daiee bahmbeenee
What do you think of the country/people?	Cosa pensa del paese/della gente?	kawsah paynsah dayl pahaysay/dayllah jayntay
What do you do?	Che lavoro fa?	kay lahvoaroa fah
I'm a student.	Sono studente.	soanoa stoodehntay
I'm here on a business trip.	Sono qui in viaggio d'affari.	soanoa kooee een veeahdjoa dahffaaree
Do you play cards/ chess?	Gioca a carte/a scacchi?	joakah ah kahrtay/ah skahkkee

The weather   *Il tempo*

What a lovely day!	**Che bella giornata!**	kay behllah joarnaatah
What awful weather!	**Che tempo orribile!**	kay tehmpoa orreebeelay
Isn't it cold/hot today?	**Che freddo/caldo fa oggi!**	kay frehddoa/kahldoa fah odjee
Is it usually as warm as this?	**Fa sempre caldo così?**	fah sehmpray kahldoa kawsee
Do you think it's going to ... to-morrow?	**Pensa che do-mani ...?**	paynsah kay domaanee
be a nice day	**sarà una bella giornata**	sahrah oonah behllah joarnaatah
rain	**pioverà**	peeovayrah
snow	**nevicherà**	nayveekayrah
What is the weather forecast?	**Come sono le previsioni del tempo?**	koamay soanoa lay preh-veezeeoanee dayl tehmpoa

cloud	**la nuvola**	lah noovolah
fog	**la nebbia**	lah nehbbeeah
frost	**il gelo**	eel jayloa
ice	**il ghiaccio**	eel geeahtchoa
lightning	**il lampo**	eel lahmpoa
moon	**la luna**	lah loonah
rain	**la pioggia**	lah peeodjah
sky	**il cielo**	eel chayloa
snow	**la neve**	lah nayvay
star	**la stella**	lah stayllah
sun	**il sole**	eel soalay
thunder	**il tuono**	eel twonoa
thunderstorm	**il temporale**	eel tehmpoaraalay
wind	**il vento**	eel vayntoa

Invitations   *Inviti*

Would you like to have dinner with us on ...?	**Vorrebbe cenare con noi ...?**	vorrehbbay chaynaaray kon noaee
May I invite you for lunch?	**Posso invitarla a pranzo?**	possoa-eenveetaarlah ah prahndzoa

DAYS OF THE WEEK, see page 151

Can you come over for a drink this evening?	Può venire a bere un bicchiere da me questa sera?	pwo vayneeray ah bayray oon beekkeeayray dah mai kooaystah sayrah
There's a party. Are you coming?	C'è un ricevimento. Viene?	chai oon reechayvee-mayntoa. veeaynay
That's very kind of you.	È molto gentile da parte sua.	ai moaltoa jaynteelay dah pahrtay sooah
I'd love to come.	Verrò con piacere.	vayrro kon peeahchayray
What time shall we come?	A che ora dobbiamo venire?	ah kay oarah doab-beeaamoa vayneeray
May I bring a friend?	Posso portare un amico (un'amica)?	possoa portaaray oon ahmeekoa (oonahmeekah)
I'm afraid we've got to go now.	Mi dispiace, ma adesso dobbiamo andare.	mee deespeeaachay mah ahdehssoa doabbeeaamoa ahndaaray
Next time you must come to visit us.	La prossima volta dovete venire da noi.	lah prosseemah voltah doavaytay vayneeray dah noaee
Thanks for the evening. It was great.	Grazie per la serata. È stata splendida.	graatseeay pair la say-raatah. ai staatah splehndeedah

Dating *Appuntamento*

Do you mind if I smoke?	La disturbo se fumo?	lah deestoorboa say foomoa
Would you like a cigarette?	Posso offrirle una sigaretta?	possoa offreerlay oonah seegahrayttah
Do you have a light, please?	Ha un fiammifero, per favore?	ah oon feeahmmeefayroa pair fahvoaray
Why are you laughing?	Perchè ride?	payrkai reeday
Is my Italian that bad?	È così cattivo il mio italiano?	ai kosee kahtteevoa eel meeoa eetahleeaanoa
Do you mind if I sit down here?	Permette che mi sieda qui?	pehrmayttay kay mee seeaydah kooee
Can I get you a drink?	Posso offrirle qualcosa da bere?	possoa offreerlay kwahlkawsah dah bayray
Are you waiting for someone?	Aspetta qualcuno?	ahspayttah kwahlkoonoa

Are you free this evening?	È libera stasera?	ai leebayrah stahsayrah
Would you like to go out with me tonight?	Uscirebbe con me stasera?	oosheerehbbay kon mai stahsayrah
Would you like to go dancing?	Le piacerebbe andare a ballare?	lay peeahchayrehbbay ahndaaray ah bahllaaray
I know a good discotheque.	Conosco una buona discoteca.	koanoaskoa oonah bwawnah deeskoataykah
Shall we go to the cinema (movies)?	Andiamo al cinema?	ahndeeaamoa ahl cheenaymah
Would you like to go for a drive?	Andiamo a fare un giro in macchina?	ahndeeaamoa ah faaray oon jeeroa een mahkkeenah
Where shall we meet?	Dove possiamo incontrarci?	doavay posseeaamoa eengkontraarchee
I'll pick you up at your hotel.	Passerò a prenderla all'albergo.	pahssayroa ah prayndayrlah ahllahlbehrgoa
I'll call for you at 8.	Passerò da lei alle 8.	pahssayroa dah laiee ahllay 8
May I take you home?	Posso accompagnarla a casa?	possoa ahkkoampahñaarlah ah kaasah
Can I see you again tomorrow?	Posso rivederla domani?	possoa reevaydayrlah doamaanee
What's your telephone number?	Qual è il suo numero di telefono?	kwahl ai eel soooa noomayroa dee taylaifoanoa

... and you might answer:

I'd love to, thank you.	Con piacere, grazie.	kon peeahchayray graatseeay
Thank you, but I'm busy.	Grazie, ma sono impegnato(a).	graatseeay mah soanoa eempayñaatoa(ah)
No, I'm not interested, thank you.	No, non mi interessa, grazie.	no noan mee eentayrehssah graatseeay
Leave me alone!	Mi lasci in pace!	mee lahshee een paachay
Thank you, it's been a wonderful evening.	Grazie, è stata una magnifica serata.	graatseeay ai staatah oonah mahñeefeekah sayraatah
I've enjoyed myself.	Mi sono divertito(a) molto.	mee soanoa deevayrteetoa(ah) moaltoa

Shopping guide

This shopping guide is designed to help you find what you want with ease, accuracy and speed. It features:

1. A list of all major shops, stores and services (p. 98);
2. Some general expressions required when shopping to allow you to be specific and selective (p. 100);
3. Full details of the shops and services most likely to concern you. Here you'll find advice, alphabetical lists of items and conversion charts listed under the headings below.

		Page
Bookshop/ Stationer's	books, magazines, newspapers, stationery	104
Camping equipment	all items required for camping	106
Chemist's (drugstore)	medicine, first-aid, cosmetics, toilet articles	108
Clothing	clothes, accessories, shoes	112
Electrical appliances	radios, cassette-recorders, shavers	119
Grocery	some general expressions, weights, measures and packaging	120
Jeweller's/ Watchmaker's	jewellery, watches, watch repairs	121
Optician	glasses, lenses, binoculars	123
Photography	cameras, films, developing accessories	124
Tobacconist's	smoker's supplies	126
Miscellaneous	souvenirs, records, cassettes, toys	127

LAUNDRY, see page 29/HAIRDRESSER, see page 30

Guida degli acquisti

Shops, stores and services   *Negozi e servizi*

Shop hours in Italy differ from summer to winter. In winter
the shops are generally open from 8 a.m. to 7 p.m. with a
lunch break between 1 and 3 p.m. During the tourist season,
shops open and close later in the afternoon (4 to 8 p.m.).
Some remain open on Sundays but most close a half day during
the week—often Monday morning or Thursday afternoon.

Swiss shops are open from 8 a.m. to noon or 12.30 p.m. and
from 1.30 to 6.30 or 7 p.m. (Saturdays until 5 p.m.) with
half-day closings similar to Italy.

Where's the nearest ...?	Dove si trova ... più vicino(a)?	doavay see trawvah ... peeoo veecheenoa(ah)
antique shop	l'antiquario	lahnteekwaareeoa
art gallery	la galleria d'arte	lah gahllayreeah dahrtay
baker's	la panetteria	lah pahnehttayreeah
bank	la banca	lah bahngkah
barber's	il barbiere	eel bahrbeeayray
beauty salon	l'istituto di bellezza	leesteetootoa dee behllehttsah
bookshop	la libreria	lah leebrayreeah
butcher's	la macelleria	lah mahchayllayreeah
cake shop	la pasticceria	lah pahsteetchayreeah
camera shop	il negozio d'apparecchi fotografici	eel naygotseeoa dahppahrehkkee foatoagraafeechee
chemist's	la farmacia	lah fahrmahcheeah
confectioner's	la pasticceria	lah pahsteetchayreeah
dairy	la latteria	lah lahttayreeah
delicatessen	la salumeria	lah sahloomayreeah
department store	il grande magazzino	eel grahnday mahgahdzeenoa
drugstore	la farmacia	lah fahrmahcheeah
dry cleaner's	la lavanderia a secco	lah lahvahndayreeah ah saykkoa
electrician	l'elettricista	laylehttreecheestah
fishmonger's	la pescheria	lah payskayreeah
flower shop	il fiorista	eel feeoareestah
furrier's	la pellicceria	lah paylleetchayreeah
greengrocer's	il negozio di frutta e verdura	eel naygotseeoa dee froottah ay vehrdoorah
grocery	il negozio di alimentari	eel naygotseeoa dee ahleemayntaaree
hairdresser's	il parrucchiere	eel pahrrookkeeayray

hardware store	il negozio di ferramenta	eel naygotseeoa dee fehrrahmayntah
health food shop	il negozio di cibi dietetici	eel naygotseeoa dee cheebeeh deeaytayteechee
ironmonger's	il negozio di ferramenta	eel naygotseeoa dee fehrrahmayntah
jeweller's	la gioielleria	lah joeeayllayreeah
launderette	la lavanderia automatica	lah lahvahndayreeah owtoamaateekah
laundry	la lavanderia	la lahvahndayreeah
library	la biblioteca	lah beebleeoataykah
market	il mercato	eel mayrkaatoa
newsagent's	il giornalaio	eel joarnahlaaeeoa
newsstand	l'edicola	laydeekoalah
optician	l'ottico	lotteekoa
pastry shop	la pasticceria	lah pahsteetchayreeah
photographer	il fotografo	eel foatoagrahfoa
police station	il posto di polizia	eel poastoa dee poaleetseeah
post office	l'ufficio postale	looffeechoa poastaalay
shoemaker's (repairs)	il calzolaio	eel kahltsoalaaeeoa
shoe shop	il negozio di scarpe	eel naygotseeoa dee skahrpay
souvenir shop	il negozio di ricordi	eel naygotseeoa dee reekordee
sporting goods shop	il negozio di articoli sportivi	eel naygotseeoa dee ahrteekoalee sporteevee
stationer's	la cartoleria	lah kahrtoalayreeah
supermarket	il supermercato	eel soopairmayrkaatoa
tailor's	la sartoria	lah sahrtoreeah
tobacconist's	la tabaccheria	lah tahbahkkayreeah
toy shop	il negozio di giocattoli	eel naygotseeoa dee joakahttoalee
travel agency	l'agenzia di viaggi	lahjayntseeah dee veeaahdjee
vegetable store	il negozio di frutta e verdura	eel naygotseeoa dee froottah ay vehrdoorah
watchmaker's	l'orologiaio	loaroaloajaaeeoa
wine merchant	il vinaio	eel veenaaeeoa

ENTRATA	ENTRANCE
USCITA	EXIT
USCITA DI SICUREZZA	EMERGENCY EXIT

General expressions *Espressioni generali*

Where? *Dove?*

Where's a good ...?	**Dov'è un buon ...?**	doavai oon bwawn
Where can I find ...?	**Dove posso trovare ...?**	doavay possoa tro-vaaray
Where's the main shopping area?	**Dov'è la zona principale dei negozi?**	doavai lah dzoanah preen-cheepaalay daiee naygotsee
How far is from here?	**Quanto dista da qui?**	kwahntoa deestah dah kooee
How do I get there?	**Come ci si può arrivare?**	koamay chee see pwo ahrreevaaray

> **SALDI**   SALE

Service *Servizio*

Can you help me?	**Può aiutarmi?**	pwo aheeootaarmee
I'm just looking.	**Do soltanto un'occhiata.**	doa soaltahntoa oonokkeeaatah
I want ...	**Desidero ...**	dayzeedayroa
Can you show me some ...?	**Può mostrarmi dei ...?**	pwo moastraarmee daiee
Do you have any ...?	**Ha dei ...?**	ah daiee
Where is the ... department?	**Dove si trova il reparto ...?**	doavay see trawvah eel raypahrtoa
Where is the lift (elevator)/escalator?	**Dov'è l'ascensore/ la scala mobile?**	doavai lahshaynsoaray/ lah skahlah mobeelay
Where do I pay?	**Dov'è la cassa?**	doavai lah kahssah

That one *Quello là*

Can you show me ...?	**Mi può mostrare ...?**	mee pwo moastraaray
this/that the one in the window/on the shelf	**questo/quello quello in vetrina/ sullo scaffale**	kooaystoa/kooaylloa kooaylloa een vaytreenah/ soolloa skahffaalay

Defining the article *Descrizione dell'articolo*

I'd like a ... one.	**Ne vorrei un ...**	nay vorraiee oon
big	**grande**	grahnday
cheap	**economico**	aykoanawmeekoa
dark	**scuro**	skooroa
good	**buono**	bwawnoa
heavy	**pesante**	paysahntay
large	**grande**	grahnday
light (weight)	**leggero**	laydjairoa
light (colour)	**chiaro**	keeaaroa
oval	**ovale**	ovaalay
rectangular	**rettangolare**	rehttahngolaaray
round	**rotondo**	rotoandoa
small	**piccolo**	peekkoaloa
square	**quadrato**	kwahdraatoa
sturdy	**solido**	soaleedoa
I don't want anything too expensive.	**Non voglio qualcosa di troppo caro.**	noan volyoa kwahlkawsah dee troppoa kaaroa

Preference *Preferenze*

Can you show me some more?	**Me ne può mostrare degli altri?**	may nay pwo moastraaray daylyee ahltree
Haven't you anything ...?	**Non ha qualcosa ...?**	noan ah kwahlkawsah
better	**migliore**	meelyoaray
cheaper	**meno caro**	maynoa kaaroa
larger	**più grande**	peeoo grahnday
smaller	**più piccolo**	peeoo peekkoaloa

How much? *Quanto?*

How much is this?	**Quanto costa questo?**	kwahntoa kostah kooaystoa
How much are they?	**Quanto costano?**	kwahntoa kostahnoa
I don't understand.	**Non capisco.**	noan kahpeeskoa
Please write it down.	**Per favore, me lo scriva.**	pair fahvoaray may loa skreevah
I don't want to spend more than ... lire.	**Non voglio spendere più di ... lire.**	noan volyoa spehndayray peeoo dee ... leeray

COLOURS, see page 113

Decision   *Decisione*

It's not quite what I want.	**Non è ciò che volevo.**	noan ai choa kay voalayvoa
No, I don't like it.	**No, non mi piace.**	noa noan mee peeaachay
I'll take it.	**Lo prendo.**	loa **prayn**doa

Ordering   *Ordinazione*

| Can you order it for me? | **Può ordinarmelo?** | pwo oardee**naar**mayloa |
| How long will it take? | **Quanto tempo ci sarà da aspettare?** | **kwahn**toa **tehm**poa chee sahrah dah ahspehtt**aa**ray |

Delivery   *Consegna*

I'll take it with me.	**Lo porto via.**	loa **poar**toa **vee**ah
Deliver it to the ... Hotel.	**Lo consegni all'Albergo ...**	loa kon**say**ñee ahllahl-**bayr**goa
Please send it to this address.	**Per favore, lo mandi a questo indirizzo.**	pair fah**voa**ray loa **mahn**dee ah koo**ays**toa eendee**reett**soa
Will I have any difficulty with the customs?	**Avrò delle difficoltà alla dogana?**	ah**vroa dayl**lay deeffee-**koal**tah **ahl**lah doa**gaa**nah

Paying   *Pagamento*

How much is it?	**Quant'è?**	kwahn**tai**
Can I pay by traveller's cheque?	**Accettate i traveller's cheque?**	ahtchehtt**aa**tay ee "traveller's cheque"
Do you accept dollars/pounds?	**Accettate dei dollari/ delle sterline?**	ahtchehtt**aa**tay **dai**ee dol-**lah**ree/**dayl**lay stayr**lee**nay
Do you accept credit cards?	**Accettate carte di credito?**	ahtchehtt**aa**tay **kahr**tay dee **kray**deetoa
Do I have to pay the VAT (sales tax)?	**Devo pagare l'I.V.A.?**	**day**voa pah**gaa**ray **lee**vah
Haven't you made a mistake in the bill?	**Non vi siete sbagliati nel fare il conto?**	noan vee see**ay**tay sbah-**lyaa**tee nayl **faa**ray eel **koan**toa

Anything else? *Qualcos'altro?*

No, thanks, that's all.	No, grazie, è tutto.	no graatseeay ai toottoa
Yes. I want ...	Sì, desidero ...	see dayzeedayroa
Show me ...	Mi mostri ...	mee moastree
May I have a bag, please?	Può darmi un sacchetto, per favore?	pwo daarmee oon sahkkehttoa pair fahvoaray

Dissatisfied *Scontento*

Can you please exchange this?	Può cambiare questo, per favore?	pwo kahmbeeaaray kooaystoa pair fahvoaray
I want to return this.	Desidero rendere questo.	dayzeedayroa rayndayray kooaystoa
I'd like a refund. Here's the receipt.	Desidero essere rimborsato. Ecco la ricevuta.	dayzeedayroa ehssayray reemboarsaatoa. ehkkoa lah reechayvootah

Posso aiutarla?	Can I help you?
Cosa desidera?	What would you like?
Che ... desidera?	What ... would you like?
colore/forma qualità/quantità	colour/shape quality/quantity
Mi dispiace, non ne abbiamo.	I'm sorry, we haven't any.
L'abbiamo esaurito.	We're out of stock.
Dobbiamo ordinarglielo?	Shall we order it for you?
Lo porta via o dobbiamo mandarglielo?	Will you take it with you or shall we send it?
Qualcos'altro?	Anything else?
Sono ... lire, per favore.	That's ... lire, please.
La cassa è laggiù.	The cashier's over there.

Bookshop—Stationer's *Libreria—Cartoleria*

In Italy, bookshops and stationer's are usually separate shops, though the latter will often sell paperbacks. Newspapers and magazines are sold at newsstands.

Where's the nearest ...?	**Dov'è ... più vicina?**	doavai ... peeoo veecheenah
bookshop	**la libreria**	lah leebrayreeah
stationer's	**la cartoleria**	lah kahrtoalayreeah
newsstand	**l'edicola**	laydeekoalah
Where can I buy an English-language newspaper?	**Dove posso comprare un giornale in inglese?**	doavay possoa kompraaray oon joarnaalay een eengglaysay
Where's the guide-book section?	**Dov'è il reparto delle guide turistiche?**	doavai eel raypahrtoa dayllay gooeeday tooreesteekay
Where do you keep the English books?	**Dov'è il reparto dei libri inglesi?**	doavai eel raypahrtoa daiee leebree eengglaysee
Do you have second-hand books?	**Avete libri d'occasione?**	ahvaytay leebree dokkahzeeooanay
I'd like a/an/some ...	**Vorrei ...**	vorraiee
address book	**un'agenda per gli indirizzi**	oonahjayndah pair lyee eendeereettsee
ball-point pen	**una biro**	oonah beeroa
book	**un libro**	oon leebroa
calendar	**un calendario**	oon kahlayndaareeoa
carbon paper	**della carta carbone**	dayllah kahrtah kahrboanay
cellophane tape	**del nastro adesivo**	dayl nahstroa ahdayzeevoa
crayons	**dei pastelli**	daiee pahstehllee
dictionary	**un dizionario**	oon deetseeoanaareeoa
Italian-English	**italiano-inglese**	eetahleeaanoa/ eengglaysay
pocket	**tascabile**	tahskaabeelay
drawing paper	**della carta da disegno**	dayllah kahrtah dah deesayñoa
drawing pins	**delle puntine**	dayllay poonteenay
envelopes	**delle buste**	dayllay boostay
eraser	**una gomma**	oonah goammah
exercise book	**un quaderno**	oon kwahdairnoa
felt-tip pen	**un pennarello**	oon paynnahrehlloa
fountain pen	**una penna stilografica**	oonah paynnah steeloagraafeekah

glue	della colla	dayllah kollah
grammar book	una grammatica	oonah grahmmahteekah
guidebook	una guida turistica	oonah gooeedah tooreesteekah
ink	dell'inchiostro	daylleengkeeostroa
(adhesive) labels	delle etichette (adesive)	dayllay ayteekehttay (ahdayzeevay)
magazine	una rivista	oonah reeveestah
map	una carta geo-grafica	oonah kahrtah jayoa-graafeekah
map of the town	una pianta della città	oonah peeahntah dayllah cheettah
road map of ...	una carta stradale di ...	oonah kahrtah strahdaalay dee
mechanical pencil	un portamine	oon poartahmeenay
newspaper	un giornale	oon joarnaalay
notebook	un taccuino	oon tahkkooeenoa
note paper	della carta da lettere	dayllah kahrtah dah lehttayray
paintbox	una scatola di colori	oonah skaatoalah dee koaloaree
paper	della carta	dayllah kahrtah
paperback	un libro tascabile	oon leebroa tahskaabeelay
paperclips	dei fermagli	daiee fayrmahlyee
paste	della colla	dayllah kollah
pen	una penna	oonah paynnah
pencil	una matita	oonah mahteetah
pencil sharpener	un temperamatite	oon taympayrahmahteetay
playing cards	delle carte da gioco	dayllay kahrtay dah jokoa
pocket calculator	una calcolatrice tascabile	oonah kahlkoalahtreechay tahskaabeelay
postcard	una cartolina	oonah kahrtoaleenah
propelling pencil	un portamine	oon poartahmeenay
refill (for a pen)	un ricambio (per biro)	oon reekahmbeeoa (pair beeroa)
rubber	una gomma	oonah goammah
ruler	una riga	oonah reegah
staples	delle graffette	dayllay grahffehttay
string	dello spago	daylloa spaagoa
thumbtacks	delle puntine	dayllay poonteenay
tissue paper	della carta velina	dayllah kahrtah vayleenah
typewriter ribbon	un nastro per mac-china da scrivere	oon nahstroa pair mahk-keenah dah skreevayray
typing paper	della carta per mac-china da scrivere	dayllah kahrtah pair mahk-keenah dah skreevayray
writing pad	un blocco per appunti	oon blokkoa pair appoontee

COLOURS, see page 113

Camping equipment   *Materiale da campeggio*

I'd like a/an/some ...	Vorrei ...	vorraiee
bottle-opener	un apribottiglia	oon ahpreebotteelyah
bucket	un secchio	oon saykkeeoa
butane gas	del gas butano	dayl gahz bootaanoa
campbed	un letto da campo	oon lehttoa dah kahmpoa
can opener	un apriscatole	oon ahpreeskaatoalay
candles	delle candele	dayllay kahndaylay
(folding) chair	una sedia (pieghevole)	oonah saydeeah (peeaygayvoalay)
charcoal	della carbonella	dayllah kahrboanayllah
clothes pegs	delle mollette da bucato	dayllay mollehttay dah bookaatoa
compass	una bussola	oonah boossoalah
cool box	una ghiacciaia	oonah geeahtchaaeeah
corkscrew	un cavatappi	oon kahvahtahppee
dishwashing detergent	del detersivo per lavare i piatti	dayl dehtehrseevoa pair lahvaaray ee peeahttee
first-aid kit	una cassetta del pronto soccorso	oonah kahssehttah dayl proantoa soakkoarsoa
fishing tackle	degli arnesi da pesca	daylyee ahrnayzee dah payskah
flashlight	una lampadina tascabile	oonah lahmpahdeenah tahskaabeelay
food box	un contenitore per il cibo	oon koantayneetoaray pair eel cheeboa
frying-pan	una padella	oonah pahdehllah
groundsheet	un telo per il terreno	oon tayloa pair eel tayrraynoa
hammer	un martello	oon mahrtehlloa
hammock	un'amaca	oonaamahkah
ice-pack	un elemento refrigerante	oon aylaymayntoa rayfreejayrahntay
kerosene	del petrolio	dayl paytrolyo
knapsack	uno zaino	oonoa dzaaeenoa
lamp	una lampada	oonah lahmpahdah
lantern	una lanterna	oonah lahntehrnah
matches	dei fiammiferi	daiee feeahmmeefayree
mattress	un materasso	oon mahtayrahssoa
methylated spirits	dell'alcool metilico	dayllahlkoal mayteeleekoa
mosquito net	una zanzariera	oonah dzahndzahreeayrah
pail	un secchio	oon saykkeeoa
paper napkins	dei tovagliolo di carta	daiee toavahlyoalee dee kahrtah
paraffin	del petrolio	dayl paytrolyo

penknife	un temperino	oon taympayreenoa
picnic basket	un cestino da picnic	oon chaysteenoa dah "picnic"
plastic bag	un sacchetto di plastica	oon sahkkehttoa dee plahsteekah
rope	della corda	dayllah koardah
rucksack	uno zaino	oonoa dzaaeenoa
saucepan	una casseruola	oonah kahssayrwoalah
scissors	un paio di forbici	oon paaeeoa dee foarbeechee
screwdriver	un cacciavite	oon kahtchahveetay
sleeping bag	un sacco a pelo	oon sahkkoa ah payloa
(folding) table	una tavola (pieghevole)	oonah taavoalah (peeaygayvoalay)
tent	una tenda	oonah tayndah
tent pegs	dei picchetti per tenda	daiee peekkehttee pair tayndah
tent pole	un palo per tenda	oon paaloa pair tayndah
tinfoil	un foglio di alluminio	oon foalyoa dee ahlloomeeneeoa
tin opener	un apriscatole	oon ahpreeskaatoalay
tongs	un paio di tenaglie	oon paaeeoa dee taynaalyay
torch	una lampadina tascabile	oonah lahmpahdeenah tahskaabeelay
vacuum flask	un thermos	oon tairmoas
washing powder	del detersivo	dayl daytehrseevoa
water flask	una borraccia	oonah boarratchah
wood alcohol	dell'alcool metilico	dayllahlkoal mayteeleekoa

Crockery *Stoviglie*

cups	delle tazze	dayllay tahttsay
mugs	dei boccali	daiee boakkaalee
plates	dei piatti	daiee peeahttee
saucers	dei piattini	daiee peeahtteenee
tumblers	dei bicchieri	daiee beekeeayree

Cutlery *Posate*

forks	delle forchette	dayllay forkehttay
knives	dei coltelli	daiee koaltehllee
spoons	dei cucchiai	daiee kookkeeaaee
teaspoons	dei cucchiaini	daiee kookkeeaheenee
(made of) plastic	(di) plastica	(dee) plahsteekah
(made of) stainless steel	(di) acciaio inossidabile	(dee) ahtchaaeeoa eenosseedaabeelay

Chemist's (drugstore) *Farmacia*

The Italian chemists' normally don't stock the great range of goods that you'll find in England or in the U.S. For example, they don't sell photographic equipment or books. For perfume, make-up, etc., you can also go to a *profumeria* (proafoomay**ree**ah).

You can recognize a chemist's by the sign outside—a green or red cross, illuminated at night. In the window you'll see a notice telling where the nearest all-night chemist's is.

This section is divided into two parts:

1. Pharmaceutical—medicine, first-aid, etc.
2. Toiletry—toilet articles, cosmetics

General *Generalità*

Where's the nearest (all-night) chemist's?	**Dov'è la farmacia (di turno) più vicina?**	doavai lah fahrmah**chee**ah (dee **toor**noa) peeoo veecheenah
What time does the chemist's open/ close?	**A che ora apre/ chiude la farmacia?**	ah kay oarah aapray/ keeooday lah fahrmah**chee**ah

1—Pharmaceutical *Medicine, primi soccorsi, ecc.*

I want something for a ...	**Desidero qualcosa per ...**	dayzee**day**roa kwahl**kaw**sah pair
cold	**il raffreddore**	eel rahffrayd**doa**ray
cough	**la tosse**	lah **toas**say
hay fever	**la febbre del fieno**	lah **fayb**bray dayl feeaynoa
insect bites	**le punture d'insetti**	lay poon**too**ray deen**seht**tee
hangover	**il mal di testa**	eel mahl dee **teh**stah
sunburn	**una scottatura solare**	oonah skoattah**too**rah soa**laa**ray
travel sickness	**il mal d'auto**	eel mahl **dow**toa
upset stomach	**il mal di stomaco**	eel mahl dee **sto**mahkoa
Can you make up this prescription for me?	**Può prepararmi questa ricetta?**	pwo praypah**raar**mee kooaystah ree**cheht**tah
Can I get it without a prescription?	**Può darmi questa medicina senza ricetta?**	pwo **daar**mee kooaystah maydee**chee**nah **sayn**tsah ree**cheht**tah

DOCTOR, see page 137

Can I have a/an/some ...?	Mi può dare ...?	mee pwo daaray
analgesic	un analgesico	oon ahnahljaizeekoa
antiseptic cream	della crema antisettica	dayllah kraimah ahntee-sehtteekah
aspirin	delle aspirine	dayllay ahspeereenay
bandage	una benda	oonah bayndah
elastic bandage	una benda elastica	oonah bayndah aylahsteekah
Band-Aids	dei cerotti	daiee chayrottee
contraceptives	degli antifecondativi	daylyee ahnteefaykoandah-teevee
corn plasters	dei cerotti calli-fughi	daiee chayrottee kahllee-foogee
cotton wool (absorbent cotton)	del cotone idrofilo	dayl koatoonay eedroa-feeloa
cough drops	delle pasticche per la tosse	dayllay pahsteekkay pair lah toassay
disinfectant	del disinfettante	dayl deeseenfehttahntay
ear drops	delle gocce per le orecchie	dayllay goatchay pair lay oraykkeeay
Elastoplast	dei cerotti	daiee chayrottee
eye drops	delle gocce per gli occhi	dayllay goatchay pair lyee okkee
gauze	della garza	dayllah gahrdzah
insect repellent/spray	una crema contro gli insetti/uno spray insetticida	oonah kraimah koantroa lyee eensehttee/oonoa "spray" eensehttee-cheedah
iodine	della tintura di iodio	dayllah teentoorah dee eeodeeoa
laxative	un lassativo	oon lahssahteevoa
mouthwash	un gargarismo	oon gahrgahreezmoa
nose drops	delle gocce nasali	dayllay goatchay naasaalee
sanitary towels (napkins)	degli assorbenti igienici	daylyee ahssoarbayntee eejayneechee
sleeping pills	dei sonniferi	daiee soanneefayree
suppositories	delle supposte	dayllay sooppostay
... tablets	delle pastiglie ...	dayllay pahsteelyay
tampons	dei tamponi igienici	daiee tahmpoanee eejayneechee
thermometer	un termometro	oon tayrmoamaytroa
throat lozenges	delle pasticche per la gola	dayllay pahsteekkay pair lah goalah
tranquillizers	dei tranquillanti	daiee trahnkooeellahntee
vitamin pills	delle vitamine	dayllay veetahmeenay

2 — Toiletry   *Articoli da toilette*

I'd like a/an/some ...	Desidero ...	dayzeedayroa
after-shave lotion	una lozione dopobarba	oonah loatseeoanay dawpoabahrbah
bath salts	dei sali da bagno	daiee saalee dah baañoa
bubble bath	un bagnoschiuma	oon baañoaskeeoomah
cream	una crema	oonah kraimah
cleansing cream	una crema detergente	oonah kraimah daytehrjayntay
foundation cream	un fondo tinta	oon foandoa teentah
moisturizing cream	una crema idratante	oonah kraimah eedrahtahntay
night cream	una crema da notte	oonah kraimah dah nottay
cuticle remover	un prodotto per togliere le pellicine	oon proadoattoa pair tolyayray lay pehlleecheenay
deodorant	un deodorante	oon dayoadoarahntay
emery board	una limetta per unghie	oonah leemehttah pair oonggeeay
eye liner	un "eye-liner"	oon "eye-liner"
eye pencil	una matita per occhi	oonah mahteetah pair okkee
eye shadow	un ombretto	oon oambrayttoa
face powder	della cipria	dayllah cheepreeah
foot cream	una crema per i piedi	oonah kraimah pair ee peeaydee
hand cream	una crema per le mani	oonah kraimah pair lay maanee
lipsalve	un burro cacao	oon boorroa kahkaaoa
lipstick	un rossetto	oon roassehttoa
make-up remover pads	dei tamponi per togliere il trucco	daiee tahmpoanee pair tolyayray eel trookkoa
nail brush	uno spazzolino da unghie	oonoa spahtsoaleenoa dah oonggeeay
nail file	una lima da unghie	oonah leemah dah oonggeeay
nail polish	uno smalto	oonoa smahltoa
nail polish remover	un solvente per le unghie	oon soalvayntay pair lay oonggeeay
nail scissors	un paio di forbicine per le unghie	oon paaeeoa dee forbeecheenay pair lay oonggeeay
perfume	un profumo	oon proafoomoa
powder	della cipria	dayllah cheepreeah
razor	un rasoio	oon rahsoaeeoa
razor blades	delle lamette	dayllay lahmayttay
rouge	del fard	dayl "fard"

safety pins	delle spille di sicurezza	dayllay speellay dee seekoorayttsah
shaving cream	una crema da barba	oonah kraimah dah bahrbah
soap	una saponetta	oonah sahpoanayttah
sun-tan cream	una crema solare	oonah kraimah soalaaray
sun-tan oil	un olio solare	oon olyoa soalaaray
talcum powder	del talco	dayl tahlkoa
tissues	dei fazzolettini di carta	daiee fahttsoalehtteenee dee kahrtah
toilet paper	della carta igienica	dayllah kahrtah eejay-neekah
toilet water	dell'acqua di colonia	dayllahkkwah dee koa-loneeah
toothbrush	uno spazzolino da denti	oonoa spahttsoaleenoa dah dehntee
toothpaste	un dentifricio	oon daynteefreechoa
tweezers	delle pinzette	dayllay peentsehttay

For your hair *Per i vostri capelli*

bobby pins	delle mollette	dayllay mollayttay
colour shampoo	uno shampoo colorante	oonoa shahmpoa koaloa-rahntay
comb	un pettine	oon paytteenay
dry shampoo	uno shampo secco	oonoa shahmpoa sehkkoa
hairbrush	una spazzola per capelli	oonah spahttsoalah pair kahpayllee
hair slide	un fermaglio	oon fayrmaalyoa
hairgrips	delle mollette	dayllay mollayttay
hair lotion	una lozione per capelli	oonah loatseeooanay pair kahpehllee
hairspray	della lacca	dayllah lahkkah
setting lotion	una lozione fissativa	oonah loatseeooanay feessahteevah
shampoo for dry/greasy (oily) hair	dello shampoo per capelli secchi/grassi	daylloa shahmpoa pair kahpehllee saykkee/grahssee

For the baby *Per il vostro bambino*

baby food	degli alimenti per bebè	daylyee ahleemaintee pair baybay
dummy (pacifier)	un succhiotto	oon sookkeeottoa
feeding bottle	un biberon	oon beebayroan
nappies (diapers)	dei pannolini	daiee pahnnoaleenee

Clothing *Abbigliamento*

If you want to buy something specific, prepare yourself in advance. Look at the list of clothing on page 116. Get some idea of the colour, material and size you want. They're all listed on the next few pages.

General *Generalità*

I'd like ...	**Vorrei ...**	vorraiee
I want ... for a 10-year-old boy/girl.	**Desidero ... per un bambino/una bambina di 10 anni.**	dayzeedayroa ... pair oon bahmbeenoa/oonah bahm-beenah dee 10 ahnnee
I want something like this.	**Voglio qualcosa come questo.**	volyoa kwahlkawsah koamay kooaystoa
I like the one in the window.	**Mi piace quello in vetrina.**	mee peeaachay kooaylloa een vaytreenah
How much is that per metre?	**Quanto costa al metro?**	kwahntoa kostah ahl maytroa

1 centimetre (cm.) = 0.39 in.	1 inch = 2.54 cm.
1 metre (m.) = 39.37 in.	1 foot = 30.5 cm.
10 metres = 32.81 ft.	1 yard = 0.91 m.

Colour *Colore*

I want something in ...	**Voglio qualcosa di colore ...**	volyoa kwahlkawsah dee koaloaray
I'd like a darker/lighter shade.	**Desidero una tonalità più scura/più chiara.**	dayzeedayroa oonah toanahleetah peeoo skoorah/peeoo keeaarah
I want something to match this.	**Voglio qualcosa per ravvivare questo.**	volyoa kwahlkawsah pair rahvveevaaray kooaystoa
I'd like the same colour as ...	**Vorrei lo stesso colore che ...**	vorraiee loa stayssoa koaloaray kai
I don't like the colour.	**Non mi piace il colore.**	noan mee peeaachay eel koaloaray

beige	**beige**	baizh
black	**nero**	nayroa
blue	**blu**	bloo
light blue	**azzurro**	ahdzoorroa
brown	**marrone**	mahrroanay
golden	**dorato**	doaraatoa
green	**verde**	vayrday
grey	**grigio**	greejoa
mauve	**lilla**	leellah
orange	**arancio**	ahrahnchoa
pink	**rosa**	rawzah
purple	**viola**	veeolah
red	**rosso**	roassoa
silver	**argentato**	ahrjayntaatoa
turquoise	**turchese**	toorkayzay
white	**bianco**	beeahngkoa
yellow	**giallo**	jahlloa
light ...	**... chiaro**	keeaaroa
dark ...	**... scuro**	skooroa

tinta unita	**a righe**	**a pallini**	**a quadri**	**fantasia**
(teentah ooneetah)	(ah reegay)	(ah pahlleenee)	(ah kwaadree)	(fahntahzeeah)

Material *Tessuto*

Do you have anything in ...?	**Ha qualcosa in ...?**	ah kwahlkawsah een
I want a cotton blouse.	**Voglio una blusa di cotone.**	volyoa oonah bloosah dee koatoanay
Is that ...?	**È un prodotto ...?**	ai oon proadoattoa
handmade	**fatto a mano**	**fahttoa ah maanoa**
imported	**importato**	eempoartaatoa
made here	**nazionale**	nahtseeoanaalay
I want something thinner.	**Desidero qualcosa di più fine.**	dayzeedayroa kwahlkawsah dee peeoo feenay
Do you have any better quality?	**Ha una qualità migliore?**	ah oonah kwahleetah meelyoaray
What's it made of?	**Di che cos'è?**	dee kay kosai

cambric	la tela battista	lah taylah bahtteestah
camel-hair	il pelo di cammello	eel payloa dee kahm-mehlloa
chiffon	lo chiffon	loa sheeffoan
corduroy	il velluto a coste	eel vayllootoa ah koastay
cotton	il cotone	eel koatoanay
crepe	il crespo	eel krayspoa
denim	la tela di cotone	lah taylah dee koatoanay
felt	il feltro	eel fayltroa
flannel	la flanella	lah flahnehllah
gabardine	il gabardine	eel gahbahrdeen
lace	il pizzo	eel peettsoa
leather	la pelle	lah pehllay
linen	il lino	eel leenoa
poplin	il popeline	eel poapayleen
satin	il raso	eel raasoa
silk	la seta	lah saytah
suede	la renna	lah rehnnah
towelling (terrycloth)	il tessuto di spugna	eel tayssootoa dee spooñah
velvet	il velluto	eel vayllootoa
velveteen	il velluto di cotone	eel vayllootoa dee koatoanay
wool	la lana	lah laanah
worsted	il pettinato	eel paytteenaatoa

Is it ...?	È ...?	ai
pure cotton/wool	puro cotone/pura lana	pooroa koatoanay/poorah laanah
synthetic	sintetico	seentayteekoa
colourfast	di colore solido	dee koaloaray soleedoa
wrinkle resistant	ingualcibile	eengwahlcheebeelay
Is it hand washable/ machine washable?	Si può lavare a mano/ in lavatrice?	see pwo lahvaaray ah maanoa/een lahvahtreechay
Will it shrink?	Si restringe al lavaggio?	see raystreenjay ahl lahvahdjoa

Size *Taglia*

I take size 38.	La mia taglia è il 38.	lah meeah tahlyah ai eel 38
Could you measure me?	Può prendermi le misure?	pwo prehndayrmee lay meezooray
I don't know the Italian sizes.	Non conosco le misure italiane.	noan koanoaskoa lay meezooray eetahleeaanay

Sizes can vary somewhat from one manufacturer to another, so be sure to try on shoes and clothing before you buy.

Women *Donne*

Dresses/Suits					
American	8	10	12	14	16	18
British	10	12	14	16	18	20
Continental	36	38	40	42	44	46

Stockings							Shoes			
American	} 8	8½	9	9½	10	10½	6	7	8	9
British							4½	5½	6½	7½
Continental	0	1	2	3	4	5	37	38	40	41

Men *Uomini*

Suits/Overcoats							Shirts			
American	} 36	38	40	42	44	46	15	16	17	18
British										
Continental	46	48	50	52	54	56	38	41	43	45

Shoes									
American	} 5	6	7	8	8½	9	9½	10	11
British									
Continental	38	39	41	42	43	43	44	44	45

A good fit? *Una buona prova?*

Can I try it on?	**Posso provarlo?**	possoa provahrloa
Where's the fitting room?	**Dov'è la cabina di prova?**	doavai lah kahbeenah dee prawvah
Is there a mirror?	**C'è uno specchio?**	chai oonoa spaykkeeoa
It fits very well.	**Va molto bene.**	vah moaltoa bainay
It doesn't fit.	**Non va bene.**	noan vah bainay
It's too ...	**È troppo ...**	ai troppoa
short/long	**corto/lungo**	koartoa/loonggoa
tight/loose	**stretto/largo**	strayttoa/lahrgoa

NUMBERS, see page 147

| How long will it take to alter? | **Quanto tempo ci vuole per le modifiche?** | kwahntoa tehmpoa chee vwolay pair lay moadee-feekay |

Clothes and accessories *Indumenti e accessori*

I'd like a/an/some ...	**Vorrei ...**	vorraiee
anorak	**una giacca a vento**	oonah jahkkah ah vayntoa
bathing cap	**una cuffia da bagno**	oonah kooffeeah dah baañoa
bathing suit	**un costume da bagno**	oon koastoomay dah baañoa
bathrobe	**un accappatoio**	oon ahkkahppahtoaeeoa
blouse	**una blusa**	oonah bloozah
bow tie	**una cravatta a farfalla**	oonah krahvahttah ah fahrfahllah
bra	**un reggiseno**	oon raydjeesaynoa
braces	**delle bretelle**	dayllay braytehllay
briefs	**uno slip**	oonoa "slip"
cap	**un berretto**	oon bayrrayttoa
cardigan	**un cardigan**	oon "cardigan"
coat	**un cappotto**	oon kahppottoa
dress	**un abito**	oon aabeetoa
dressing gown	**una vestaglia**	oonah vehstahlyah
evening dress (woman's)	**un abito da sera**	oon aabeetoa dah sayrah
frock	**un abito**	oon aabeetoa
garter belt	**un reggicalze**	oon raydjeekahltsay
girdle	**un busto**	oon boostoa
gloves	**dei guanti**	daiee gwahntee
handbag	**una borsetta**	oonah boarsayttah
handkerchief	**un fazzoletto**	oon fahtsoalehttoa
hat	**un cappello**	oon kahppehlloa
jacket	**una giacca**	oonah jahkkah
jeans	**dei jeans**	daiee "jeans"
jersey	**una maglietta**	oonah mahlyehttah
jumper (Br.)	**un maglione**	oon mahlyoanay
kneesocks	**dei calzettoni**	daiee kahltsehttoanee
nightdress	**una camicia da notte**	oonah kahmeechah dah nottay
overalls	**una tuta**	oonah tootah
pair of ...	**un paio di ...**	oon paaeeoa dee
panties	**uno slip**	oonoa "slip"
pants (Am.)	**dei pantaloni**	daiee pahntahloanee
panty girdle	**una guaina**	oonah gwaaeenah
panty hose	**dei collant**	daiee kollahnt

pullover	un pullover	oon "pullover"
roll-neck (turtle-neck)	a collo alto	ah kolloa ahltoa
round	a girocollo	ah jeeroakolloa
V-neck	con scollatura a punta	kon skollahtoorah ah poontah
pyjamas	un pigiama	oon peejaamah
raincoat	un impermeabile	oon eempayrmayaabeelay
scarf	una sciarpa	oonah shahrpah
shirt	una camicia	oonah kahmeechah
shorts	uno short	oonoa "short"
skirt	una gonna	oonah goannah
slip	una sottoveste	oonah soattoavehstay
socks	dei calzini	daiee kahltseenee
stockings	delle calze da donna	dayllay kahltsay dah donnah
suit (man's)	un completo	oon koamplaytoa
suit (woman's)	un tailleur	oon "tailleur"
suspenders (Am.)	delle bretelle	dayllay braytehllay
sweater	un maglione	oon mahlyoanay
sweatshirt	una blusa	oonah bloozah
swimming trunks/ swimsuit	un costume da bagno	oon koastoomay dah baañoa
T-shirt	una maglietta di cotone	oonah mahlyehttah dee koatoanay
tie	una cravatta	oonah krahvahttah
tights	dei collant	daiee kollahnt
tracksuit	una tuta sportiva	oonah tootah sporteevah
trousers	dei pantaloni	daiee pahntahloanee
umbrella	un ombrello	oon oambrehlloa
underpants	delle mutande/uno slip	dayllay mootahnday/oonoa "slip"
undershirt	una canottiera	oonah kahnotteeayrah
vest (Am.)	un panciotto	oon pahnchottoa
vest (Br.)	una canottiera	oonah kahnotteeayrah
waistcoat	un panciotto	oon pahnchottoa

belt	la cintura	lah cheentoorah
button	il bottone	eel boattoanay
pocket	la tasca	lah tahskah
press stud (snap fastener)	il bottone a pressione	eel boattoanay ah praysseeoanay
sleeve	la manica	lah maaneekah
zip (zipper)	la cerniera	lah chehrneeayrah

Shoes   *Scarpe*

I'd like a pair of ...	Vorrei un paio di ...	vorraiee oon paaeeoa dee
boots	stivali	steevaalee
moccasins	mocassini	moakahsseenee
plimsolls (sneakers)	scarpe da tennis	skahrpay dah tainnees
sandals	sandali	sahndahlee
shoes	scarpe	skahrpay
flat	basse	bahssay
with a heel	con i tacchi	koan ee tahkkee
slippers	pantofole	pahntofoalay
These are too ...	Queste sono troppo ...	kwaystay soanoa troppoa
narrow/wide	strette/larghe	strayttay/lahrgay
large/small	grandi/piccole	grahndee/peekkoalay
Do you have a larger/ smaller size?	Ha un numero più grande/più piccolo?	ah oon noomayroa peeoo grahnday/peeoo peekkoaloa
Do you have the same in black?	Ha le stesse in nero?	ah lay stehssay een nayroa
cloth/leather/ rubber/suede	in tela/pelle/ gomma/camoscio	een taylah/pehllay/ goammah/kahmoshoa
Is it genuine leather?	È vera pelle?	ai vayrah pehllay
I need some shoe polish/shoelaces.	Mi serve del lucido/ dei lacci.	mee sairvay dayl loocheedoa/daiee lahtchee

Shoes worn out? Here's the key to getting them fixed again:

Can you repair these shoes?	Mi può riparare queste scarpe?	mee pwo reepahraaray kooaystay skahrpay
Can you stitch this?	Può attaccare questo?	pwo ahttahkkaaray kooaystoa
I want new soles and heels.	Desidero suole e tacchi nuovi.	dayzeedayroa swolay ay tahkkee nwawvee
When will they be ready?	Quando saranno pronte?	kwahndoa sahrahnnoa proantay
I need them ...	Ne ho bisogno ...	nay oa beezoañoa
as soon as possible	il più presto possibile	eel peeoo prehstoa posseebeelay
tomorrow	domani	doamaanee

COLOURS, see page 113

Electrical appliances *Apparecchi elettrici*

In Italy you will usually find 220-volt current, though some older buildings, particularly in Rome, have 125-volt outlets.

What's the voltage?	**Qual è il voltaggio?**	kwahl ai eel voaltahdjoa
Do you have a battery for this?	**Ha una pila per questo?**	ah oonah peelah pair kooaystoa
This is broken. Can you repair it?	**È rotto. Me lo può riparare?**	ai roattoa. may loa pwo reepahraaray
Can you show me how it works?	**Può mostrarmi come funziona?**	pwo moastraarmee koamay foontseeoanah
I'd like (to hire) a video cassette.	**Vorrei (noleggiare) una video cassetta.**	vorraiee (noalaydjaaray) oonah veedayoa kahssehttah
I'd like a/an/some ...	**Vorrei ...**	vorraiee
adaptor	**una presa multipla**	oonah prayzah moolteeplah
amplifier	**un amplificatore**	oon ahmpleefeekahtoaray
bulb	**una lampadina**	oonah lahmpahdeenah
clock-radio	**una radio-sveglia**	oonah raadeeoa-svaylyah
electric toothbrush	**uno spazzolino da denti elettrico**	oonoa spatsoaleenoa dah dayntee aylehttreekoa
extension lead (cord)	**una prolunga**	oonah proaloonggah
hair dryer	**un asciugacapelli**	oon ashoogahkahpayllee
headphones	**una cuffia (d'ascolto)**	oonah kooffeeah (dahskoaltoa)
(travelling) iron	**un ferro da stiro (da viaggio)**	oon fehrroa dah steeroa (dah veeahdjoa)
lamp	**una lampada**	oonah lahmpahdah
plug	**una spina**	oonah speenah
portable ...	**... portatile**	... poartaateelay
radio	**una radio**	oonah raadeeoa
car radio	**un'autoradio**	oonowtoaraadeeoa
record player	**un giradischi**	oon jeerahdeeskee
shaver	**un rasoio elettrico**	oon rahsoaeeoa aylehttreekoa
speakers	**degli altoparlanti**	daylyee ahltoapahrlahntee
(cassette) tape recorder	**un registratore (a cassette)**	oon rayjeestrahtoaray (ah kassehttay)
(colour) television	**un televisore (a colori)**	oon taylayveezoaray (ah koaloaree)
transformer	**un trasformatore**	oon trahsfoarmahtoaray
video-recorder	**un video registratore**	oon veedayoa rayjeestrahtoaray

Grocery *Negozio di alimentari*

I'd like some bread, please.	**Vorrei del pane, per favore.**	vorraiee dayl paanay pair fahvoaray
What sort of cheese do you have?	**Che formaggi avete?**	kay foarmahdjee ahvaytay
A piece of that one/ the one on the shelf.	**Un pezzo di quello/ quello sullo scaffale.**	oon pehtsoa dee kooaylloa/ kooaylloa soolloa skahf-faalay
I'll have one of those, please.	**Vorrei uno di quelli, per favore.**	vorraiee oonoa dee kooayllee pair fahvoaray
May I help myself?	**Posso servirmi?**	possoa sayrveermee
I'd like …	**Vorrei …**	vorraiee
a kilo of apples	**un chilo di mele**	oon keeloa dee maylay
half a kilo of tomatoes	**mezzo chilo di pomodori**	mehdzoa keeloa dee pomodawree
100 grams of butter	**100 grammi (un etto) di burro**	chehntoa grahmmee (oon ehttoa) dee boorroa
a litre of milk	**un litro di latte**	oon leetroa dee lahttay
half a dozen eggs	**mezza dozzina di uova**	mehdzah doadzeenah dee wawvah
4 slices of ham	**4 fette di prosciutto**	4 fehttay dee proashoottoa
a packet of tea	**un pacchetto di tè**	oon pahkkehttoa dee tai
a jar of jam	**un vasetto di marmellata**	oon vahzehttoa dee marmehllaatah
a tin (can) of peaches	**una scatola di pesche**	oonah skaatoalah dee payskay
a tube of mustard	**un tubetto di mostarda**	oon toobehttoa dee moastahrdah
a box of chocolates	**una scatola di cioccolatini**	oonah skaatoalah dee chokkoalahteenee

1 kilogram or kilo (kg.) = 1000 grams (g.)
100 g. = 3.5 oz.   ½ kg. = 1.1 lbs.
200 g. = 7.0 oz.   1 kg. = 2.2 lbs.
1 oz. =   28.35 g.
1 lb. = 453.60 g.

1 litre (l.) = 0.88 imp. quarts = 1.06 U.S. quarts
1 imp. quart = 1.14 l.   1 U.S. quart = 0.95 l.
1 imp. gallon = 4.55 l.   1 U.S. gallon = 3.8 l.

FOOD, see also page 63

Jeweller's—Watchmaker's   *Gioielleria—Orologeria*

Could I please see that?	**Potrei vedere quello, per favore?**	potraiee vaydayray kooayl-loa pair fahvoaray
Do you have anything in gold?	**Avete qualcosa in oro?**	ahvaytay kwahlkawsah een oroa
How many carats is this?	**Di quanti carati è?**	dee kwahntee kahraatee ai
Is this real silver?	**È vero argento?**	ai vayroa ahrjayntoa
Can you repair this watch?	**Può riparare questo orologio?**	pwo reepahraaray kooay-stoa oaroaolojoa
I'd like a/an/some ...	**Vorrei ...**	vorraiee
alarm clock	**una sveglia**	oonah svaylyah
bangle	**un braccialetto**	oon brahtchahlehttoa
battery	**una pila**	oonah peelah
bracelet	**un braccialetto**	oon brahtchahlehttoa
chain bracelet	**un braccialetto a catena**	oon brahtchahlehttoa ah kahtaynah
charm bracelet	**un braccialetto a ciondoli**	oon brahtchahlehttoa ah choandoalee
brooch	**una spilla**	oonah speellah
chain	**una catenina**	oonah kahtayneenah
charm	**un ciondolo**	oon choandoaloa
cigarette case	**un portasigarette**	oon portahseegahrayttay
cigarette lighter	**un accendino**	oon ahtchayndeenoa
clip	**un fermaglio**	oon fayrmaalyoa
clock	**un orologio**	oon oaroaolojoa
cross	**una croce**	oonah kroachay
cuckoo clock	**un orologio a cucù**	oon oaroaolojoa ah kookoo
cuff links	**dei gemelli**	daiee jaymehllee
cutlery	**delle posate**	dayllay poasaatay
earrings	**degli orecchini**	daylyee oaraykkeenee
gem	**una pietra preziosa**	oonah peeaytrah pray-tseeoasah
jewel box	**un portagioielli**	oon portahjoeeehllee
music box	**un carillon**	oon kahreeyon
necklace	**una collana**	oonah koallaanah
pendant	**un pendente**	oon payndayntay
pocket watch	**un orologio da tasca**	oon oaroaolojoa dah tahskah
powder compact	**un portacipria**	oon portahcheepreeah
ring	**un anello**	oon ahnehlloa
engagement ring	**un anello di fidanzamento**	oon ahnehlloa dee feedahntsahmayntoa

signet ring	un anello con stemma	oon ahnehlloa kon stehmmah
wedding ring	una fede nuziale	oonah fayday nootseeaalay
rosary	un rosario	oon rawzaareeoa
silverware	dell'argenteria	dayllahrjayntayreeah
tie clip	un fermacravatte	oon fayrmahkrahvahttay
tie pin	uno spillo per cravatta	oonoa speelloa pair krahvahttah
watch	un orologio	oon oaroalojoa
automatic	automatico	owtoamaateekoa
digital	digitale	deejeetaalay
quartz	al quarzo	ahl kwahrtsoa
with a second hand	con lancetta dei secondi	kon lahnchehttah daiee saykoandee
watchstrap	un cinturino per orologio	oon cheentooreenoa pair oaroalojoa
wristwatch	un orologio braccialetto	oon oaroalojoa brahtchahlehttoa

alabaster	l'alabastro	lahlahbahstroa
amber	l'ambra	lahmbrah
amethyst	l'ametista	lahmayteestah
copper	il rame	eel raamay
coral	il corallo	eel koarahlloa
crystal	il cristallo	eel kreestahlloa
cut glass	il vetro tagliato	eel vaytroa tahlyaatoa
diamond	il diamante	eel deeahmahntay
emerald	lo smeraldo	loa smayrahldoa
enamel	lo smalto	loa smahltoa
gold	l'oro	loroa
gold plate	placcato d'oro	plahkkaatoa doroa
ivory	l'avorio	lahvoreeoa
jade	la giada	lah jaadah
onyx	l'onice	loneechay
pearl	la perla	lah pehrlah
pewter	il peltro	eel payltroa
platinum	il platino	eel plaateenoa
ruby	il rubino	eel roobeenoa
sapphire	lo zaffiro	loa dzahffeeroa
silver	l'argento	lahrjayntoa
silver plate	placcato d'argento	plahkkaatoa dahrjayntoa
stainless steel	l'acciaio inossidabile	lahtchaaeeoa eenoasseedaabeelay
topaz	il topazio	eel toapaatseeoa
turquoise	il turchese	eel toorkayzay

Optician   *Ottico*

I've broken my glasses.	**Ho rotto gli occhiali.**	oa **roa**ttoa lyee okkee**aa**lee
Can you repair them for me?	**Può ripararmeli?**	pwo reepahr**aa**rmaylee
When will they be ready?	**Quando saranno pronti?**	**kwahn**doa sahrahn**no**a pro**an**tee
Can you change the lenses?	**Può cambiare le lenti?**	pwo kahmbee**aa**ray lay **leh**ntee
I want tinted lenses.	**Desidero delle lenti colorate.**	dayzee**d**ayroa **day**llay **leh**ntee koaloa**raa**tay
The frame is broken.	**La montatura è rotta.**	lah moantah**t**oorah ai **roa**ttah
I'd like a spectacle case.	**Vorrei un astuccio per occhiali.**	vorr**aie**e oon ahs**toot**choa pair okkee**aa**lee
I'd like to have my eyesight checked.	**Vorrei farmi control-lare la vista.**	vorr**aie**e **fahr**mee koan-troa**llaa**ray lah **vee**stah
I'm short-sighted/long-sighted.	**Sono miope/presbite.**	**soa**noa mee**oa**pay/**preh**-zbeetay
I want some contact lenses.	**Desidero delle lenti a contatto.**	dayzee**d**ayroa **day**llay **leh**ntee ah koan**taht**toa
I've lost one of my contact lenses.	**Ho perso una lente a contatto.**	oa **peh**rsoa **oo**nah **leh**ntay ah koan**taht**toa
Could you give me another one?	**Può darmene un'altra?**	pwo **daar**mehneh **oo**nahltrah
I have hard/soft lenses.	**Ho delle lenti a con-tatto dure/morbide.**	oa **day**llay **leh**ntee ah koan**taht**toa **doo**ray/**mor**beeday
Have you any con-tact-lens liquid?	**Avete del liquido per lenti a contatto?**	ah**vay**tay dayl lee**koo**eedoa pair **leh**ntee ah koan**taht**toa
I'd like to buy a pair of sunglasses.	**Vorrei degli occhiali da sole.**	vorr**aie**e **day**lyee okkee**aa**lee dah **soa**lay
May I look in a mirror?	**Posso guardarmi in uno specchio?**	**pos**soa gwahr**d**aarmee een **oo**noa spehk**kee**oa
I'd like to buy a pair of binoculars.	**Vorrei acquistare un binocolo.**	vorr**aie**e akkooees**taa**ray oon beeno**koa**loa

Photography *Fotografia*

I want a(n) ... camera.	**Voglio una macchina fotografica ...**	volyoa oonah **mahkkeenah** foatoagraafeekah
automatic	**automatica**	owtoa**maa**teekah
inexpensive	**economica**	aykoanomeekah
simple	**semplice**	saym**plee**chay
Show me some cine (movie) cameras, please.	**Per favore, mi faccia vedere alcune cine-prese.**	pair fah**voa**ray mee **faht**-chah vay**day**ray ahl**koo**nay cheenay**pray**zay
I'd like to have some passport photos taken.	**Vorrei che mi facesse delle fotografie d'identità.**	vorraiee kay mee faht-**chays**say day**llay** foatoa-grah**fee**ay deedayn**tee**tah

Film *Pellicola*

I'd like a film for this camera.	**Vorrei una pellicola per questa macchina fotografica.**	vorraiee oonah pehllee-koalah pair kooaystah **mahk**-keenah foatoagraafeekah
black and white	**in bianco e nero**	een bee**ahng**koa ay **nay**roa
colour	**a colori**	ah koa**loa**ree
colour negative	**per negativo a colori**	pair naygah**tee**voa ah koa**loa**ree
colour slide	**per diapositive**	pair deeahpoazee**tee**vay
cartridge	**un rotolo**	oon rotoaloa
roll film	**una bobina**	oonah boa**bee**nah
video cassette	**una video cassetta**	oonah **vee**dayoa kahs**sayt**tah
24/36 exposures	**ventiquattro/trenta-sei pose**	vaynteek**waht**troa/**trayn**-tahsehee poazay
this size	**questo formato**	kooaystoa foar**maa**toa
this ASA/DIN number	**questo numero ASA/DIN**	kooaystoa **noo**mayroa aasah/deen
artificial light type	**per luce artificiale**	pair **loo**chay ahrteefee-**chaa**lay
daylight type	**par luce naturale**	pair **loo**chay nahtoo**raa**lay
fast (high-speed)	**rapido**	**raa**peedoa
fine grain	**a grana fine**	ah **graa**nah **fee**nay

Processing *Sviluppo*

How much do you charge for developing?	**Quanto fate pagare per lo sviluppo?**	**kwahn**toa **faa**tay pahgaa-ray pair loa sveeloooppoa

NUMBERS, see page 147

I want ... prints of each negative.	Voglio ... stampe per ogni negativa.	volyoa ... stahmpay pair oañee naygahteevah
with a mat finish	su carta opaca	soo kahrtah oapaakah
with a glossy finish	su carta lucida	soo kahrtah loocheedah
Will you please enlarge this?	Mi può ingrandire questo, per favore?	mee pwo eenggrahndeeray kooaystoa pair fahvoaray
When will the photos be ready?	Quando saranno pronte le fotografie?	kwahndoa sahrahnnoa prontay lay foatoagrahfeeay

Accessories and repairs *Accessori e riparazioni*

I want a/an/some ...	Vorrei ...	vorraiee
battery	una pila	oonah peelah
cable release	uno scatto	oonoa skahttoa
camera case	un astuccio (per macchina fotografica)	oon ahstootchoa (pair mahkkeenah foatoagraafeekah)
(electronic) flash	un flash (elettronico)	oon "flash" (aylayttroneekoa)
filter	un filtro	oon feeltroa
for black and white	per bianco e nero	pair beeahngkoa ay nayroa
for colour	per foto a colori	pair foatoa ah koaloaree
lens	un obiettivo	oon oabeeaytteevoa
telephoto lens	un teleobiettivo	oon taylayoabeeaytteevoa
wide-angle lens	un grandangolare	oon grahndahngoalaaray
lens cap	un cappuccio (per obiettivo)	oon kahppootchoa (pair oabeeaytteevoa)
Can you repair this camera?	Può riparare questa macchina fotografica?	pwo reepahraaray kooaystah mahkkeenah foatoagraafeekah
The film is jammed.	La pellicola è bloccata.	lah pehlleekoalah ai bloakkaatah
There's something wrong with the ...	... non funziona.	noan foontseeoanah
exposure counter	il contatore di esposizioni	eel koantahtoaray dee ayspoazeetseeoanee
film winder	la leva d'avanzamento della pellicola	lah layvah dahvahntsahmayntoa dayllah pehlleekoalah
flash attachment	l'attaccatura del flash	lahttahkkahtoorah dayl "flash"
light meter	l'esposimetro	layspoazeemaytroa
rangefinder	il telemetro	eel taylaymaytroa
shutter	l'otturatore	loattoorahtoaray

SHOPPING GUIDE

Tobacconist's   *Tabaccheria*

Tobacco is a state monopoly in Italy. You recognize licensed
tobacconist's by a large white "T" on a black background.
Cigarettes are also sold in some cafés and newsstands.

A packet of cigarettes, please.	**Un pacchetto di sigarette, per favore.**	oon pahkkayttoa dee seegahrayttay pair fahvoaray
Do you have any American/English cigarettes?	**Avete sigarette americane/inglesi?**	ahvaytay seegahrayttay ahmayreekaanay/eengglaysee
I'd like a carton.	**Ne vorrei una stecca.**	nay vorraiee oonah staykkah
Give me a/some ..., please.	**Per favore, mi dia ...**	pair fahvoaray mee deeah
candy	**delle caramelle**	dayllay kahrahmaillay
chewing gum	**della gomma da masticare**	dayllah goammah dah mahsteekaaray
chocolate	**del cioccolato**	dayl choakkoalaatoa
cigarette case	**un portasigarette**	oon portahseegahrayttay
cigarette holder	**un bocchino**	oon boakkeenoa
cigarettes	**delle sigarette**	dayllay seegahrayttay
filter-tipped/	**con filtro/**	kon feeltroa/
without filter	**senza filtro**	sayntsah feeltroa
light/dark tobacco	**tabacco chiaro/scuro**	tahbahkkoa keeaaroa/skooroa
mild/strong	**leggere/forti**	laydjayray/fortee
menthol	**al mentolo**	ahl mayntoaloa
king-size	**formato lungo**	foarmaatoa loonggoa
cigars	**dei sigari**	daiee seegahree
lighter	**un accendino**	oon ahtchayndeenoa
lighter fluid/gas	**della benzina/del gas per accendino**	dayllah bayndzeenah/dayl gahz pair ahtchayndeenoa
matches	**dei fiammiferi**	daiee feeahmmeefayree
pipe	**una pipa**	oonah peepah
pipe cleaners	**dei nettapipe**	daiee nayttahpeepay
pipe tobacco	**del tabacco da pipa**	dayl tahbahkkoa dah peepah
pipe tool	**un curapipe**	oon koorahpeepay
postcard	**una cartolina**	oonah kahrtoaleenah
stamps	**dei francobolli**	daiee frahngkoaboallee
sweets	**delle caramelle**	dayllay karahmaillay
wick	**uno stoppino**	oonoa stoppeenoa

Guida degli acquisti

Miscellaneous *Diversi*

Souvenirs *Oggetti ricordo*

Here are some suggestions for articles you might like to bring
back as a souvenir or a gift. Italy is particularly noted for
its top fashions for men and women, for articles made of
silk, leather, olive wood and alabaster, for pottery and
embroidered clothes and accessories. Hand-made jewellery
of amber, gold and silver are particularly appreciated.

antiques	l'antichità	lahnteekeetah
ceramics	la ceramica	lah chayraameekah
doll	la bambola	lah bahmboalah
flask of Chianti	il fiasco di Chianti	eel feeaaskoa dee keeahntee
glassware	gli articoli di vetro	lyee ahrteekoalee dee vehtroa
jewellery	i gioielli	ee joeeehllee
knitwear	la maglieria	lah mahlyayreeah
leather work	la pelletteria	lah payllayttayreeah
needlework	il ricamo	eel reekaamoa
porcelain	la porcellana	lah poarchayllaanah
silk	la seta	lah saitah
woodwork	il lavoro in legno	eel lahvoaroa een lehñoa

Some typical products of Switzerland are:

chocolate	il cioccolato	eel choakkoalaatoa
cuckoo clock	l'orologio a cucù	loaroalojoa ah kookoo
fondue forks/pot	le forchette/il pento-lino per la fonduta	lay foarkayttay/eel payntoa-leenoa pair lah foan-dootah
watch	l'orologio	loaroaloojoa

Records—Cassettes *Dischi—Cassette*

Do you have any records by ...?	Avete dischi di ...?	ahvaytay deeskee dee
I'd like a ...	Vorrei ...	vorraiee
cassette	una cassetta	oonah kahssayttah
video cassette	una video cassetta	oonah veedayoa kahs-sayttah
compact disc	un disco compatto	oon deeskoa koampahttoa

| Have you any songs by ...? | **Avete delle canzoni di ...?** | ahvaytay **day**llay kahn-**tso**anee dee |
| Can I listen to this record? | **Posso ascoltare questo disco?** | **pos**soa ahskoal**taa**ray koo**ays**toa **dees**koa |

L.P. (33 rpm)	**33 giri**	trayntah**tray** jeeree
E.P. (45 rpm)	**super 45 giri**	**soo**pair kwahrahntah-**cheeng**kooay **jee**ree
single	**45 giri**	kwahrahntah**cheeng**kooay jeeree

chamber music	**musica da camera**	**moo**zeekah dah **kaa**mayrah
classical music	**musica classica**	**moo**zeekah **klahs**seekah
folk music	**musica folcloristica**	**moo**zeekah folkloree-**stee**kah
instrumental music	**musica strumentale**	**moo**zeekah stroomayn-**taa**lay
jazz	**jazz**	"jazz"
light music	**musica leggera**	**moo**zeekah layd**jair**ah
orchestral music	**musica sinfonica**	**moo**zeekah seen**fo**neekah
pop music	**musica pop**	**moo**zeekah pop

Toys *Giocattoli*

I'd like a toy/game ...	**Vorrei un giocattolo/un gioco ...**	vor**raiee** oon joakaht**too**aloa/oon **joa**koa
for a boy	**per un bambino**	pair oon bahm**bee**noa
for a 5-year-old girl	**per una bambina di 5 anni**	pair **oo**nah bahm**bee**nah dee 5 **ahn**nee
beach ball	**un pallone (da spiaggia)**	oon pahl**loa**nay (dah spee**ahd**jah)
bucket and spade (pail and shovel)	**un secchiello e una paletta**	oon sayk**kee**ay**lloa** ay **oo**nah pah**layt**tah
building blocks (bricks)	**un gioco di costruzioni**	oon **joa**koa dee koastroo-**tsee**oanee
card game	**delle carte da gioco**	**day**llay **kahr**tay dah **joa**koa
chess set	**degli scacchi**	**day**lyee **skahk**kee
doll	**una bambola**	**oo**nah **bahm**boalah
electronic game	**un gioco elettronico**	oon **joa**koa aylayt**tro**neekoa
flippers	**delle pinne**	**day**llay **peen**nay
roller skates	**dei pattini a rotelle**	**daiee** pah**ttee**nee ah roteh**lla**y
snorkel	**la maschera da subacqueo**	lah **mah**skayrah dah soobahk**koo**ayoa

Your money: banks—currency

Italy's monetary unit is the *lira* (**lee**rah), plural *lire* (**lee**ray), abbreviated to *L.* or *Lit.* There are coins of 10, 20, 50, 100, 200 and 500 lire. Banknotes come in denomination of 500, 1,000, 2,000, 5,000, 10,000, 50,000 and 100,000 lire.

In Switzerland, the basic unit currency is the *franco* (**frahng**koa) divided into 100 *centesimi* (chayn**tay**zeemee). There are coins of 5, 10, 20 and 50 centimes and of 1, 2 and 5 francs. There are banknotes of 10, 20, 50, 100, 500 and 1,000 francs.

Though hours can vary, banks in Italy are generally open from 8.30 to 1 p.m. and from 2.30 to 3.30 p.m., Monday to Friday.

In Switzerland banks are generally open from 8.30 or 9 a.m. to noon and from 1.30 or 2 to 4.30 or 5 p.m., Monday to Friday. Main branches often remain open during the lunch hours.

In both countries you will find currency-exchange offices *(uffici cambio)* which are often open outside regular banking hours.

Credit cards may be used in an increasing number of hotels, restaurants, shops, etc. Signs are posted indicating which cards are accepted.

Traveller's cheques are accepted by hotels, travel agents and many shops, although the exchange rate is invariably better at a bank. Don't forget to take your passport when going to cash a traveller's cheque. Eurocheques are also accepted.

Where's the nearest bank?	Dov'è la banca più vicina?	doavai lah bahngkah peeoo veecheenah
Where is the currency exchange office?	Dov'è l'ufficio cambio?	doavai looffeechoa kahmbeeoa

At the bank *In banca*

I want to change some dollars/pounds.	Desidero cambiare dei dollari/delle sterline.	dayzeedayroa kahmbee**aa**ray da**ie**e dolla**hree**/**dayl**lay stayr**lee**nay
I want to cash a traveller's cheque/Eurocheque.	Voglio incassare un traveller's cheque/un eurocheque.	vol**yoa** eengkahss**aa**ray oon "traveller's cheque"/oon "eurocheque"
What's the exchange rate?	Qual è il corso del cambio?	kwahl ai eel **koar**soa dayl **kahm**beeoa
How much commission do you charge?	Quanto trattiene di commissione?	**kwahn**toa traht**tee**aynay dee koammees**seeoa**nay
Can you cash a personal cheque?	Può cambiare un assegno personale?	pwo kahmbee**aa**ray oon ahs**say**ñoa payrsoan**aa**lay
Can you telex my bank in London?	Può mandare un telex alla mia banca a Londra?	pwo mahn**daa**ray oon "telex" **ahl**lah **mee**ah **bahng**kah ah **loan**drah
I have a/an/some ...	Ho ...	oa
bank card	una carta d'identità bancaria	**oo**nah **kahr**tah deedayn**tee**teeah bahng**kaa**reeah
credit card	una carta di credito	**oo**nah **kahr**tah dee **kray**deetoa
introduction from ...	una lettera di presentazione di ...	**oo**nah **leht**tayrah dee prayzayntahtsee**oa**nay dee
letter of credit	una lettera di credito	**oo**nah **leht**tayrah dee **kray**deetoa
I'm expecting some money from New York. Has it arrived?	Aspetto del denaro da New York. È arrivato?	ahs**peht**toa dayl day**naa**roa dah "New York". ai ahrree**vaa**toa
Please give me ... notes (bills) and some small change.	Per favore, mi dia ... banconote e della moneta.	pair fah**voa**ray mee **dee**ah ... bahngkoa**no**tay ay **dayl**lah moa**nay**tah

Depositing—Withdrawing *Depositi—Prelevamenti*

I want to credit this to my account.	Desidero accreditare questo sul mio conto.	dayzeedayroa ahkkraydee**taa**ray koo**ays**toa sool **mee**oa **koan**toa
I want to ...	Desidero ...	dayzeedayroa
open an account	aprire un conto	ah**pree**ray oon **koan**toa
withdraw ... lire	prelevare ... lire	praylayvaaray ... **lee**ray

NUMBERS, see page 147

I want to credit this to Mr...'s account.	Desidero accreditare questo sul conto del signor ...	dayzeedayroa ahkkraydeetaaray kooaystoa sool koantoa dayl seeñoar
Where should I sign?	Dove devo firmare?	doavay dayvoa feermaaray

Business terms   *Termini d'affari*

My name is ...	Mi chiamo ...	mee keeaamoa
Here's my card.	Ecco il mio bigliettino.	ehkkoa eel meeoa beelyaytteenoa
I have an appointment with ...	Ho un appuntamento con ...	oa oon appoontahmayntoa kon
Can you give me an estimate of the cost?	Può farmi un preventivo?	pwo faarmee oon prayvvaynteevoa
What's the rate of inflation?	Qual è il tasso di inflazione?	kwahl ai eel tahssoa dee eenflahtseeoanay
Can you provide me with an interpreter/ a secretary?	Può procurarmi un interprete/una segretaria?	pwo prokooraarmee oon eentehrprehtay/oonah saygraytaareeah
Where can I make photocopies?	Dove posso fare delle fotocopie?	doavay possoa faaray dayllay fotokawpeeay

amount	l'importo	leempoartoa
balance	il bilancio	eel beelahnchoa
capital	il capitale	eel kahpeetaalay
cheque book	il libretto d'assegni	eel leebrehttoa dahssayñee
contract	il contratto	eel koantrahttoa
expenses	le spese	lay spaysay
interest	l'interesse	leentayrehssay
investment	l'investimento	leenvaysteemayntoa
invoice	la fattura	lah fahttoorah
loss	la perdita	lah payrdeetah
mortgage	l'ipoteca	leepoataykah
payment	il pagamento	eel pahgahmayntoa
percentage	la percentuale	lah payrchayntooaalay
profit	il profitto	eel proafeettoa
purchase	l'acquisto	lahkooeestoa
sale	la vendita	lah vayndeetah
share	l'azione	lahtseeoanay
transfer	il trasferimento	eel trahsfayreemayntoa
value	il valore	eel vahloaray

At the post office

Post offices in Italy bear the sign *PT* and are normally open from 8.15 a.m. to 1 or 2 p.m., Monday to Friday, Saturday till 12 noon or 1 p.m. Offices in major towns and tourist resorts stay open longer, but often for urgent matters only. Stamps are also sold at tobacconist's *(tabaccaio)* and at some hotel desks. Letter boxes (mailboxes) are red in Italy, and yellow in Switzerland.

Swiss post offices are recognized by a *PTT* sign and are open from 7.30 a.m. to noon and from 1.45 to 6.30 p.m., Monday to Friday, Saturday till 11 a.m.

Note that telephone service in Italy is generally separated from the post office.

Where's the nearest post office?	Dov'è l'ufficio postale più vicino?	doavai looffeechoa poa-staalay peeoo veecheenoa
What time does the post office open/close?	A che ora apre/chiude l'ufficio postale?	ah kay oarah aapray/keeooday looffeechoa poastaalay
A stamp for this letter/postcard, please.	Un francobollo per questa lettera/cartolina, per favore.	oon frahngkoaboalloa pair kooaystah lehttayrah/kahrtoaleenah pair fahvoaray
I want 2 ... -lire stamps.	Vorrei 2 francobolli da ... lire.	vorraiee 2 frahngkoaboallee dah ... leeray
What's the postage for a letter to London?	Qual è l'affrancatura per una lettera per Londra?	kwahl ai lahffrahngkahtoorah pair oonah lehttayrah pair loandrah
What's the postage for a postcard to Los Angeles?	Qual è l'affrancatura per una cartolina per Los Angeles?	kwahl ai lahffrahngkahtoorah pair oonah kahrtoaleenah pair "Los Angeles"
Where's the letter box (mailbox)?	Dov'è la cassetta delle lettere?	doavai lah kahssehttah dayllay lehttayray
I want to send this parcel.	Vorrei spedire questo pacco.	vorraiee spaydeeray kooaystoa pahhkkoa

I want to send this by ...	**Desidero inviare questo per ...**	dayzeedayroa eenveeaaray kooaystoa pair
airmail	**via aerea**	veeah ahayrayah
express (special delivery)	**espresso**	aysprehssoa
registered mail	**raccomandata**	rahkkoamahndaatah
At which counter can I cash an international money order?	**A quale sportello posso riscuotere un vaglia internazionale?**	ah kwaalay sportehlloa possoa reeskwotayray oon vaalyah eentayrnahtseeoanaalay
Where's the poste restante (general delivery)?	**Dov'è lo sportello del fermo posta?**	doavai loa spoartehlloa dayl fayrmoa postah
Is there any mail for me? My name is ...	**C'è della posta per me? Mi chiamo ...**	chai dayllah postah pair may? mee keeaamoa

FRANCOBOLLI	STAMPS
PACCHI	PARCELS
VAGLIA POSTALI	MONEY ORDERS

Telegrams *Telegrammi*

In Italy and Switzerland, you can either go directly to the post-office to send a telegram or phone it in. Some telegraph offices are open 24 hours a day.

I want to send a telegram/telex.	**Vorrei inviare un telegramma/telex.**	vorraiee eenveeaaray oon taylaygrahmmah/"telex"
May I please have a form?	**Può darmi un modulo?**	pwo daarmee oon modooloa
How much is it per word?	**Quanto costa ogni parola?**	kwahntoa kostah oñee pahrolah
How long will a cable to Boston take?	**Quanto tempo ci vorrà per inviare un telegramma a Boston?**	kwahntoa tehmpoa chee vorrah pair eenveeaaray oon taylaygrahmmah ah boston
How much will this telex cost?	**Quanto costerà questo telex?**	kwahntoa koastayrah kooaystoa "telex"

Telephoning *Per telefonare*

The telephone system in Italy and Switzerland is virtually entirely automatic. International or long-distance calls can be made from phone boxes, or ask at your hotel. Local calls in Italy can also be made from cafés, where you might have to pay after the call or to buy a *gettone* (token) to put into the phone.

Telephone numbers are given in pairs in Italy so that 12 34 56 would be expressed in Italian, twelve, thirty-four, fifty-six.

Where's the telephone?	**Dov'è il telefono?**	doa**vai** eel taylay**foa**noa
I'd like a telephone token.	**Vorrei un gettone (telefonico).**	vor**rai**ee oon jayt**toa**nay (taylayfoa**nee**koa)
Where's the nearest telephone booth?	**Dov'è la cabina telefonica più vicina?**	doa**vai** lah kah**bee**nah taylayfoa**nee**kah peeoo vee**chee**nah
May I use your phone?	**Posso usare il suo telefono?**	**pos**soa oo**zaa**ray eel **soo**oa taylay**foa**noa
Do you have a telephone directory for Rome?	**Ha un elenco telefonico di Roma?**	ah oon ay**layng**koa taylay**foa**neekoa dee **roam**ah
What's the dialling (area) code for …?	**Qual è il prefisso di …?**	kwahl ai eel pray**fees**soa dee
How do I get the international operator?	**Come si ottiene il servizio internazionale?**	**koa**may see ot**tee**aynay eel sayr**veet**seeoa eentayrnaht**seeoa**naalay

Operator *Centralinista*

Good morning, I want Venice 12 34 56.	**Buon giorno. Desidero il 12 34 56 di Venezia.**	bwon **joar**noa. dayzee**dayr**oa eel 12 34 56 dee vay**nait**seeah
Can you help me get this number?	**Mi può aiutare a ottenere questo numero?**	mee pwo aheeoo**taa**ray ah ot**tay**nayray koo**ay**stoa **noo**mayroa

NUMBERS, see page 147

I want to place a ...	Vorrei fare ...	vorraiee faaray
personal (person-to-person) call	una telefonata con preavviso	oonah taylayfoanaatah kon prayahvveezoa
reversed charge (collect) call	una telefonata a carico del destinatario	oonah taylayfoanaatah ah kaareekoa dayl daysteenahtaareeoa

Speaking *Al telefono*

Hello. This is ... speaking.	Pronto. Qui parla ...	prontoa. kooee pahrlah
I want to speak to ...	Vorrei parlare a ...	vorraiee pahrlaaray ah
I want extension ...	Mi dia la linea interna ...	mee deeah lah leenayah eentehrnah
Speak louder/more slowly, please.	Parli più forte/più lentamente, per favore.	pahrlee peeoo fortay/peeoo layntahmayntay pair fahvoaray

Bad luck *Sfortuna*

Would you please try again later?	Per favore, vuol provare di nuovo più tardi?	pair fahvoaray vwawl proavaaray dee nwawvoa peeoo tahrdee
Operator, you gave me the wrong number.	Signorina, mi ha dato il numero sbagliato.	seeñoareenah mee ah daatoa eel noomayroa zbahlyaatoa
Operator, we were cut off.	Signorina, la comunicazione si è interrotta.	seeñoareenah lah komooneekahtseeoanay see ai eentehrroattah

Telephone alphabet

A	Ancona	ahngkoanah	N	Napoli	naapoalee
B	Bari	baaree	O	Otranto	oatrahntoa
C	Catania	kahtaaneeah	P	Palermo	pahlehrmoa
D	Domodossola	doamoadossoalah	Q	Quarto	kwahrtoa
E	Empoli	aympoalee	R	Roma	roamah
F	Firenze	feerehntsay	S	Sassari	sahssahree
G	Genova	jainoavah	T	Torino	tawreenoa
H	Hotel	oatehl	U	Udine	oodeenay
I	Imperia	eempayreeah	V	Venezia	vaynaitseeah
J	i lunga	ee loonggah	W	v doppia	vee doappeeah
K	kappa	kahppah	X	ix	eekss
L	Livorno	leevoarnoa	Y	i greca	ee graykah
M	Milano	meelaanoa	Z	zeta	dzaitah

Not there   *La persona è assente*

When will he/she be back?	**Quando ritornerà?**	kwahndoa reetoarnehrah
Will you tell him/her I called? My name is ...	**Vuol dirgli/dirle che ho telefonato? Mi chiamo ...**	vwawl **deerlyee/deerlay** kay oa taylayfoanaatoa. mee keeaamoa
Would you ask him/her to call me?	**Può chiedergli/ chiederle di tele- fonarmi?**	pwo keeaidayrlyee/ keeaidayrlay dee taylay- foanaarmee
Would you please take a message?	**Per favore, può trasmettere un messaggio?**	pair fahvoaray pwo trahzmayttayray oon mayssahdjoa

Charges   *Costo della telefonata*

| What was the cost of that call? | **Quanto è costata la telefonata?** | kwahntoa ai kostaatah lah taylayfoanaatah |
| I want to pay for the call. | **Desidero pagare la telefonata.** | dayzeedayroa pahgaaray lah taylayfoanaatah |

C'è una telefonata per lei.	There's a telephone call for you.
Che numero chiama?	What number are you calling?
La linea è occupata.	The line's engaged.
Non risponde.	There's no answer.
Ha chiamato il numero sbagliato.	You've got the wrong number.
Il telefono non funziona.	The phone is out of order.
Un momento!	Just a moment.
Resti in linea.	Hold on, please.
Egli/Ella è fuori in questo momento.	He's/She's out at the moment.

Doctor

To be at ease, make sure your health insurance policy covers any illness or accident while on holiday. If not, ask your insurance representative, automobile association or travel agent for details of special health insurance.

General *Generalità*

Can you get me a doctor?	**Può chiamarmi un medico?**	pwo keeahmaarmee oon maideekoa
Is there a doctor here?	**C'è un medico qui?**	chai oon maideekoa kooee
I need a doctor, quickly!	**Mi serve un medico— presto!**	mee sayrvay oon maideekoa— prehstoa
Where can I find a doctor who speaks English?	**Dove posso trovare un medico che parla inglese?**	doavay possoa troavaaray oon maideekoa kay pahrlah eengglaysay
Where's the surgery (doctor's office)?	**Dov'è l'ambulatorio del medico?**	doavai lahmboolahtoreeoa dayl maideekoa
What are the surgery (office) hours?	**Quali sono le ore di consultazione?**	kwahlee soanoa lay oaray dee koansooltahtseeoanay
Could the doctor come to see me here?	**Il medico può venire a visitarmi qui?**	eel maideekoa pwo vayneeray ah veezeetaarmee kooee
What time can the doctor come?	**Quando può venire il medico?**	kwahndoa pwo vayneeray eel maideekoa
Can you recommend a/an ...?	**Può consigliarmi ...?**	pwo koanseelyaarmee
general practitioner	**un medico generico**	oon maideekoa jehnayreekoa
children's doctor	**un pediatra**	oon paydeeaatrah
eye specialist	**un oculista**	oon okooleestah
gynaecologist	**un ginecologo**	oon jeenaykoloagoa
Can I have an appointment ...?	**Può fissarmi un appuntamento ...?**	pwo feessaarmee oon ahppoontahmayntoa
right now	**subito**	soobeetoa
tomorrow	**domani**	doamaanee
as soon as possible	**il più presto possibile**	eel peeoo prehstoa posseebeelay

CHEMIST'S (PHARMACY), see page 108

Parts of the body *Parti del corpo*

English	Italian	Pronunciation
appendix	l'appendice	lahppayndeechay
arm	il braccio	eel brahtchoa
artery	l'arteria	lahrtaireeah
back	la schiena	lah skeeainah
bladder	la vescica	lah vaysheekah
bone	l'osso	lossoa
bowels	l'intestino	leentaysteenoa
breast	il petto	eel pehttoa
chest	il torace	eel toaraachay
ear	l'orecchio	loaraykkeeoa
eye(s)	l'occhio (gli occhi)	lokkeeoa (lyee okkee)
face	il viso	eel veezoa
finger	il dito della mano	eel deetoa dayllah maanoa
foot	il piede	eel peeayday
genitals	i genitali	ee jayneetaalee
gland	la ghiandola	lah geeahndoalah
hand	la mano	lah maanoa
head	la testa	lah tehstah
heart	il cuore	eel kworay
intestines	l'intestino	leentaysteenoa
jaw	la mascella	lah mahshehllah
joint	l'articolazione	lahrteekoalahtseeoanay
kidney	il rene	eel rainay
knee	il ginocchio	eel jeenokkeeoa
leg	la gamba	lah gahmbah
lip	il labbro	eel lahbbroa
liver	il fegato	eel faygahtoa
lung	il polmone	eel poalmoanay
mouth	la bocca	lah boakkah
muscle	il muscolo	eel mooskoaloa
neck	il collo	eel kolloa
nerve	il nervo	eel nehrvoa
nervous system	il sistema nervoso	eel seestaimah nehrvoasoa
nose	il naso	eel naasoa
rib	la costola	lah kostoalah
shoulder	la spalla	lah spahllah
skin	la pelle	lah pehllay
spine	la spina dorsale	lah speenah doarsaalay
stomach	lo stomaco	loa stomahkoa
tendon	il tendine	eel tehndeenay
throat	la gola	lah goalah
toe	il dito del piede	eel deetoa dayl peeayday
tongue	la lingua	lah leenggwah
tonsils	le tonsille	lay toanseellay
vein	la vena	lah vaynah

Accident—Injury *Incidente—Ferita*

There has been an accident.	C'è stato un incidente.	chai staatoa oon eencheedayntay
My child has had a fall.	Il mio bambino/ la mia bambina è caduto(a).	eel meeoa bahmbeenoa/ lah meeah bahmbeenah ai kahdootoa(ah)
He/She has hurt his/ her head.	Lui/Lei si è fatto(a) male alla testa.	looee/layee see ai fahttoa(ah) maalay ahllah tehstah
He's/She's unconscious.	È svenuto(a).	ai zvaynootoa(ah)
He's/She's bleeding heavily.	Perde molto sangue.	payrday moaltoa sahnggooay
He's/She's (seriously) injured.	È (gravemente) ferito(a).	ai (grahvaimayntay) fayreetoa(ah)
His/Her arm is broken.	Si è rotto(a) il braccio.	see ai rottoa(ah) eel brahtchoa
His/Her ankle is swollen.	Ha la caviglia gonfia.	ah lah kahveelyah goanfeeah
I've been stung.	Sono stato punto.	soanoa staatoa poontoa
I've got something in my eye.	Ho qualcosa nell'occhio.	oa kwahlkawsah nehllokkeeoa
I've got a/an ...	Ho ...	oa
blister	una vescica	oonah vaysheekah
boil	un foruncolo	oon foaroongkoaloa
bruise	una contusione	oonah koantoozeeoanay
burn	una scottatura	oonah skottahtoorah
cut	un taglio	oon taalyoa
graze	un'escoriazione	oonayskoareeahtseeoanay
insect bite	una puntura d'insetto	oonah poontoorah deensehttoa
lump	un bernoccolo	oon bayrnokkoaloa
rash	un esantema	oon ayzahntehmah
sting	una puntura	oonah poontoorah
swelling	un gonfiore	oon goanfeeoaray
wound	una ferita	oonah fayreetah
Could you have a look at it?	Può esaminarlo?	pwo ayzahmeenaarloa
I can't move my ...	Non posso muovere ...	noan possoa mwovayray
It hurts.	Mi fa male.	mee fah maalay

Dove fa male?	Where does it hurt?
Che genere di dolore è?	What kind of pain is it?
debole/acuto/lancinante costante/a intervalli	dull/sharp/throbbing constant/on and off
È ...	It's ...
rotto/distorto slogato/lacerato	broken/sprained dislocated/torn
Voglio che faccia una radiografia.	I want you to have an X-ray taken.
Sarà ingessato.	You'll get a plaster.
Ha fatto infezione.	It's infected.
È stato vaccinato(a) contro il tetano?	Have you been vaccinated against tetanus?
Le darò un antisettico/ un antinevralgico.	I'll give you an antiseptic/ a painkiller.

Illness   *Malattia*

I'm not feeling well.	**Non mi sento bene.**	noan mee **sayn**toa **bai**nay
I'm ill.	**Mi sento male.**	mee **sayn**toa **maa**lay
I feel ...	**Mi sento ...**	mee **sayn**toa
dizzy	**stordito(a)**	stoar**dee**toa(ah)
nauseous	**la nausea**	lah **now**zayah
shivery	**rabbrividire**	rahbbreevee**dee**ray
I've got a fever.	**Ho la febbre.**	oa lah **fehb**bray
My temperature is 38 degrees.	**Ho la febbre a 38.**	oa lah **fehb**bray ah 38
I've been vomiting.	**Ho vomitato.**	oa voamee**taa**toa
I'm constipated/ I've got diarrhoea.	**Sono costipato(a)/ Ho la diarrea.**	**soa**noa koas**tee**paa**toa(ah)/ oa lah deeah**rray**ah
My ... hurt(s).	**Ho male al/alla ...**	oa **maa**lay ahl/**ahl**lah
I have a nosebleed.	**Mi sanguina il naso.**	mee **sahng**gooeenah eel **naa**soa

NUMBERS, see page 147

I've got (a/an) ...	Ho ...	oa
asthma	l'asma	lahzmah
backache	il mal di schiena	eel mahl dee skeeainah
cold	il raffreddore	eel rahffrayddoaray
cough	la tosse	lah tossay
cramps	i crampi	ee krahmpee
earache	il mal d'orecchi	eel mahl doaraykkee
hay fever	la febbre del fieno	lah fehbbray dayl feeehnoa
headache	il mal di testa	eel mahl dee tehstah
indigestion	un'indigestione	ooneendeejaysteeoanay
palpitations	delle palpitazioni	dayllay pahlpeetahtseeoanee
rheumatism	i reumatismi	ee rayoomahteezmee
sore throat	il mal di gola	eel mahl dee goalah
stiff neck	il torcicollo	eel torcheekolloa
stomach ache	il mal di stomaco	eel mahl dee stomahkoa
sunstroke	un colpo di sole	oon koalpoa dee soalay
I have difficulties breathing.	Ho difficoltà a respirare.	oa deeffeekoltah ah rayspeeraaray
I have a pain in my chest.	Ho un dolore nel torace.	oa oon doaloaray nehl toaraachay
I had a heart attack ... years ago.	Ho avuto un attacco cardiaco ... anni fa.	oa ahvootoa oon ahttahkkoa kahrdeeahkoa ... ahnnee fah
My blood pressure is too high/too low.	La mia pressione è troppo alta/troppo bassa.	lah meeah prehsseeoanay ai troppoa ahltah/troppoa bahssah
I'm allergic to ...	Sono allergico a ...	soanoa ahllayrjeekoa ah
I'm a diabetic.	Ho il diabete.	oa eel deeahbehtay

Women's section *Sezione femminile*

I have period pains.	Ho delle mestruazioni dolorose.	oa dayllay maystrooahtseeoanee doaloarawsay
I have a vaginal infection.	Ho un'infezione vaginale.	oa ooneenfaytseeoanay vahjeenaalay
I'm on the pill.	Prendo la pillola.	prehndoa lah peelloalah
I haven't had my period for 2 months.	Non ho avuto le mestruazioni per 2 mesi.	noan oa ahvootoa lay maystrooahtseeoanee pair 2 maisee
I'm (3 months) pregnant.	Sono incinta (di 3 mesi).	soanoa eencheentah (dee 3 maisee)

Da quanto tempo si sente così?	How long have you been feeling like this?
È la prima volta che ha questo disturbo?	Is this the first time you've had this?
Le misuro la pressione/la febbre.	I'll take your blood pressure/temperature.
Tiri su la manica.	Roll up your sleeve, please.
Si spogli (fino alla vita).	Please undress (down to the waist).
Per favore, si sdrai qui.	Please lie down over there.
Apra la bocca.	Open your mouth.
Respiri profondamente.	Breathe deeply.
Tossisca, prego.	Cough, please.
Dove sente il dolore?	Where do you feel the pain?
Lei ha ...	You've got (a/an) ...
l'appendicite	appendicitis
un avvelenamento da cibi	food poisoning
una cistite	cystitis
la gastrite	gastritis
un'infiammazione a ...	inflammation of ...
l'influenza	flu
l'itterizia	jaundice
una malattia venerea	venereal disease
il morbillo	measles
la polmonite	pneumonia
Le farò un'iniezione.	I'll give you an injection.
Desidero un campione del sangue/dell'urina/delle feci.	I want a specimen of your blood/urine/stools.
Deve restare a letto per ... giorni.	You must stay in bed for ... days.
Deve consultare uno specialista.	I want you to see a specialist.
Deve andare all'ospedale per un controllo generale.	I want you to go to the hospital for a general check-up.
Deve essere operato(a).	You'll have to have an operation.

Prescription—Treatment *Ricetta—Cura*

This is my usual medicine.	**Questa è la mia medicina abituale.**	kooaystah ai lah **mee**ah maydee**chee**nah ahbeetoo-**aa**lay
Can you give me a prescription for this?	**Può farmi una ricetta per questo?**	pwo **faar**mee oonah ree-**chay**ttah pair kooay**stoa**
Can you prescribe a/an/some ...?	**Può prescrivermi ...?**	pwo pray**skree**vayrmee
antidepressant	**un antidepressivo**	oon ahnteedayprehs**see**voa
sleeping pills	**dei sonniferi**	daiee soan**nee**fayree
tranquillizer	**un tranquillante**	oon trahngkooeel**lahn**tay
I'm allergic to antibiotics/penicillin.	**Sono allergico(a) agli antibiotici/alla penicillina.**	**soa**noa ahllayr**jee**koa(ah) **ahl**yee ahnteebeeoa**tee**chee/ **ahl**lah paineecheel**lee**nah
I don't want anything too strong.	**Non voglio qualcosa troppo forte.**	noan **vol**yoa kwahl**kaw**sah **trop**poa **foar**tay
How many times a day should I take it?	**Quante volte al giorno devo prenderla?**	**kwahn**tay **vol**tay ahl **joar**noa **day**voa **prehn**dayrlah
Must I swallow them whole?	**Devo inghiottirle intere?**	**day**voa eengghee**oat**teerlay een**tay**ray

---

Che cura fa?	What treatment are you having?
Che medicine prende?	What medicine are you taking?
Per iniezioni o via orale?	By injection or orally?
Prenda ... cucchiaini di questa medicina ...	Take ... teaspoons of this medicine ...
Prenda una compressa con un bicchiere d'acqua ...	Take one pill with a glass of water ...
ogni ... ore	every ... hours
... volte al giorno	... times a day
prima/dopo ogni pasto	before/after each meal
al mattino/alla sera	in the morning/at night
in caso di dolore	if there is any pain
per ... giorni	for ... days

CHEMIST'S (PHARMACY), see page 108

Fee   *Onorario*

How much do I owe you?	**Quanto le devo?**	kwahntoa lay dayvoa
May I have a receipt for my health insurance?	**Posso avere una ricevuta per la mia assicurazione malattia?**	possoa ahvayray oonah reechayvootah pair lah meeah asseekoorahtseeoanay mahlahtteeah
Can I have a medical certificate?	**Posso avere un certificato medico?**	possoa ahvayray oon chayrteefeekaatoa maideekoa
Would you fill in this health insurance form, please?	**Potrebbe compilare questo modulo per l'assicurazione malattie, per favore?**	potrehbbay koampeelaaray kooaystoa moadooloa pair lasseekoorahtseeoanay mahlahtteeay pair fahvoaray

Hospital   *Ospedale*

What are the visiting hours?	**Quali sono gli orari di visita?**	kwahlee soanoa lyee oraaree dee veezeetah
When can I get up?	**Quando posso alzarmi?**	kwahndoa possoa ahltsaarmee
When will the doctor come?	**Quando verrà il dottore?**	kwahndoa vayrrah eel dottawray
I'm in pain.	**Ho male.**	oa maalay
I can't eat/I can't sleep.	**Non ho appetito/ Non riesco a dormire.**	noan oa ahppayteetoa/ noan reeehskoa ah doarmeeray
Can I have a pain-killer/some sleeping pills?	**Posso avere un calmante/dei sonniferi?**	possoa ahvayray oon kahlmahntay/daiee soanneefayree
Where is the bell?	**Dov'è il campanello?**	doavai eel kahmpahnehlloa

nurse	**l'infermiera**	leenfayrmeeayrah
patient	**il/la paziente**	eel/lah pahtseeaintay
anaesthetic	**l'anestetico**	lahnaystaiteekoa
blood transfusion	**la trasfusione di sangue**	lah trahsfoozeeoanay dee sahnggooay
injection	**l'iniezione**	leeneeaytseeoanay
operation	**l'operazione**	loapayrahtseeoanay
bed	**il letto**	eel lehttoa
bedpan	**la padella**	lah pahdehllah
thermometer	**il termometro**	eel tayrmomaytroa

Dentist *Dentista*

Can you recommend a good dentist?	**Può consigliarmi un buon dentista?**	pwo koanseelyahrmee oon bwawn daynteestah
Can I make an (urgent) appointment to see Dr ...?	**Desidero un appuntamento (urgente) con il dottor/la dottoressa ...**	dayzeedayroa oon ahppoontahmayntoa (oorjehntay) kon eel doattoar/lah doatoarehssah
Can't you possibly make it earlier than that?	**Non è possibile prima?**	noan ai poasseebeelay preemah
I have a broken tooth.	**Mi sono rotto un dente.**	mee soanoa rottoa oon dehntay
I have a toothache.	**Ho mal di denti.**	oa mahl dee dehntee
I have an abscess.	**Ho un ascesso.**	oa oon ahshehssoa
This tooth hurts.	**Mi fa male questo dente.**	mee fah maalay kooaystoa dehntay
at the top	**in alto**	een ahltoa
at the bottom	**in basso**	een bahssoa
in the front	**davanti**	dahvahntee
at the back	**dietro**	deeehtroa
Can you fix it temporarily?	**Può curarlo provvisoriamente?**	pwo kooraarloa proavvee-zoareeahmayntay
I don't want it extracted.	**Non voglio un'estrazione.**	noan volyoa oonaystrah-tseeoanay
Could you give me an anaesthetic?	**Potrebbe farmi l'anestesia?**	potrehbbay faarmee lahnaystayzeeah
I've lost a filling.	**L'otturazione si è staccata.**	loattoorahtseeoanay see ai stahkkaatah
The gum ...	**La gengiva ...**	lah jaynjeevah
is very sore	**è infiammata**	ai eenfeeahmmaatah
is bleeding	**sanguina**	sahnggooeenah
I've broken this denture.	**Ho rotto questa dentiera.**	oa roattoa kooaystah daynteeehrah
Can you repair this denture?	**Può ripararmi questa dentiera?**	pwo reepahraarmee kooaystah daynteeehrah
When will it be ready?	**Quando sarà pronta?**	kwahndoa sahrah proantah

Reference section

Where do you come from? *Da dove viene?*

Africa	l'Africa	laafreekah
Asia	l'Asia	laazeeah
Australia	l'Australia	lowstraaleeah
Europe	l'Europa	layooropah
North America	l'America del Nord	lahmaireekah dayl nord
South America	l'America del Sud	lahmaireekah dayl sood
Algeria	l'Algeria	lahljayreeah
Austria	l'Austria	lowstreeah
Belgium	il Belgio	eel behljoa
Canada	il Canada	eel kahnahdah
China	la Cina	lah cheenah
Denmark	la Danimarca	lah dahneemahrkah
England	l'Inghilterra	leengeeltehrrah
Finland	la Finlandia	lah feenlahndeeah
France	la Francia	lah frahnchah
Germany	la Germania	lah jayrmaaneeah
Great Britain	la Gran Bretagna	lah grahn braytaañah
Greece	la Grecia	lah graichah
India	l'India	leendeeah
Ireland	l'Irlanda	leerlahndah
Israel	Israele	eesrahaylay
Italy	l'Italia	leetaaleeah
Japan	il Giappone	eel jahppoanay
Luxembourg	il Lussemburgo	eel loossaymboorgoa
Morocco	il Marocco	eel mahrokkoa
Netherlands	l'Olanda	lolahndah
New Zealand	la Nuova Zelanda	lah nwawvah dzaylahndah
Norway	la Norvegia	lah norvayjah
Portugal	il Portogallo	eel portogahlloa
Scotland	la Scozia	lah skotseeah
South Africa	il Sudafrica	eel soodaafreekah
Soviet Union	l'Unione Sovietica	looneeoanay soaveeeh-teekah
Spain	la Spagna	lah spaañah
Sweden	la Svezia	lah svehtseeah
Switzerland	la Svizzera	lah sveettsayrah
Tunisia	la Tunisia	lah tooneezeeah
Turkey	la Turchia	lah toorkeeah
United States	gli Stati Uniti	lyee staatee ooneetee
Wales	il Galles	eel gahllayss
Yugoslavia	la Iugoslavia	lah eeoogoaslaaveeah

REFERENCE SECTION

Informazioni varie

Numbers *Numeri*

0	zero	dzehroa
1	uno	oonoa
2	due	dooay
3	tre	tray
4	quattro	kwahttroa
5	cinque	cheengkooay
6	sei	sehee
7	sette	sehttay
8	otto	ottoa
9	nove	nawvay
10	dieci	deeaichee
11	undici	oondeechee
12	dodici	doadeechee
13	tredici	traydeechee
14	quattordici	kwahttordeechee
15	quindici	kooeendeechee
16	sedici	saydeechee
17	diciassette	deechahssehttay
18	diciotto	deechottoa
19	diciannove	deechahnnawvay
20	venti	vayntee
21	ventuno	vayntoonoa
22	ventidue	vaynteedooay
23	ventitre	vaynteetray
24	ventiquattro	vaynteekwahttroa
25	venticinque	vaynteecheengkooay
26	ventisei	vaynteesehee
27	ventisette	vaynteesehttay
28	ventotto	vayntottoa
29	ventinove	vaynteenawvay
30	trenta	trayntah
31	trentuno	trayntoonoa
32	trentadue	trayntahdooay
33	trentatre	trayntatray
40	quaranta	kwahrahntah
41	quarantuno	kwahrahntoonoa
42	quarantadue	kwahrahntahdooay
43	quarantatre	kwahrahntahtray
50	cinquanta	cheengkwahntah
51	cinquantuno	cheengkwahntoonoa
52	cinquantadue	cheengkwahntahdooay
53	cinquantatre	cheengkwahntahtray
60	sessanta	sayssahntah
61	sessantuno	sayssahntoonoa
62	sessantadue	sayssahntahdooay

63	**sessantatre**	saysssahntahtray
70	**settanta**	sayt**tahn**tah
71	**settantuno**	sayttahn**toon**oa
72	**settantadue**	sayttahntah**dooay**
73	**settantatre**	sayttahntah**tray**
80	**ottanta**	ot**tahn**tah
81	**ottantuno**	ottahn**toon**oa
82	**ottantadue**	ottahntah**dooay**
83	**ottantatre**	ottahntah**tray**
90	**novanta**	noa**vahn**tah
91	**novantuno**	noavahn**toon**oa
92	**novantadue**	noavahntah**dooay**
93	**novantatre**	noavahntah**tray**
100	**cento**	**chehn**toa
101	**centouno**	chehntoa**oon**oa
102	**centodue**	chehntoa**dooay**
110	**centodieci**	chehntoa**dee**eaichee
120	**centoventi**	chehntoa**vayn**tee
130	**centotrenta**	chehntoa**trayn**tah
140	**centoquaranta**	chehntoak**wahrahn**tah
150	**centocinquanta**	chehntoacheeng**kwahn**tah
160	**centosessanta**	chehntoasays**sahn**tah
170	**centosettanta**	chehntoasayt**tahn**tah
180	**centottanta**	chehntot**tahn**tah
190	**centonovanta**	chehntoanoa**vahn**tah
200	**duecento**	dooay**chehn**toa
300	**trecento**	tray**chehn**toa
400	**quattrocento**	kwahttroa**chehn**toa
500	**cinquecento**	cheengkooay**chehn**toa
600	**seicento**	sehee**chehn**toa
700	**settecento**	sehttay**chehn**toa
800	**ottocento**	otto**chehn**toa
900	**novecento**	noavay**chehn**toa
1000	**mille**	**meel**lay
1100	**millecento**	meellay**chehn**toa
1200	**milleduecento**	meellaydooay**chehn**toa
2000	**duemila**	dooay**meel**ah
5000	**cinquemila**	cheengkooay**meel**ah
10,000	**diecimila**	deeaichee**meel**ah
50,000	**cinquantamila**	cheengkwahntah**meel**ah
100,000	**centomila**	chehntoa**meel**ah
1,000,000	**un milione**	oon meel**yoa**nay
1,000,000,000	**un miliardo**	oon meel**yahr**doa

first/second	**primo/secondo**	preemoa/saykoandoa
third/fourth	**terzo/quarto**	tehrtsoa/kwahrtoa
fifth/sixth	**quinto/sesto**	kooeentoa/sehstoa
seventh/eighth	**settimo/ottavo**	sehtteemoa/ottaavoa
ninth/tenth	**nono/decimo**	nonoa/dehcheemoa
once	**una volta**	oonah voltah
twice	**due volte**	dooay voltay
three times	**tre volte**	tray voltay
a half	**un mezzo**	oon mehddzoa
half a ...	**mezzo ...**	mehddzoa
half of ...	**metà di ...**	maytah dee
half (adj.)	**mezzo**	mehddzoa
a quarter	**un quarto**	oon kwahrtoa
one third	**un terzo**	oon tehrtsoa
a pair of	**un paio di**	oon paaeeoa dee
a dozen	**una dozzina**	oonah doaddzeenah
one per cent	**uno per cento**	oonoa pair chehntoa
3.4%	**3,4%**	tray veergoalah kwahttroa pair chehntoa
1981	**millenovecent-ottantuno**	meellay-noavaychehnt-ottahntoonoa
1992	**millenovecento-novantadue**	meellay-noavaychehntoa-noavahntahdooay
2003	**duemilatre**	dooaymeelahtray

Year and age *Anno ed età*

year	**l'anno**	lahnnoa
leap year	**l'anno bisestile**	lahnnoa beesaysteelay
decade	**il decennio**	eel dehchehnneeoa
century	**il secolo**	eel saikoloa
this year	**quest'anno**	kooaystahnnoa
last year	**l'anno scorso**	lahnnoa skoarsoa
next year	**l'anno prossimo**	lahnnoa prosseemoa
each year	**ogni anno**	oñee ahnnoa
2 years ago	**2 anni fa**	2 ahnnee fah
in one year	**in un anno**	een oon ahnnoa
in the eighties	**negli anni ottanta**	naylyee ahnnee ottahntah
the 16th century	**il sedicesimo secolo**	eel sehdeechayzeemoa saikoloa
in the 20th century	**nel ventesimo secolo**	nayl vayntayzeemoa saikoloa

How old are you?	**Quanti anni ha?**	kwahntee ahnnee ah
I'm 30 years old.	**Ho trent'anni.**	oa trayntahnnee
He/She was born in 1960.	**Lui/Lei è nato(a) nel millenovecento-sessanta.**	looee/laiee ai nahtoa(ah) nayl meellay-noavaychehn-toa-sayssahntah
What is his/her age?	**Quanti anni ha?**	kwahntee ahnnee ah
Children under 16 are not admitted.	**Vietato ai minori di sedici anni.**	veeaytaatoa ahee meenoa-ree dee saydeechee ahnnee

Seasons *Stagioni*

spring/summer	**la primavera/l'estate**	lah preemahvayrah/laystaatay
autumn/winter	**l'autunno/l'inverno**	lowtoonnoa/leenvehrnoa
in spring	**in primavera**	een preemahvayrah
during the summer	**durante l'estate**	doorahntay laystaatay
in autumn	**in autunno**	een owtoonnoa
during the winter	**durante l'inverno**	doorahntay leenvehrnoa
high season	**alta stagione**	ahltah stahjoanay
low season	**bassa stagione**	bahssah stahjoanay

Months *Mesi*

January	**gennaio***	jehnnaaeeoa
February	**febbraio**	fehbbraaeeoa
March	**marzo**	mahrtsoa
April	**aprile**	ahpreelay
May	**maggio**	mahdjoa
June	**giugno**	jooñoa
July	**luglio**	loolyoa
August	**agosto**	ahgoastoa
September	**settembre**	sayttehmbray
October	**ottobre**	oattoabray
November	**novembre**	noavehmbray
December	**dicembre**	deechehmbray
in September	**in settembre**	een sayttehmbray
since October	**da ottobre**	dah oattoabray
the beginning of January	**l'inizio di gennaio**	leeneetseeoa dee jehnnaaeeoa
the middle of February	**la metà di febbraio**	lah maytah dee fehbbraaeeoa
the end of March	**la fine di marzo**	lah feenay dee mahrtsoa

----

* The names of months aren't capitalized in Italian.

Days and Date *Giorni e data*

What day is it today?	**Che giorno è oggi?**	kay joarnoa ai odjee
Sunday	**domenica***	doamayneekah
Monday	**lunedì**	loonaydee
Tuesday	**martedì**	mahrtaydee
Wednesday	**mercoledì**	mehrkoalaydee
Thursday	**giovedì**	joavaydee
Friday	**venerdì**	vaynayrdee
Saturday	**sabato**	saabahtoa
It's ...	**È ...**	ai
July 1	**il primo luglio**	eel preemoa loolyoa
March 10	**il 10 marzo**	eel deeaichee mahrtsoa
in the morning	**al mattino**	ahl mahtteenoa
during the day	**durante il giorno**	doorahntay eel joarnoa
in the afternoon	**nel pomeriggio**	nayl poamayreedjoa
in the evening	**alla sera**	ahllah sayrah
at night	**la notte**	lah nottay
the day before yesterday	**ieri l'altro**	eeairee lahltroa
yesterday	**ieri**	eeairee
today	**oggi**	odjee
tomorrow	**domani**	doamaanee
the day after tomorrow	**dopodomani**	dopoadoamaanee
the day before	**il giorno prima**	eel joarnoa preemah
the next day	**il giorno seguente**	eel joarnoa saygooayntay
two days ago	**due giorni fa**	dooay joarnee fah
in three days' time	**fra tre giorni**	frah tray joarnee
last week	**la settimana scorsa**	lah saytteemaanah skoarsah
next week	**la settimana prossima**	lah saytteemaanah prosseemah
for a fortnight (two weeks)	**per quindici giorni**	pair kooeendeechee joarnee
birthday	**il compleanno**	eel koamplayahnnoa
day off	**il giorno di riposo**	eel joarnoa dee reeposoa
holiday	**il giorno festivo**	eel joarnoa faysteevoa
holidays/vacation	**le vacanze**	lay vahkahntsay
week	**la settimana**	lah saytteemaanah
weekend	**il fine settimana**	eel feenay saytteemaanah
working day	**il giorno feriale**	eel joarnoa fayreeaalay

* The names of days aren't capitalized in Italian.

Public holidays   *Giorni festivi*

While there may be additional regional holidays in Italy, only national holidays are cited below.

January 1	**Capodanno**	New Year's Day
January 6	**Epifania**	Epiphany
April 25	**Anniversario della Liberazione (1945)**	Liberation Day
May 1	**Festa del Lavoro**	Labour Day
August 15	**Ferragosto**	Assumption Day
November 1	**Ognissanti**	All Saints' Day
December 8	**L'Immacolata Concezione**	Immaculate Conception
December 25	**Natale**	Christmas Day
December 26	**Santo Stefano**	St. Stephen's Day
Movable date:	**Lunedì di Pasqua (Pasquetta)**	Easter Monday

Except for the 25th April, all the Italian holidays are celebrated in the Ticino, as well as the 19th March *(San Giuseppe),* 1st August (National Holiday), and the usual holidays *Ascensione* (Ascension Day), *Lunedì di Pentecoste* (Whit Monday) and *Corpus Domini.*

Greetings and wishes   *Saluti e auguri*

Merry Christmas!	**Buon Natale!**	bwawn nahtaalay
Happy New Year!	**Buon anno!**	bwawn ahnnoa
Happy Easter!	**Buona Pasqua!**	**bwaw**nah pahskwah
Happy birthday!	**Buon compleanno!**	bwawn koamplayahnnoa
Best wishes!	**Tanti auguri!**	**tahn**tee ahoogooree
Congratulations!	**Congratulazioni!**	koangrahtoolahtseeoanee
Good luck/All the best!	**Buona fortuna!**	**bwaw**nah foartoonah
Have a good trip!	**Buon viaggio!**	bwawn veeahdjoa
Have a good holiday!	**Buone vacanze!**	**bwaw**nay vahkahntsay
Best regards from ...	**I migliori saluti da ...**	ee meel**yoa**ree sahlootee dah
My regards to ...	**I miei saluti a ...**	ee mee**aiee** sahlootee ah

What time is it?   *Che ore sono?*

Excuse me. Can you tell me the time?	**Mi scusi. Può dirmi che ore sono?**	mee skoozee. pwo deermee kay oaray soanoa
It's five past one.	**È l'una e cinque.**	ai loonah ay cheengkooay
It's ...	**Sono le ...**	soanoa lay
ten past two	**due e dieci**	dooay ay deeaichee
a quarter past three	**tre e un quarto**	tray ay oon kwahrtoa
twenty past four	**quattro e venti**	kwahttroa ay vayntee
twenty-five past five	**cinque e venticinque**	cheengkooay ay vayntee-cheengkooay
half past six	**sei e mezza**	sehee ay mehddzah
twenty-five to eight	**sette e trentacinque**	sehttay ay trayntah-cheengkooay
twenty to eight	**otto meno venti**	ottoa mainoa vayntee
a quarter to nine	**nove meno un quarto**	navvay mainoa oon kwahrtoa
ten to ten	**dieci meno dieci**	deeaichee mainoa deeaichee
five to eleven	**undici meno cinque**	oondeechee mainoa cheengkooay
twelve o'clock (noon/midnight)	**dodici (mezzogiorno/ mezzanotte)**	doadeechee (mehdzoajoarnoa/ mehdzahnottay)
in the morning	**del mattino**	dayl mahtteenoa
in the afternoon	**del pomeriggio**	dayl poamayreedjoa
in the evening	**della sera**	dayllah sayrah
The train leaves at ...	**Il treno parte alle ...**	eel traynoa pahrtay ahllay
13.04 (1.04 p.m.)	**tredici e quattro***	traydeechee ay kwahttroa
0.40 (0.40 a.m.)	**zero e quaranta**	dzehroa ay kwahrahntah
in five minutes	**fra cinque minuti**	frah cheengkooay meenootee
in a quarter of an hour	**fra un quarto d'ora**	frah oon kwahrtoa doarah
half an hour ago	**mezz'ora fa**	mehdzoarah fah
about two hours	**circa due ore**	cheerkah dooay oaray
more than 10 minutes	**più di dieci minuti**	peeoo dee deeaichee meenootee
less than 30 seconds	**meno di trenta secondi**	mainoa dee trayntah saykoandee
The clock is fast/ slow.	**L'orologio è avanti/ indietro.**	loaroalojoa ai ahvahntee/ eendeeaytroa

---

* In ordinary conversation, time is expressed as shown above. However, official time uses a 24-hour clock which means that after noon hours are counted from 13 to 24.

Common abbreviations   *Abbreviazioni correnti*

A.A.T.	Azienda Autonoma di Soggiorno, Cura e Turismo	local tourist board
a.	arrivo	arrival
ab.	abitanti	inhabitants, population
a.C.	avanti Cristo	B.C.
A.C.I.	Automobile Club d'Italia	Italian Automobile Association
a.D.	anno Domini	A.D.
A.G.I.P.	Azienda Generale Italiana Petroli	Italian National Oil Company
alt.	altitudine	altitude
C.I.T.	Compagnia Italiana Turismo	Italian Travel Agency
c.m.	corrente mese	of this month
C.P.	casella postale	post office box
C.so	Corso	avenue
d.C.	dopo Cristo	A.D.
ecc.	eccetera	etc.
E.N.I.T.	Ente Nazionale italiano per il Turismo	National Tourist Organization
F.F.S.	Ferrovie Federali Svizzere	Swiss Federal Railways
F.S.	Ferrovie dello Stato	Italian State Railways
I.V.A.	Imposta sul Valore Aggiunto	value added tax (sales tax)
Mil.	militare	military
p.	partenza; pagina	departure; page
P.T.	Poste & Telecomunicazioni	Post & Telecommunications
P.za	Piazza	square
R.A.I.	Radio Audizioni Italiane	Italian Broadcasting Company
Rep.	Repubblica	republic
sec.	secolo	century
Sig.	Signor	Mr.
Sig.a	Signora	Mrs.
Sig.na	Signorina	Miss
S.p.a.	Società per azioni	Ltd., Inc.
S.P.Q.R.	Senatus Populusque Romanus	The Senate and the People of Rome (Latin)
S.r.l.	Società a responsabilità limitata	limited liability company
S./S.ta	San(to)/Santa	Saint
S.S.	Sua Santità	His Holiness
T.C.I.	Touring Club Italiano	Italian Touring Association
V.le	Viale	avenue
V.U.	Vigili Urbani	city police

Signs and notices *Cartelli*

Affittasi	To let, for hire
Al completo	Full/No vacancies
Aperto da ... a ...	Open from ... to ...
Ascensore	Lift (elevator)
Attenti al cane	Beware of the dog
Caldo	Hot
Cassa	Cash desk
Chiudere la porta	Close the door
Chiuso	Closed
Chiuso per ferie/per riposo settimanale	Closed for holiday/Weekly closing day
Entrare senza bussare	Enter without knocking
Entrata	Entrance
Entrata libera	Free entrance
Freddo	Cold
Fuori servizio	Out of order
I trasgressori saranno puniti a norma di legge	Trespassers will be prosecuted
Informazioni	Information
In sciopero	On strike
In vendita	For sale
Libero	Vacant
Non disturbare	Do not disturb
Non toccare	Do not touch
Occupato	Occupied
Pericolo (di morte)	Danger (of death)
Pista per ciclisti	Path for cyclists
Pittura fresca	Wet paint
Privato	Private
Prudenza	Caution
Riservato	Reserved
Saldi	Sales
Signore	Ladies
Signori	Gentlemen
Spingere	Push
Strada privata	Private road
Suonare, per favore	Please ring
Svendita	Sales
Tirare	Pull
Uscita	Exit
Uscita di sicurezza	Emergency exit
Vietato ...	... forbidden
Vietato fumare	No smoking
Vietato l'ingresso	No entrance
Vietato toccare	Do not touch

Emergency *Emergenza*

Call the police	**Chiami la polizia**	keeaamee lah poaleetseeah
DANGER	**PERICOLO**	payreekoaloa
FIRE	**AL FUOCO**	ahl fwawkoa
Gas	**Gas**	gaz
Get a doctor	**Chiami un medico**	keeaamee oon maideekoa
Go away	**Se ne vada**	say nay vaadah
HELP	**AIUTO**	aheeootoa
Get help quickly	**Chiami aiuti, presto**	keeaamee aheeootee prehstoa
I'm ill	**Mi sento male**	mee sayntoa maalay
I'm lost	**Mi sono perso(a)**	mee soanoa pehrsoa(ah)
Leave me alone	**Mi lasci in pace**	mee laashee een paachay
LOOK OUT	**ATTENZIONE**	ahttayntseeoanay
Poison	**Veleno**	vaylaynoa
POLICE	**POLIZIA**	poaleetseeah
Quick	**Presto**	prehstoa
STOP	**FERMATEVI**	fayrmaataayvee
Stop that man/ woman	**Fermate quell'uomo/ quella donna**	fayrmaatay kooayllwomoa/ kooayllah donnah
STOP THIEF	**AL LADRO**	ahl laadroa

Emergency telephone numbers *Chiamate di emergenza*

Italy:	Police, all-purpose emergency number	113
	Road assistance (Automobile Club d'Italia)	116
Switzerland:	Police, all-purpose emergency number	117
	Fire	118

Lost! *In caso di perdite o di furti*

Where's the ...?	**Dov'è ...?**	doavai
lost-property (lost and found) office	**l'ufficio oggetti smarriti**	looffeechoa oadjehttee zmahrreetee
police station	**il posto di polizia**	eel poastoa dee poaleetseeah
I want to report a theft.	**Devo denunciare un furto.**	dayvoa daynoonchaaray oon foortoa
My ... has been stolen.	**Mi hanno rubato ...**	mee ahnnoa roobaatoa
I've lost my ...	**Ho perso ...**	oa pehrsoa
handbag	**la mia borsetta**	lah meeah boarsayttah
passport	**il mio passaporto**	eel meeoa pahssahpoartoa
wallet	**il mio portafogli**	eel meeoa portahfoalyee

CAR ACCIDENTS, see page 78

Conversion tables

Centimetres and inches

To change centimetres into inches, multiply by .39.

To change inches into centimetres, multiply by 2.54.

	in.	feet	yards
1 mm.	0.039	0.003	0.001
1 cm.	0.39	0.03	0.01
1 dm.	3.94	0.32	0.10
1 m.	39.40	3.28	1.09

	mm.	cm.	m.
1 in.	25.4	2.54	0.025
1 ft.	304.8	30.48	0.305
1 yd.	914.4	91.44	0.914

(32 metres = 35 yards)

Temperature

To convert centigrade into degrees Fahrenheit, multiply centigrade by 1.8 and add 32.

To convert degrees Fahrenheit into centigrade, subtract 32 from Fahrenheit and divide by 1.8.

Kilometres into miles

1 kilometre (km.) = 0.62 miles

km.	10	20	30	40	50	60	70	80	90	100	110	120	130
miles	6	12	19	25	31	37	44	50	56	62	68	75	81

Miles into kilometres

1 mile = 1.609 kilometres (km.)

miles	10	20	30	40	50	60	70	80	90	100
km.	16	32	48	64	80	97	113	129	145	161

Fluid measures

1 litre (l.) = 0.88 imp. quart or = 1.06 U.S. quart

1 imp. quart = 1.14 l.	1 U.S. quart = 0.95 l.
1 imp. gallon = 4.55 l.	1 U.S. gallon = 3.8 l.

litres	5	10	15	20	25	30	35	40	45	50
imp. gal.	1.1	2.2	3.3	4.4	5.5	6.6	7.7	8.8	9.9	11.0
U.S. gal.	1.3	2.6	3.9	5.2	6.5	7.8	9.1	10.4	11.7	13.0

Weights and measures

1 kilogram or kilo (kg.) = 1000 grams (g.)

100 g. = 3.5 oz.	½ kg. = 1.1 lb.
200 g. = 7.0 oz.	1 kg. = 2.2 lb.

1 oz. = 28.35 g.
1 lb. = 453.60 g.

CLOTHING SIZES, see page 115/YARDS AND INCHES, see page 112

A very basic grammar

Articles

There are two genders in Italian—masculine (masc.) and feminine (fem.).

1. Definite article (the):

	singular	plural
masc.	l' before a vowel	gli
	lo before z or s + consonant	gli
	il before all other consonants	i
	l'amico (the friend)	gli amici (the friends)
	lo studente (the student)	gli studenti (the students)
	il treno (the train)	i treni (the trains)
fem.	l' before a vowel	le
	la before a consonant	le
	l'arancia (the orange)	le arance (the oranges)
	la casa (the house)	le case (the houses)

2. Indefinite article (a/an):

masc.	un (uno before z or s + consonant*)
	un piatto (a plate)
	uno specchio (a mirror)
fem.	una (un' before a vowel)
	una strada (a street)
	un'amica (a girl friend)

3. Partitive (some/any)

In affirmative sentences and some interrogatives, **some** and **any** are expressed by **di + definite article,** which has the following contracted forms:

masc.	dell' before a vowel	degli
	dello before z or s + consonant	degli
	del before other consonants	dei
fem.	dell' before a vowel	delle
	della before a consonant	delle

---

*When s is followed by a vowel, the masculine articles are il/i (definite) and un (indefinite).

For other contractions of preposition + definite article, see page 163.

Desidero del vino	I want some wine.
Vorrei delle sigarette.	I'd like some cigarettes.
Ha degli amici a Roma?	Have you any friends in Rome?

Nouns

Nouns ending in **o** are generally masculine. To form the plural, change **o** to **i**.

il tavolo (the table) **i tavoli** (the tables)

Nouns ending in **a** are usually feminine. To form the plural, change **a** to **e**.

la casa (the house) **le case** (the houses)

Nouns ending in **e**—no rule as to gender. Learn each noun individually. Plurals are formed by changing the **e** to **i**.

il piede (the foot) **i piedi** (the feet)
la notte (the night) **le notti** (the nights)

Adjectives

They agree with the noun they modify in number and gender. There are two basic types—ending in **o** and ending in **e**.

	singular	plural
masc.	**leggero** light (in weight)	**leggeri**
	grande big	**grandi**
fem.	**leggera**	**leggere**
	grande	**grandi**

They usually follow the noun but certain common adjectives precede the noun.

un caro amico (a dear friend)
una strada lunga (a long street)

Demonstratives

this	**questo/questa** (contracted to **quest'** before a vowel)
these	**questi/queste** (no contraction)
that	**quell', quello, quel** (masc.)/**quell', quella*** (fem.)
those	**quegli, quei** (masc.)/ **quelle** (fem.)

Possessive adjectives and pronouns

These agree in number and gender *with the nouns they modify* (or replace). They are almost always used with the definite article.

	masculine		feminine	
	singular	plural	singular	plural
my, mine	**il mio**	**i miei**	**la mia**	**le mie**
your, yours	**il tuo**	**i tuoi**	**la tua**	**le tue**
his, her, hers, its	**il suo**	**i suoi**	**la sua**	**le sue**
our, ours	**il nostro**	**i nostri**	**la nostra**	**le nostre**
your, yours	**il vostro**	**i vostri**	**la vostra**	**le vostre**
their, theirs	**il loro**	**i loro**	**la loro**	**le loro**
**your, yours (sing.)	**il suo**	**i suoi**	**la sua**	**le sue**
**your, yours (plur.)	**il loro**	**i loro**	**la loro**	**le loro**

Thus, depending on the context, **il suo cane** can mean *his, her* or *your dog*, **la sua casa**, *his, her* or *your house*.

Personal pronouns

	Subject	Direct Object	Indirect Object	After a Preposition
I	**io**	**mi**	**mi**	**me**
you	**tu**	**ti**	**ti**	**te**
he, it (masc.)	**lui/egli**	**lo**	**gli**	**lui**
she, it (fem.)	**lei/ella**	**la**	**le**	**lei**
we	**noi**	**ci**	**ci**	**noi**
you	**voi**	**vi**	**vi**	**voi**
they (masc.)	**loro/essi**	**li**	**loro**	**loro**
they (fem.)	**loro/esse**	**le**	**loro**	**loro**

* These forms follow the same system as **dell'/dello/della**, etc. (see p. 163).
** This is the formal form—used in addressing people you do not know well.

Note: There are two forms for "you" in Italian: **tu** (singular) is used when talking to relatives, close friends and children (and between young people); the plural of **tu** is **voi**. **Lei** (singular) and **Loro** (plural) are used in all other cases (with the 3rd person singular/plural of the verb).

Verbs

Here we are concerned only with the infinitive and the present tense.

Learn these two **auxiliary verbs**:

essere (to be)	avere (to have)
io* sono (I am)	**io* ho** (I have)
tu sei (you are)	**tu hai** (you have)
lui, lei è (he, she, it is)	**lui, lei ha** (he, she, it has)
lei è (you are)	**lei ha** (you have)
noi siamo (we are)	**noi abbiamo** (we have)
voi siete (you are)	**voi avete** (you have)
essi/esse sono (they are)	**essi/esse hanno** (they have)

C'è/Ci sono are equivalent to "there is/there are":

C'è una lettera per Lei.   There's a letter for you.
Ci sono due pacchi per lui.   There are two parcels for him.

Regular verbs follow one of three patterns (conjugations) depending on the ending of the infinitive.

	ends in **-are**	ends in **-ere**	ends in **-ire**
Infinitive:	**amare** (to love)	**vendere** (to sell)	**partire** (to leave)
io*	**amo**	**vendo**	**parto**
tu	**ami**	**vendi**	**parti**
lui, lei	**ama**	**vende**	**parte**
noi	**amiamo**	**vendiamo**	**partiamo**
voi	**amate**	**vendete**	**partite**
essi/esse	**amano**	**vendono**	**partono**

* The subject pronouns are seldom used except for emphasis.

Irregular verbs: As in all languages, these have to be learned. Here are four you'll find useful.

Infinitive:	andare (to go)	potere (to be able)	volere (to want)	fare (to make)
io	vado	posso	voglio	faccio
tu	vai	puoi	vuoi	fai
lui/lei	va	può	vuole	fa
noi	andiamo	possiamo	vogliamo	facciamo
voi	andate	potete	volete	fate
essi/esse	vanno	possono	vogliono	fanno

Negatives

Negatives are formed by putting **non** before the verb.

Non vado a Roma.   I am not going to Rome.

Questions

In Italian, questions are often formed by simply changing the inflexion of your voice. Remember that the personal pronoun is rarely used, either in affirmative sentences or in questions.

Parlo italiano.   I speak Italian.
Parla italiano?   Do you speak Italian?

Prepositions

There is a list of prepositions on page 14. Note the following contractions:

Definite Article	a at, to	da by, from	di of	in in	su on	con with
+ il	al	dal	del	nel	sul	col
+ l'	all'	dall'	dell'	nell'	sull'	coll'
+ lo	allo	dallo	dello	nello	sullo	con lo
+ la	alla	dalla	della	nella	sulla	con la
+ i	ai	dai	dei	nei	sui	coi/con i
+ gli	agli	dagli	degli	negli	sugli	con gli
+ le	alle	dalle	delle	nelle	sulle	con le

Dictionary
and alphabetical index

English–Italian

f feminine	m masculine	pl plural

a un(a) 159
abbey abbazia f 81
abbreviation abbreviazione f 154
able, to be potere 163
about *(approximately)* circa 153
above sopra 15, 63
absces ascesso m 145
absorbent cotton cotone idrofilo m 109
accept, to accettare 62, 102
accessories accessori m/pl 116, 125
accident incidente m 78, 79, 139
accommodation alloggio m 22
account conto m 130, 131
ache dolore m, male m 141
adaptor presa multipla f 119
address indirizzo m 21, 31, 76, 79, 102
address book agenda per gli indirizzi f 104
adhesive adesivo(a) 105
admission entrata f 82, 89, 155
Africa Africa f 146
after dopo 14, 77
afternoon pomeriggio m 151, 153
after-shave lotion lozione dopobarba f 110
age età f 149; anni m 150
ago fa 149, 151
air conditioner condizionatore d'aria m 28
air conditioning aria condizionata f 23
airmail via aerea 133
airplane aereo m 65
airport aeroporto m 16, 21, 65

alabaster alabastro m 122
alarm clock sveglia f 121
alcohol alcool m 107
alcoholic alcolico(a) 59
Algeria Algeria f 146
allergic allergico(a) 141, 143
almond mandorla f 54
alphabet alfabeto m 8
also anche 15
amazing sorprendente 84
amber ambra f 122
ambulance ambulanza f 79
American americano(a) 93, 126
American plan pensione completa f 24
amethyst ametista f 122
amount importo m 62, 131
amplifier amplificatore m 119
anaesthetic anestetico m 144
analgesic analgesico m 109
anchovy acciuga f 41, 46
and e 15
animal animale m 85
ankle caviglia f 139
anorak giacca a vento f 116
another un(') altro(a) 123
answer, to rispondere 136
antibiotic antibiotico m 143
antidepressant antidepressivo m 143
antiques antichità f/pl 83
antique shop antiquario m 98
antiseptic antisettico(a) 109
antiseptic antisettico m 140
any del, della 14
anyone qualcuno(a) 11
anything qualcosa 17, 25, 113

aperitif aperitivo *m* 56
appendicitis appendicite *f* 142
appendix appendice *f* 138
appetizer antipasto *m* 41
apple mela *f* 54, 63
appliance apparecchio *m* 119
appointment appuntamento *m* 30, 131, 137, 145
apricot albicocca *f* 54
April aprile *m* 150
archaeology archeologia *f* 83
architect architetto *m* 83
area code prefisso *m* 134
arm braccio *m* 138, 139
arrival arrivo *m* 16, 65
arrive, to arrivare 65, 68, 130
art arte *f* 83
artery arteria *f* 138
art gallery galleria d'arte *f* 81, 98
artichoke carciofo *m* 41, 52
artificial artificiale 124
artist artista *m/f* 81, 83
ashtray portacenere *m* 27, 36
Asia Asia *f* 146
ask for, to chiedere 25, 61, 136
asparagus asparago *m* 52
aspirin aspirina *f* 109
assorted assortito(a) 41
asthma asma *f* 141
at a 14, 163
at least come minimo 24
at once subito 15; immediatamente 31
aubergine melanzana *f* 52
August agosto *m* 150
aunt zia *f* 93
Australia Australia *f* 146
Austria Austria *f* 146
automatic automatico(a) 20, 122, 124
autumn autunno *m* 150
average medio(a) 91
awful orribile 84

B

baby bambino *m* 24, 111; bebè *m* 111
baby food alimenti per bebè *m/pl* 111
babysitter babysitter *f* 27
back schiena *f* 138
backache mal di schiena *m* 141
bacon pancetta *f* 38
bacon and eggs uova e pancetta *m/pl* 38
bad cattivo(a) 13, 95

bag borsa *f* 18; sacchetto *m* 103
baggage bagagli *m/pl* 18, 26, 31, 71
baggage cart carrello portabagagli *m* 18, 71
baggage check deposito bagagli *m* 67, 71
baggage locker custodia automatica dei bagagli *f* 18, 67, 71
baked al forno 47, 50
baker's panetteria *f* 98
balance *(account)* bilancio *m* 131
balcony balcone *m* 23
ball *(inflated)* pallone *m* 128
ballet balletto *m* 88
ball-point pen biro *f* 104
banana banana *f* 54, 63
bandage benda *f* 109
Band-Aid cerotto *m* 109
bangle braccialetto *m* 121
bangs frangia *f* 30
bank *(finance)* banca *f* 98, 129
bank card carta d'identità bancaria *f* 130
banknote banconota *f* 130
bar bar *m* 33, 67; *(chocolate)* stecca *f* 64
barbecued alla graticola, alla griglia 50
barber's barbiere *m* 30, 98
basil basilico *m* 53
basketball pallacanestro *f* 89
bath *(hotel)* bagno *m* 23, 25, 27
bathing cap cuffia da bagno *f* 116
bathing hut cabina *f* 91
bathing suit costume da bagno *m* 116
bathrobe accappatoio *m* 116
bathroom bagno *m* 27
bath salts sali da bagno *m/pl* 110
bath towel asciugamano *m* 27
battery pila *f* 119, 121, 125; *(car)* batteria *f* 75, 78
be, to essere 162; trovarsi 11
beach spiaggia *f* 90
bean fagiolo *m* 52
beard barba *f* 31
beautiful bello(a) 13, 84
beauty salon istituto di bellezza *m* 30, 98
bed letto *m* 24, 144
bed and breakfast camera e colazione *f* 24
bedpan padella *f* 144
beef manzo *m* 48

beer birra f 59, 64
beet(root) barbabietola f 52
before (place) davanti a 14; (time) prima di 14, 151
begin, to iniziare 80, 88; incominciare 87
beginner principiante m/f 91
beginning inizio m 150
behind dietro 14, 77
beige beige 113
Belgium Belgio m 146
bell (electric) campanello m 144
bellboy fattorino m 26
below al di sotto 15; sotto 63
belt cintura f 117
bend (road) curva f 79
berth cuccetta f 69, 70, 71
best migliore 152
better migliore 13, 25, 101, 113
between tra, fra 15
bicycle bicicletta f 74
big grande 13, 101
bill conto m 31, 62, 102; (banknote) banconota f 130
billion (Am.) miliardo m 148
binoculars binocolo m 123
bird uccello m 85
birth nascita f 25
birthday compleanno m 151, 152
biscuit (Br.) biscotto m 64
bitter amaro(a) 61
black nero(a) 113
black and white bianco e nero 124, 125
blackberry mora f 54
blackcurrant ribes nero m 54
bladder vescica f 138
blanket coperta f 27
bleed, to perdere sangue 139; sanguinare 145
blind (window) persiana f 29
blister vescica f 139
block, to otturare 28
blood sangue m 142
blood pressure pressione f 141
blood transfusion trasfusione di sangue f 144
blouse blusa f 116
blow-dry asciugatura col fono f 30
blue blu, azzurro(a) 113
blueberry mirtillo m 54
boar (wild) cinghiale m 51
boarding house pensione f 19, 22

boat battello m 74
bobby pin molletta f 111
body corpo m 138
boil foruncolo m 139
boiled lesso(a) 47, 50
boiled egg uovo alla coque m 38
bone osso m 138
book libro m 11, 104
book, to prenotare 69
booking office ufficio prenotazioni m 19, 67
booklet blocchetto m 72
bookshop libreria f 98, 104
boot stivale m 118
born nato(a) 150
botanical gardens giardino botanico m 81
botany botanica f 83
bottle bottiglia f 17, 57
bottle-opener apribottiglia m 106
bottom basso m 145
bowels intestino m 138
bow tie cravatta a farfalla f 116
box scatola f 120
boxing pugilato m 89
boy (child) bambino m 112, 128
boyfriend ragazzo m 93
bra reggiseno m 116
bracelet braccialetto m 121
braces (suspenders) bretelle f/pl 116
braised brasato(a) 50
brake freno m 78
brake fluid olio dei freni m 75
brandy brandy m 59
bread pane m 36, 38, 64
break, to rompere 29, 119, 123, 145; rompersi 139, 145
break down, to avere un guasto 78
breakdown guasto m 78
breakdown van carro attrezzi m 78
breakfast colazione f 24, 34, 38
breast petto m 138
breathe, to respirare 141
bridge ponte m 85
briefs slip m 116
bring, to portare 12
bring down, to portare giù 31
British britannico(a) 93
broken rotto(a) 29, 119, 140
brooch spilla f 121
brother fratello m 93
brown marrone 113
bruise contusione f 139
brush spazzola f 111

Brussels sprouts cavolini di Bruxelles *m/pl* 52
bubble bath bagnoschiuma *m* 110
bucket secchio *m* 106; secchiello *m* 128
build, to costruire 83
building edificio *m* 81, 83
building blocks/bricks gioco di costruzioni *m* 128
bulb lampadina *f* 28, 75, 119
burn scottatura *f* 139
burn out, to *(bulb)* bruciare 28
bus autobus *m* 18, 19, 65, 72, 73; pullman *m* 72, 80
business affari *m/pl* 16, 131
business trip viaggio d'affari *m* 93
bus stop fermata dell'autobus *f* 72, 73
busy impegnato(a) 96
but ma, però 15
butane gas gas butano *m* 32, 106
butcher's macelleria *f* 98
butter burro *m* 36, 38, 64
button bottone *m* 29, 117
buy, to comprare 82, 104; acquistare 123

C

cabana cabina *f* 91
cabbage cavolo *m* 52
cabin *(ship)* cabina *f* 74
cable telegramma *m* 133
cable car funivia *f* 74
cable release scatto *m* 125
café caffè *m* 33
caffein-free decaffeinato 38, 60
cake dolce *m* 55; torta *f* 55, 64
cake shop pasticceria *f* 98
calculator calcolatrice *f* 105
calendar calendario *m* 104
call *(phone)* telefonata *f* 135, 136
call, to chiamare 11, 78, 156; telefonare 136
cambric tela battista *f* 114
camel-hair pelo di cammello *m* 114
camera macchina fotografica *f* 124, 125
camera case astuccio (per macchina fotografica) *m* 125
camera shop negozio di apparecchi fotografici *m* 98
camp, to campeggiare 32
campbed letto da campo *m* 106
camping campeggio *m* 32

camping equipment materiale da campeggio *m* 106
camp site campeggio *m* 32
can *(of peaches)* scatola *f* 120
can *(to be able)* potere 11, 12, 163
Canada Canada *m* 146
cancel, to annullare 65
candle candela *f* 106
candy caramella *f* 126
can opener apriscatole *m* 106
cap berretto *m* 116
caper cappero *m* 53
capital *(finance)* capitale *m* 131
car macchina *f* 19, 20, 75, 76, 78; automobile *f* 78
carafe caraffa *f* 57
carat carato *m* 121
caravan roulotte *f* 32
caraway cumino *m* 53
carbon paper carta carbone *f* 104
carburettor carburatore *m* 78
card carta *f* 93; *(visiting)* bigliettino *m* 131
card game carte da gioco *f/pl* 128
cardigan cardigan *m* 116
car hire autonoleggio *m* 19, 20
car park parcheggio *m* 77
car racing corsa automobilistica *f* 89
car radio autoradio *f* 119
car rental autonoleggio *m* 20
carrot carota *f* 52
carry, to portare 21
cart carrello *m* 18
carton *(of cigarettes)* stecca (di sigarette) *f* 17
cartridge *(camera)* rotolo *m* 124
case *(instance)* caso *m* 143; *(cigarettes etc)* astuccio *m* 123, 125
cash, to incassare 130; riscuotere 133
cash desk cassa *f* 103, 155
cashier cassiere(a) *m/f* 103
cassette cassetta *f* 119, 127
castle castello *m* 81
catacomb catacomba *f* 81
catalogue catalogo *m* 82
cathedral cattedrale *f* 81
Catholic cattolico(a) 84
cauliflower cavolfiore *m* 52
caution prudenza *f* 155
cave grotta *f* 81
celery sedano *m* 52
cellophane tape nastro adesivo *m* 104

cemetery cimitero m 81
centimetre centimetro m 112
centre centro m 19, 21, 76, 81
century secolo m 149
ceramics ceramica f 83, 127
cereal cereali m/pl 38
certificate certificato m 144
chain catena f 79
chain (jewellery) catenina f 121
chain bracelet braccialetto a catena
   m 121
chair sedia f 36, 106
chamber music musica da camera f
   128
change (money) moneta f 77, 130;
   resto m 62
change, to cambiare 61, 65, 68, 73,
   75, 123; (money) 18, 130
chapel cappella f 81
charcoal carbonella f 106
charge tariffa f 20; prezzo m 89;
   costo m 136
charge, to fare pagare 24; (commission) trattenere 130
charm (trinket) ciondolo m 121
charm bracelet braccialetto a cion-
   doli m 121
cheap buon mercato 13; economi-
   co(a) 101
check assegno m 130; (restaurant)
   conto m 62
check, to controllare 75, 123; (luggage) far registrare 71
check book libretto d'assegni m 131
check in, to (airport) presentarsi 65
check out, to partire 31
checkup (medical) controllo m 142
cheers! salute! cin-cin! 56
cheese formaggio m 53, 63, 64
chef chef m 40
chemist's farmacia f 98, 108
cheque assegno m 130
cheque book libretto d'assegni m 131
cherry ciliegia f 54
chess scacchi m/pl 93, 128
chest torace m 138, 141
chestnut castagna f 54
chewing gum gomma da masticare f
   126
chicken pollo m 51, 63
chick-pea cece m 52
chicory indivia f 52; (Am.) cicoria f
   52
chiffon chiffon m 114

child bambino(a) m/f 24, 61, 82, 93,
   139
children's doctor pediatra m/f 137
China Cina f 146
chips patatine fritte f/pl 63, 64
chives cipollina f 53
chocolate cioccolato m 126, 127;
   (hot) cioccolata (calda) f 38, 60
chocolate bar stecca di cioccolato f
   64
choice scelta f 40
chop braciola f 48
Christmas Natale m 152
church chiesa f 81, 84
cigar sigaro m 126
cigarette sigaretta f 17, 95, 126
cigarette case portasigarette m 121,
   126
cigarette lighter accendino m 121
cine camera cinepresa f 124
cinema cinema m 86, 96
cinnamon cannella f 53
circle (theatre) galleria f 87
city città f 81
clam vongola f 45, 47
classical classico(a) 128
clean pulito(a) 61
clean, to pulire 29, 76
cleansing cream crema detergente f
   110
cliff scogliera f 85
clip fermaglio m 121
clock orologio m 121, 153
clock-radio radio-sveglia f 119
close (near) vicino(a) 78, 98
close, to chiudere 11, 82, 108, 132
closed chiuso(a) 155
clothes abiti m/pl 29; indumenti
   m/pl 116
clothes peg molletta da bucato f 106
clothing abbigliamento m 112
cloud nuvola f 94
clove chiodo di garofano m 53
coach (bus) pullman m 72
coat cappotto m 116
coconut noce di cocco f 54
cod baccalà m 46, 47; (fresh) mer-
   luzzo m 46
coffee caffè m 38, 60, 64
coin moneta f 83
cold freddo(a) 13, 25, 61, 94, 155
cold (illness) raffreddore m 108, 141
cold cuts affettati m/pl 64
colour colore m 103, 112, 124, 125

colour chart tabella dei colori f 30
colour negative negativo a colori m 124
colour shampoo shampoo colorante m 111
colour slide diapositiva f 124
colour television (set) televisore a colori m 119
comb pettine m 111
come, to venire 36, 92, 95, 137, 146
comedy commedia f 86
commission commissione f 130
common (frequent) corrente 154
compact disc disco compatto m 127
compartment scompartimento m 70
compass bussola f 106
complaint reclamo m 61
concert concerto m 88
concert hall sala dei concerti f 81, 88
conductor (orchestra) maestro m 88
confectioner's pasticceria f 98
confirm, to confermare 65
confirmation conferma f 23
congratulations congratulazioni f/pl 152
connection (train) coincidenza f 65, 68
constant costante 140
constipated costipato(a) 140
contact lens lente a contatto f 123
contain, to contenere 37
contraceptive antifecondativo m 109
contract contratto m 131
control controllo m 16
convent convento m 81
cookie biscotto m 64
cool box ghiacciaia f 106
copper rame m 122
coral corallo m 122
corduroy velluto a coste m 114
cork tappo m 61
corkscrew cavatappi m 106
corner angolo m 21, 36, 77
corn plaster cerotto callifugo m 109
cost preventivo m 131
cost, to costare 10, 80, 133, 136
cotton cotone m 114
cotton wool cotone idrofilo m 109
cough tosse f 108, 141
cough, to tossire 142
cough drops pasticche per la tosse f/pl 109
counter sportello m 133
countryside campagna f 85

court house palazzo di giustizia m 81
cousin cugino(a) m/f 93
cover charge coperto m 62
crab granchio m 46
cramp crampo m 141
crayfish gambero m 46
crayon pastello m 104
cream panna f 55, 60; (toiletry) crema f 110
credit credito m 130
credit, to accreditare 130, 131
credit card carta di credito f 20, 31, 62, 102, 130
crockery stoviglie f/pl 107
crisps patatine fritte f/pl 64
cross croce f 121
crossing (by sea) traversata f 74
crossroads incrocio m 77
cruise crociera f 74
crystal cristallo m 122
cuckoo clock orologio a cucù m 121
cucumber cetriolo m 52
cuff link gemelli m/pl 121
cuisine cucina f 35
cup tazza f 36, 107
currency valuta f 129
currency exchange office ufficio cambio m 18, 67, 129
current corrente f 90
curtain tenda f 28
curve (road) curva f 79
custard crema f 55
customs dogana f 16, 122
cut (wound) taglio m 139
cut off, to (phone) interrompere 135
cut glass vetro tagliato m 122
cuticle remover prodotto per togliere le pellicine m 110
cutlery posate f/pl 107, 121
cuttlefish seppia f 47
cycling ciclismo m 89
cystitis cistite f 142

D

dairy latteria f 98
dance, to ballare 88, 96
danger pericolo m 155, 156
dangerous pericoloso(a) 90
dark buio(a) 25; scuro(a) 101, 112, 113
date data f 25, 151; (fruit) dattero m 54
daughter figlia f 93
day giorno m 16, 20, 24, 32, 80, 151

daylight luce naturale f 124
day off giorno di riposo m 151
death morte f 155
decade decennio m 149
December dicembre m 150
decision decisione f 25, 102
deck (ship) ponte m 74
deck-chair sedia a sdraio f 91
declare, to dichiarare 16, 17
deer cervo m 51
delay ritardo m 69
delicatessen salumeria f 98
delicious delizioso(a) 62
deliver, to consegnare 102
delivery consegna f 102
denim tela di cotone f 114
dentist dentista m/f 145
denture dentiera f 145
deodorant deodorante m 110
department (museum, shop) reparto m 83, 100
department store grande magazzino m 98
departure partenza f 65
deposit (car hire) cauzione f 20; (bank) deposito m 130
deposit, to (bank) depositare 130
dessert dessert m 40, 55; dolce m 39, 55
detour (traffic) deviazione f 79
develop, to sviluppare 124
diabetes diabete m 141
diabetic diabetico(a) m/f 37
dialling code prefisso m 134
diamond diamante m 122
diaper pannolino m 111
diarrhoea diarrea f 140
dictionary dizionario m 104
diet dieta f 37
difficult difficile 13
difficulty difficoltà f 28, 102, 141
digital digitale 122
dine, to cenare 94
dining-car carrozza ristorante f 66, 68, 71
dining-room sala da pranzo f 27
dinner cena f 34
direct diretto(a) 65
direct, to indicare 12
direction direzione f 76
director (theatre) regista m 86
directory (phone) elenco m 134
disabled andicappato(a) 82
disc disco m 77, 127

discotheque discoteca f 88, 96
disease malattia f 142
dish piatto m 36, 37, 40
dishwashing detergent detersivo per lavare i piatti m 106
disinfectant disinfettante m 109
dislocate, to slogare 140
dissatisfied scontento(a) 103
district (town) quartiere m 81
disturb, to disturbare 155
diversion (traffic) deviazione f 79
dizzy stordito(a) 140
do, to fare 163
doctor medico m 79, 137; dottore m (dottoressa f) 144, 145
doctor's office ambulatorio m 137
dog cane m 155
doll bambola f 127, 128
dollar dollaro m 18, 130
door porta f 155
double doppio(a) 59
double bed letto matrimoniale m 23
double room camera doppia f 19, 23
down giù 15
downstairs di sotto 15
down there laggiù 77
downtown centro m 81
dozen dozzina f 120, 149
draught beer birra alla spina f 59
drawing paper carta da disegno f 104
drawing pin puntina f 104
dress abito m 116
dressing gown vestaglia f 116
drink bevanda f 40, 56, 59, 60, 61; bicchiere m 95
drink, to bere 35, 36
drinking water acqua potabile f 32
drip, to (tap) sgocciolare 28
drive, to guidare, andare 21, 76
driving licence patente f 20
drop (liquid) goccia f 109
drugstore farmacia f 98, 108
dry secco(a) 30, 57, 111
dry cleaner's lavanderia a secco f 29, 98; tintoria f 38
dry shampoo shampoo secco m 111
duck anatra f 48
dull (pain) debole 140
dummy succhiotto m 111
during durante 14, 150, 151
duty (customs) dazio m 17
duty-free shop negozio duty-free m 19
dye tintura f 30, 111

E

each ogni 149
ear orecchio m 138
earache mal d'orecchi m 141
ear drops gocce per le orecchie f/pl 109
early presto 13, 31
earring orecchino m 121
east est m 77
Easter Pasqua f 152
easy facile 13
eat, to mangiare 36
eel anguilla f 44
egg uovo m (pl uova f) 38, 64
eggplant melanzana f 52
eight otto 147
eighteen diciotto 147
eighth ottavo(a) 149
eighty ottanta 148
elastic elastico(a) 109
elastic bandage benda elastica f 109
Elastoplast cerotto m 109
electrical elettrico(a) 119
electrical appliance apparecchio elettrico m 119
electrician elettricista m 98
electricity elettricità f 32
electronic elettronico(a) 125, 128
elevator ascensore m 27, 100
eleven undici 147
embark, to imbarcare 74
emerald smeraldo m 122
emergency emergenza f 156
emergency exit uscita di sicurezza f 27, 99, 155
emery board limetta per unghie f 110
empty vuoto(a) 13
enamel smalto m 122
end fine f 150
endive cicoria f 52; (Am.) indivia f 52
engagement ring anello di fidanzamento m 121
engine (car) motore m 78
England Inghilterra f 146
English inglese 11, 80, 82, 84, 104, 105, 126, 137
enjoyable piacevole 31
enjoy oneself, to divertirsi 96
enlarge, to ingrandire 125
enough abbastanza 14
enquiry informazione f 68
enter, to entrare 155
entrance entrata f 67, 99, 155
entrance fee entrata f 82

envelope busta f 27, 104
equipment equipaggiamento m, tenuta f 91; materiale m 106
eraser gomma f 104
escalator scala mobile f 100
escalope scaloppina f 49
Europe Europa f 146
evening sera f 87, 96, 151, 153; serata f 95, 96
evening dress abito da sera m 88, 116
everything tutto 31
examine, to esaminare 139
excellent eccellente 84
exchange, to cambiare 103
exchange rate corso del cambio m 18, 130
excursion gita f 80
excuse, to scusare 10
exercise book quaderno m 104
exhaust pipe tubo di scappamento m 78
exhibition esposizione f 81
exit uscita f 67, 99, 155
expect, to aspettare 130
expense spesa f 131
expensive caro(a) 13, 19, 24, 101
exposure (photography) posa f 124
exposure counter contatore di esposizioni m 125
express espresso 133
expression espressione f 9
expressway autostrada f 76
extension cord/lead prolunga f 119
extra supplemento m 40
extract, to (tooth) estrarre 145
eye occhio m (pl occhi) 138, 139
eye drops gocce per gli occhi f/pl 109
eye pencil matita per occhi f 110
eye shadow ombretto m 110
eyesight vista f 123
eye specialist oculista m/f 137

F

face viso m 138
face-pack maschera di bellezza f 30
face powder cipria f 110
factory fabbrica f 81
fair fiera f 81
fall caduta f 139; (autumn) autunno m 150
family famiglia f 93
fan ventilatore m 28

DICTIONARY

Dizionario

fan belt cinghia del ventilatore f 75
far lontano(a) 13
fare prezzo m 21
farm fattoria f 85
fast rapido(a) 124
fat (meat) grasso m 37
father padre f 93
faucet rubinetto m 28
February febbraio m 150
fee (doctor) onorario m 144
feeding bottle biberon m 111
feel, to (physical state) sentirsi 140
felt feltro m 114
felt-tip pen pennarello m 104
fennel finocchio m 52
ferry traghetto m 74
fever febbre f 140
few pochi(e) 14; (a) alcuni(e) 14
field campo m 85
fifteen quindici 147
fifth quinto(a) 149
fifty cinquanta 147
fig fico m 54
file (tool) lima f 110
fill in, to compilare 26, 144
fillet filetto m 48
filling (tooth) otturazione f 145
filling station stazione di rifornimento f 75
film (movie) film m 86; (camera) pellicola f 124, 125
filter filtro m 125
filter-tipped con filtro 126
find, to trovare 10, 11, 100, 137
fine (OK) bene 25
fine arts belle arti f/pl 83
finger dito m 138
fire fuoco m 156
first primo(a) 68, 73, 149
first-aid kit cassetta del pronto soccorso f 106
first class prima classe f 69
first course primo piatto m 40
first name nome m 25
fish pesce m 46
fish, to pescare 90
fishing pesca f 90
fishing tackle arnese da pesca m 106
fishmonger's pescheria f 98
fit, to andare bene 115
fitting room cabina di prova f 115
five cinque 147
fix, to riparare 75; curare 145
fizzy (mineral water) gasato(a) 60

flannel flanella f 114
flash (photography) flash m 125
flash attachment attaccatura del flash f 125
flashlight lampadina tascabile f 106
flask fiasco m 127
flat basso(a) 118
flat (apartment) appartamento m 22
flat tyre foratura f 75; gomma sgonfia f 78
flea market mercato delle pulci m 81
flight volo m 65
flight number numero del volo m 65
flippers pinne f/pl 128
floor piano m 27
floor show varietà m 88
florist's fiorista m/f 98
flour farina f 37
flower fiore m 85
flu influenza f 142
fog nebbia f 94
folding chair sedia pieghevole f 107
folding table tavola pieghevole f 107
folk music musica folcloristica f 128
food cibo m 37, 61; alimento m 111
food box contenitore per il cibo m 142
food poisoning avvelenamento da cibo m 142
foot piede m 138
football calcio m 89
foot cream crema per i piedi f 110
footpath sentiero m 85
for per 15, 143
forbid, to vietare 155
forecast previsione f 94
foreign straniero(a) 59
forest foresta f 85
fork forchetta f 36, 61, 107, 127
form (document) modulo m 133; scheda f 25, 26
fortnight quindici giorni m/pl 151
fortress fortezza f 81
forty quaranta 147
foundation cream fondo tinta m 110
fountain fontana f 81
fountain pen penna stilografica f 104
four quattro 147
fourteen quattordici 147
fourth quarto(a) 149
frame (glasses) montatura f 123
France Francia f 146
free libero(a) 13, 70, 82, 96, 155

DICTIONARY

French bean fagiolino *m* 52
French fries patatine fritte *f/pl* 63
fresh fresco(a) 54, 61
Friday venerdì *m* 151
fried fritto(a) 47, 50
fried egg uovo fritto *m* 38
friend amico(a) *m/f* 95
fringe frangia *f* 30
frock abito *m* 116
from da 14, 163
front davanti 75
fruit frutta *f* 54
fruit cocktail macedonia di frutta *f* 54
fruit juice succo di frutta *m* 38, 60
frying-pan padella *f* 106
full pieno(a) 13; completo(a) 155; intero(a) 80
full board pensione completa *f* 20
full insurance assicurazione completa *f* 20
furniture mobilio *m* 83
furrier's pellicceria *f* 98

G

gabardine gabardine *m* 114
gallery galleria *f* 81, 98
game gioco *m* 128; *(food)* cacciagione *f* 50
garage garage *m* 26, 78
garden giardino *m* 81, 85
garlic aglio *m* 53
gas gas *m* 156
gasoline benzina *f* 75, 78
gastritis gastrite *f* 142
gauze garza *f* 109
general generale 26, 100
general delivery fermo posta *m* 133
general practitioner medico generico *m* 137
genitals genitali *m/pl* 138
gentleman signore *m* 155
genuine vero(a) 118
geology geologia *f* 83
Germany Germania *f* 146
get, to *(find)* trovare 10, 21, 32; *(call)* chiamare 31, 137; *(obtain)* ottenere 134; procurarsi 89, 90
get back, to ritornare 80
get off, to scendere 73
get to, to andare a 19; arrivare a 70
get up, to alzarsi 144
gherkin cetriolino *m* 52, 64
gin and tonic gin e tonico *m* 60

girdle busto *m* 116
girl *(child)* bambina *f* 112, 128
girlfriend ragazza *f* 93
give, to dare 12, 123, 135
glad *(to know you)* piacere 92
gland ghiandola *f* 138
glass bicchiere *m* 36, 57, 60, 61, 143
glasses occhiali *m/pl* 123
glassware articolo di vetro *m* 127
gloomy malinconico(a) 84
glossy *(finish)* lucido(a) 125
glove guanto *m* 116
glue colla *f* 105
go, to andare 95, 96, 163
go away, to andarsene 156
gold oro *m* 121, 122
golden dorato(a) 113
gold plate placcato d'oro *m* 122
golf golf *m* 89
good buono(a) 13, 101
good-bye arrivederci 9
goods merci *f/pl* 16
goose oca *f* 51
gooseberry uva spina *f* 54
go out, to uscire 96
gram grammo *m* 120
grammar book grammatica *f* 105
grandfather nonno *m* 93
grandmother nonna *f* 93
grape uva *f* 54, 64
grapefruit pompelmo *m* 54
grapefruit juice succo di pompelmo *m* 38, 60
gray grigio(a) 113
graze escoriazione *f* 139
greasy grasso(a) 30, 111
Great Britain Gran Bretagna *f* 146
Greece Grecia *f* 146
green verde 113
green bean fagiolino *m* 52
greengrocer's negozio di frutta e verdura *m* 98
green salad insalata verde *f* 52
greeting saluto *m* 9, 152
grey grigio(a) 113
grilled alla griglia 47; ai ferri 50
grocery negozio di alimentari *m* 98, 120
group gruppo *m* 82
guide guida *f* 80
guidebook guida turistica *f* 82, 104, 105
gum *(teeth)* gengiva *f* 145
gynaecologist ginecologo(a) *m/f* 137

Dizionario

H

hair capelli m/pl 30, 111
hairbrush spazzola per capelli f 111
haircut taglio dei capelli m 30
hairdresser's parrucchiere m 27, 30, 98
hair dryer asciugacapelli m 119
hair lotion lozione per capelli f 111
hair slide fermaglio m 111
hairspray lacca f 30, 111
half metà f, mezzo m 149
half a day mezza giornata f 80
half a dozen mezza dozzina f 120
half an hour mezz'ora f 153
half board mezza pensione f 24
half price (ticket) metà tariffa f 69
hall (large room) sala f 81, 88
ham prosciutto m 41, 48, 63, 64
hammer martello m 106
hammock amaca f 106
hand mano f 138
handbag borsetta f 116, 156
hand cream crema per le mani f 110
handicrafts artigianato m 83
handkerchief fazzoletto m 116
handmade fatto(a) a mano 113
hanger attaccapanni m 27
hangover mal di testa m 108
happy felice, buon(a) 152
harbour porto m 81
hard duro(a) 123
hard-boiled egg uovo sodo m 38
hardware shop negozio di ferramenta m 99
hare lepre f 51
hat cappello m 116
have, to avere 162
hay fever febbre del fieno f 108, 141
hazelnut nocciola f 54
he egli, lui 161
head testa f 138, 139
headache mal di testa m 141
headlight faro m 79
headphones cuffia (d'ascolto) f 119
health salute f 56
health food shop negozio di cibi dietetici m 99
health insurance assicurazione malattie f 144
heart cuore m 138
heart attack attacco cardiaco m 141
heating riscaldamento m 23, 28
heavy pesante 13, 101
heel tacco m 118

height altitudine f 85
helicopter elicottero m 74
hello! (phone) pronto 135
help aiuto m 156
help, to aiutare 13, 21, 100, 134; (oneself) servirsi 120
her suo, sua (pl suoi, sue) 161
herbs odori m/pl 53
here qui, ecco 13
herring aringa f 46
high alto(a) 90, 141
high season alta stagione f 150
high tide alta marea f 90
hill collina f 85
hire noleggio m 20, 74
hire, to noleggiare 19, 20, 74, 90, 91, 119; affittare 155
his suo, sua (pl suoi, sue) 161
history storia f 83
hitchhike, to fare l'autostop 74
hold on! (phone) resti in linea! 136
hole buco m 29
holiday giorno festivo m 151
holidays vacanze f/pl 151; ferie f/pl 155
home address domicilio m 25
honey miele m 38
hors d'oeuvre antipasto m 41
horse riding corsa di cavalli f 89
hospital ospedale m 144
hot caldo(a) 14, 25, 38, 94
hotel albergo m 19, 21, 22; hotel m 22, 80
hotel guide guida degli alberghi f 19
hotel reservation prenotazione d'albergo f 19
hot water acqua calda f 23, 28
hot-water bottle borsa dell'acqua calda f 27
hour ora f 153
house casa f 83, 85
how come 10
how far quanto dista 10, 76, 85, 100
how long quanto tempo 10, 24
how many quanti 10
how much quanto 10, 24
hundred cento 148
hungry, to be aver fame 12, 35
hurry (to be in a) avere fretta 21
hurt, to fare male 139, 145; (oneself) farsi male 139
husband marito m 93
hydrofoil aliscafo m 74

I

I io 161
ice ghiaccio m 94
ice-cream gelato m 55, 64
ice-cream parlour gelateria f 33
ice cube cubetto di ghiaccio m 27
iced coffee caffè freddo m 60
ice pack elemento refrigerante m 106
iced tea tè freddo m 60
ill malato(a) 140
illness malattia f 160
important importante 12
impressive impressionante 84
in in 13, 163
include, to comprendere 20, 24, 32, 62, 80; includere 31
India India f 146
indigestion indigestione f 141
indoor (swimming pool) coperto(a) 90
inexpensive economico(a) 35, 124
infection infezione f 141
inflammation infiammazione f 142
inflation inflazione f 131
inflation rate tasso d'inflazione m 131
influenza influenza f 142
information informazione f 67, 155
injection iniezione f 142, 144
injure, to ferire 139
injured ferito(a) 79, 139
injury ferita f 139
ink inchiostro m 105
inn locanda f 22, 33; osteria f 33
inquiry informazione f 68
insect bite puntura d'insetto f 108, 139
insect repellent crema contro gli insetti f 109
insect spray spray insetticida m 109
inside dentro 15
instead invece 37
instrumental (music) strumentale 128
insurance assicurazione f 20, 79, 144
interest interesse m 80, 131
interested, to be interessarsi 83, 96
interesting interessante 84
international internazionale 133, 134
interpreter interprete m/f 131
intersection incrocio m 77
introduce, to presentare 92
introduction presentazione f 92, 130
investment investimento m 131
invitation invito m 94
invite, to invitare 94

invoice fattura f 131
iodine tintura di iodio f 109
Ireland Irlanda f 146
iron (laundry) ferro da stiro m 119
iron, to stirare 29
ironmonger's negozio di ferramenta m 99
Israel Israele m 146
Italian italiano(a) 10, 11, 95, 104, 114
Italy Italia f 146
its suo, sua (pl suoi, sue) 161
ivory avorio m 122

J

jacket giacca f 116
jade giada f 122
jam marmellata f 38
jam, to incastrare 28; bloccare 125
January gennaio m 150
Japan Giappone m 146
jar vasetto m 120
jaundice itterizia f 142
jaw mascella f 138
jeans jeans m/pl 116
jersey maglietta f 116
jewel gioiello m 121
jeweller's gioielleria f 99, 121
jewellery gioielli m/pl 127
joint articolazione f 138
journey percorso m 72
juice succo m 38, 60
July luglio m 150
jumper (sweater) maglione m 116
June giugno m 151
just (only) soltanto 100

K

keep, to tenere 62
kerosene petrolio m 106
key chiave f 26
kidney rognone m 48; rene m 138
kilogram chilogrammo m 120
kilometre chilometro m 20
kind gentile 95
kind (type) genere m 140
knapsack zaino m 106
knee ginocchio m 138
kneesocks calzettoni m/pl 116
knife coltello m 36, 61, 107
knitwear maglieria f 127
knock, to bussare 155
know, to sapere 16; conoscere 96, 114

DICTIONARY

Dizionario

L

label etichetta *f* 105
lace pizzo *m* 114
lady signora *f* 155
lake lago *m* 81, 85, 90
lamb agnello *m* 48
lamp lampada *f* 46
landmark punto di riferimento *m* 85
landscape paesaggio *m* 92
lantern lanterna *f* 106
large grande 101, 118
lark allodola *f* 51
last ultimo(a) 13, 68, 73; scorso(a) 149, 151
last name cognome *m* 25
late tardi 13
later più tardi 135
laugh, to ridere 95
launderette lavanderia automatica *f* 99
laundry *(place)* lavanderia *f* 29, 99; *(clothes)* biancheria *f* 29
laundry service servizio di lavanderia *m* 23
laxative lassativo *m* 109
lead *(theatre)* ruolo principale *m* 86
lead piombo *m* 75
leap year anno bisestile *m* 149
leather pelle *f* 114, 118
leather goods pelletteria *f* 127
leave, to partire 31, 68, 74, 162; lasciare 156; *(deposit)* depositare 26, 71
leek porro *m* 52
left sinistro(a) 21, 63, 69, 77
left-luggage office deposito bagagli *m* 67, 71
leg gamba *f* 138
lemon limone *m* 37, 38, 54, 55, 60, 64
lemonade limonata *f* 60
lemon juice succo di limone *m* 60
lens *(glasses)* lente *f* 123; *(camera)* obiettivo *m* 125
lens cap cappuccio per obiettivo *m* 125
lentil lenticchia *f* 52
less meno 14
lesson lezione *f* 91
let, to *(hire out)* affittare 155
letter lettera *f* 132
letter box cassetta delle lettere *f* 132
letter of credit lettera di credito *m* 130
lettuce lattuga *f* 52

level crossing passaggio a livello *m* 79
library biblioteca *f* 81, 99
lie down, to sdraiarsi 142
life belt cintura di salvataggio *f* 74
life boat canotto di salvataggio *m* 74
lifeguard bagnino *m* 90
lift ascensore *m* 27, 100
light leggero(a) 13, 55, 57, 101, 128; *(colour)* chiaro(a) 101, 112, 113
light luce *f* 28, 124; *(cigarette)* fiammifero *m* 95
lighter accendino *m* 126
lighter fluid benzina per accendino *f* 126
lighter gas gas per accendino *m* 126
light meter esposimetro *m* 125
like, to volere 12, 20, 23; desiderare 103; piacere 25, 61, 92, 96, 102, 112
lime cedro *m* 54
line linea *f* 73, 136
linen *(cloth)* lino *m* 114
lip labbro *m* 138
lipsalve burro cacao *m* 110
lipstick rossetto *m* 110
liqueur liquore *m* 59
liquid liquido *m* 123
listen, to ascoltare 128
litre litro *m* 57, 75, 120
little *(a)* un po' 14
live, to vivere 83
liver fegato *m* 48, 138
lobster aragosta *f* 46
local locale 36, 60
London Londra *f* 130
long lungo(a) 115
long-sighted presbite 123
look, to guardare 123
look for, to cercare 12
look out! attenzione! 156
loose *(clothes)* largo(a) 115
lose, to perdere 123, 156
loss perdita *f* 131
lost perduto(a) 12; perso(a) 156
lost and found office ufficio oggetti smarriti *m* 67, 156
lost property office ufficio oggetti smarriti *m* 67, 156
lot *(a)* molto 14
lotion lozione *f* 110
loud *(voice)* forte 135
love, to amare 162

lovely bello(a) 94
low basso(a) 90, 141
lower inferiore 69, 70
low season bassa stagione f 150
low tide bassa marea f 90
luck fortuna f 152
luggage bagagli m/pl 18, 26, 31, 71
luggage locker custodia automatica
  dei bagagli f 18, 67, 71
luggage trolley carrello portabagagli
  m 18, 71
lump (bump) bernoccolo m 139
lunch pranzo m 34, 80, 94
lung polmone m 138

M

mackerel sgombro m 47
magazine rivista f 105
magnificent magnifico(a) 84
maid cameriera f 26
mail, to spedire 28
mail posta f 28, 133
mailbox cassetta delle lettere f 132
main principale 80
make, to fare 131, 163
make up, to rifare 28; preparare 108
make-up remover pad tampone per
  togliere il trucco m 110
man uomo m (pl uomini) 115
manager direttore m 26
manicure manicure f 30
many molti(e) 14
map carta geografica f 76, 105;
  pianta f 105
March marzo m 150
marinated marinato(a) 47
marjoram maggiorana f 63
market mercato m 81, 99
marmalade marmellata d'arance f
  38
married sposato(a) 93
marrow midollo m 48
mass (church) messa f 84
mat (finish) opaco(a) 125
match fiammifero m 106, 126;
  (sport) partita f, incontro m 89
match, to (colour) ravvivare 112
material (cloth) tessuto m 113
matinée spettacolo del pomeriggio
  m 87
mattress materasso m 106
mauve lilla 113
May maggio m 150
may (can) potere 11, 12, 163

meadow prato m 85
meal pasto m 24, 34, 62, 143
mean, to significare 10, 25
means mezzo m 74
measles morbillo m 142
measure, to prendere le misure 114
meat carne f 48, 49, 61
meatball polpetta f 48
mechanic meccanico m 78
mechanical pencil portamine m 105
medical medico(a) 144
medicine medicina f 83, 143
medium (meat) a puntino 50
meet, to incontrare 96
melon melone m 54
mend, to riparare 75; (clothes) ram-
  mendare 29
menthol (cigarettes) mentolo m 126
menu menù m 36, 39, 40
message messaggio m 28, 136
methylated spirits alcool metilico m
  106
metre metro m 112
mezzanine (theatre) galleria f 87
middle mezzo m 69; metà f 87, 150
midnight mezzanotte f 153
mileage chilometraggio m 20
milk latte m 38, 60, 64
milkshake frullato di latte m 60
million milione m 148
mineral water acqua minerale f 60
minister (religion) pastore m 84
minute minuto m 153
mirror specchio m 115, 123
miscellaneous diverso(a) 127
Miss Signorina f 9
miss, to mancare 18, 29, 61
mistake errore m 31, 61, 62
mixed misto(a) 55
moccasin mocassino m 118
modified American plan mezza pensione f 24
moisturizing cream crema idratante f
  110
moment momento m 136
monastery monastero m 81
Monday lunedì m 151
money denaro m 129, 130
money order vaglia m 133
month mese m 16, 150
monument monumento m 81
moon luna f 94
moped motorino m 74
more più 14

morning mattino *m* 151, 153
mortgage ipoteca *f* 131
mosque moschea *f* 84
mosquito net zanzariera *f* 106
motel motel *m* 22
mother màdre *f* 93
motorbike moto *f* 74
motorboat barca a motore *f* 91
motorway autostrada *f* 76
mountain montagna *f* 85
moustache baffi *m/pl* 31
mouth bocca *f* 138
mouthwash gargarismo *m* 109
move, to muovere 139
movie film *m* 86
movie camera cinepresa *f* 124
movies cinema *m* 86, 96
Mr. Signor *m* 9
Mrs. Signora *f* 9
much molto(a) 14
mug boccale *m* 107
muscle muscolo *m* 138
museum museo *m* 81
mushroom fungo *m* 52
music musica *f* 83, 128
musical commedia musicale *f* 86
mussel cozza *f* 46
must, to dovere 23, 31, 37, 61, 95
mustard senape *f* 37, 64
my mio, mia (*pl* miei, mie) 161

N

nail (*human*) unghia *f* 110
nail file lima da unghie *f* 110
nail polish smalto *m* 110
nail polish remover solvente per le
    unghie *m* 110
nail scissors forbicine per le unghie
    f/pl 110
name nome *m* 23, 25, 79; cognome
    m 25
napkin tovagliolo *m* 36, 105, 106
nappy pannolino *m* 111
narrow stretto(a) 118
nationality cittadinanza *f* 25; nazio-
    nalità *f* 92
natural naturale 83
natural history storia naturale *f* 83
nausea nausea *f* 140
near vicino(a) 13; vicino a 14
nearby qui vicino 77, 84
nearest il (la) più vicino(a) 78, 98
neat (*drink*) liscio(a) 56, 59
neck collo *m* 30, 138

necklace collana *f* 121
need, to aver bisogno 29, 118; essere
    necessario 90; servire 118
needle ago *m* 27
needlework ricamo *m* 127
negative negativo *m* 125
nephew nipote *m* 93
nerve nervo *m* 138
nervous nervoso(a) 138
never mai 15
new nuovo(a) 13
newsagent's giornalaio *m* 99
newspaper giornale *m* 104, 105
newsstand edicola *f* 19, 67, 99,
    104
New Year Capodanno *m* 152
New Zealand Nuova Zelanda *f* 146
next prossimo(a) 65, 68, 73, 76,
    149; seguente 151
next to accanto a 14, 77
niece nipote *f* 93
night notte *f* 24, 151
nightclub night-club *m* 88
night cream crema da notte *f* 110
nightdress camicia da notte *f* 116
nine nove 147
nineteen diciannove 147
ninety novanta 148
ninth nono(a) 149
no no 9
noisy rumoroso(a) 25
nonalcoholic analcolico(a) 60
none nessuno(a) 15
nonsmoker non fumatori *m/pl* 36, 70
noon mezzogiorno *m* 31, 153
normal normale 30
north nord *m* 77
North America America del Nord *f*
    140
nose naso *m* 138
nosebleed emorragia nasale *f* 140
nose drops gocce nasali *f/pl* 109
not non 15, 163
note (*banknote*) banconota *f* 130
notebook taccuino *m* 105
note paper carta da lettere *m* 105
nothing nulla 15, 17; niente 15
notice (*sign*) cartello *m* 155
November novembre *m* 150
now adesso 15
number numero *m* 26, 65, 135,
    136, 147
nurse infermiera *f* 144
nutmeg noce moscata *f* 53

O

occupied occupato(a) 13, 155
October ottobre *m* 150
octopus polpo *m* 46
offer, to offrire 95
office ufficio *m* 19, 67, 99, 132, 133, 156
oil olio *m* 37, 64, 75, 111
oily grasso(a) 30, 111
old vecchio(a), anziano(a) 13
old town città vecchia *f* 81
olive oliva *f* 41
omelet frittata *f* 42
on su 14, 163
once una volta 149
one uno(a) 147
one-way *(ticket)* andata *f* 69
on foot a piedi 76
onion cipolla *f* 52
only soltanto 15, 80
on request a richiesta 73
on time in orario 68
onyx onice *m* 122
open aperto(a) 13, 82, 155
open, to aprire 10, 17, 82, 108, 131, 132, 142
open-air all'aperto 90
opera opera *f* 88
opera house teatro dell'opera *m* 81, 88
operation operazione *f* 144
operator centralinista *m/f* 134
operetta operetta *f* 88
opposite di fronte 77
optician ottico *m* 99, 123
or o 15
oral orale 143
orange arancio 113
orange arancia *f* 54, 64
orange juice succo d'arancia *m* 38, 60
orangeade aranciata *f* 60
orchestra orchestra *f* 88; *(seats)* poltrona *f* 87
orchestral music musica sinfonica *f* 128
order *(goods, meal)* ordinazione *f* 40, 102
order, to *(goods, meal)* ordinare 61, 102, 103
oregano origano *m* 53
ornithology ornitologia *f* 83
our nostro(a) 161
out of order fuori servizio 155

out of stock esaurito(a) 103
outlet *(electric)* presa *f* 27
outside fuori 15; all'aperto 36
oval ovale 101
over there laggiù 69
overalls tuta *f* 116
overdone troppo cotto(a) 61
overheat, to *(engine)* surriscaldare 78
overtake, to sorpassare 79
owe, to dovere 144
overwhelming sbalorditivo(a) 84
oyster ostrica *f* 41, 46

P

pacifier succhiotto *m* 111
packet pacchetto *m* 120, 126
page pagina *f* 77
page *(hotel)* fattorino *m* 26
pail secchio *m* 106; secchiello *m* 128
pain dolore *m* 140, 141; male *m* 144
painkiller antinevralgico *m* 140; calmante *m* 144
paint pittura *f* 155
paint, to dipingere 83
paintbox scatola di colori *f* 105
painter pittore *m* 83
painting pittura *f* 83
pair paio *m* 116, 118, 149
pajamas pigiama *m* 117
palace palazzo *m* 81
palpitation palpitazione *f* 141
panties slip *m* 116
pants *(trousers)* pantaloni *m/pl* 116
panty girdle guaina *f* 116
panty hose collant *m* 116
paper carta *f* 105
paperback libro tascabile *m* 105
paper napkin tovagliolo di carta *m* 107
paraffin *(fuel)* petrolio *m* 106
parcel pacco *m* 132
pardon? prego? 10
parents genitori *m/pl* 93
park parco *m* 81
park, to parcheggiare 26, 77
parking parcheggio *m* 77, 79
parking disc disco di sosta *m* 77
parking meter parchimetro *m* 77
parliament parlamento *m* 81
parsley prezzemolo *m* 53
part parte *f* 138
partridge pernice *f* 51

party (social gathering) ricevimento m 95
pass (mountain) passo m 85
pass, to (car) sorpassare 79
passport passaporto m 16, 17, 25, 26, 156
passport photo fotografia d'identità f 124
pass through, to essere di passaggio 16
pasta pasta f 44
paste (glue) colla f 105
pastry pasticcino m 64
pastry shop pasticceria f 99
patch, to (clothes) rappezzare 29
path sentiero m 85; pista f 155
patient paziente m/f 144
pay, to pagare 31, 62, 102
payment pagamento m 102, 131
pea pisello m 52
peach pesca f 54
peak picco m 85
peanut arachide f 54
pear pera f 54
pearl perla f 122
pedestrian pedonale 79
peg (tent) picchetto m 107
pen penna f 105
pencil matita f 105
pencil sharpener temperamatite m 105
pendant pendente m 121
penicillin penicillina f 143
penknife temperino m 107
pensioner pensionato m 82
people gente f 93
pepper pepe m 37; (sweet) peperone m 52
per cent per cento 149
percentage percentuale f 131
perch pesce persico m 46
per day per un giorno 20, 89; al giorno 32
perform, to (theatre) rappresentare 86
perfume profumo m 110
perfume shop profumeria f 108
perhaps forse 15
per hour all'ora 77; per un'ora 89
period (monthly) mestruazioni f/pl 141
period pains mestruazioni dolorose f/pl 141
permanent wave permanente f 30

permit permesso m 90
per night per una notte 24
per person per persona 32
person persona f 32
personal personale 17
personal call telefonata con preavviso f 135
personal cheque assegno personale m 130
person-to-person call telefonata con preavviso f 135
petrol benzina f 75, 78
pewter peltro m 122
pheasant fagiano m 51
photo fotografia f 82, 124, 125
photocopy fotocopia f 131
photograph, to fotografare, fare delle fotografie 82
photographer fotografo m 99
photography fotografia f 124
phrase espressione f 11
pick up, to prendere 80, 96
pickles sottaceti m/pl 41, 64
picnic picnic m 63
picnic basket cestino da picnic m 107
picture quadro m 83; (photo) fotografia f 82
piece pezzo m 120
pig porcellino m, porchetta f 46
pigeon piccione m 51
pill pillola f 141; compressa f 143
pillow guanciale m 27
pin spillo m 111, 122
pineapple ananas m 54
pink rosa 113
pipe pipa f 126
pipe cleaner nettapipe m 126
pipe tobacco tabacco da pipa m 126
pipe tool curapipe m 126
pizza pizza f 42, 63
pizza parlour pizzeria f 33
place luogo m 25; posto m 76
place of birth luogo di nascita m 25
plane aereo m 65
planetarium planetario m 82
plaster, to ingessare 140
plastic plastica f 107
plastic bag sacchetto di plastica m 107
plate piatto m 36, 61, 107
platform (station) binario m 67, 68, 69, 70
platinum platino m 122

play *(theatre)* commedia f 86
play, to interpretare 86; suonare 88; giocare 89, 93
playground parco giochi m 32
playing card carte da gioco f/pl 105
please per favore, per piacere 9
plimsolls scarpe da tennis f/pl 118
plug *(electric)* spina f 28
plum prugna f 54, 64
pneumonia polmonite f 142
poached affogato(a) 47
pocket tasca f 117
pocket watch orologio da tasca m 121
point punto m 80
point, to *(show)* indicare 11
poison veleno m 156
poisoning avvelenamento m 142
pole *(ski)* bastone m 91
police polizia f 78, 156
police station posto di polizia m 99, 156
polish *(nails)* smalto m 110
pond stagno m 85
pop music musica pop f 28
poplin popeline m 114
porcelain porcellana f 127
pork maiale m 48
port porto m 74; *(wine)* porto m 59
portable portatile 119
porter facchino m 18, 26, 71
portion porzione f 37, 61
Portugal Portogallo m 146
possible possibile 137
post *(letters)* posta f 28, 133
post, to spedire 28
postage affrancatura f 132
postage stamp francobollo m 28, 126, 132
postcard cartolina f 105, 126, 132
poste restante fermo posta m 133
post office ufficio postale m 99, 132
potato patata f 52
pottery terracotta f 83
poultry pollame m 50
pound *(money)* sterlina f 18, 130; *(weight)* libbra f 120
powder cipria f 110
powder compact portacipria m 121
prawns scampi m/pl 47
preference preferenza f 101
pregnant incinta 141
premium *(gasoline)* super 75
prescribe, to prescrivere 143

prescription ricetta f 108, 143
press, to *(iron)* stirare a vapore 29
press stud bottone a pressione m 117
pressure pressione f 75, 142
price prezzo m 24
priest prete m 84
print *(photo)* stampa f 125
private privato(a) 80, 91, 155
processing *(photo)* sviluppo m 124
profession professione f 25
profit profitto m 131
programme programma m 87
prohibit, to vietare 79, 91, 155
pronunciation pronuncia f 6
propelling pencil portamine m 105
Protestant protestante 84
provide, to procurare 131
prune prugna secca f 54
public holiday giorno festivo m 152
pull, to tirare 155
pullover pullover m 117
pumpkin zucca f 52
puncture foratura f 75
purchase acquisto m 131
pure puro(a) 114
purple viola 113
push, to spingere 155
put, to mettere 24
pyjamas pigiama m 117

Q

quail quaglia f 51
quality qualità f 103, 113
quantity quantità f 14, 103
quarter quarto m 149; *(part of town)* quartiere m 81
quarter of an hour quarto d'ora m 153
quartz quarzo m 122
question domanda f 10, 163
quick rapido(a) 13; presto 156
quickly presto 137, 156
quiet tranquillo(a) 23, 25
quince cotogna f 54

R

rabbi rabbino m 84
rabbit coniglio m 51
race course/track ippodromo m 90
racket *(sport)* racchetta f 90
radiator radiatore m 78
radio *(set)* radio f 23, 28, 119
radish ravanello m 52

railroad crossing passaggio a livello
m 79
railway ferrovia f 154
railway station stazione f 19, 21,
67, 70
rain pioggia f 94
rain, to piovere 94
raincoat impermeabile m 117
raisin uva passa f 54
rangefinder telemetro m 125
rare (meat) al sangue 50, 61
rash esantema m 139
raspberry lampone m 54
rate tariffa f 20; tasso m 131
razor rasoio m 110
razor blade lametta f 110
reading-lamp lampada f 27
ready pronto(a) 29, 118, 123, 125,
145
real vero(a) 121
rear dietro 75
receipt ricevuta f 103, 144
reception ricevimento m 23
receptionist capo ricevimento m 26
recommend, to consigliare 35, 36,
40, 80, 86, 88, 137, 145
record (disc) disco m 127, 128
record player giradischi m 119
rectangular rettangolare 101
red rosso(a) 57, 113
redcurrant ribes m 54
red mullet triglia f 46
reduction riduzione f 24, 82
refill ricambio m 105
refund, to rimborsare 103
regards saluti m/pl 152
register, to (luggage) far registrare 71
registered mail raccomandato(a) 133
registration registrazione f 25
registration form scheda f 25, 26
regular (petrol) normale 75
religion religione f 83
religious service funzione religiosa f
84
rent, to noleggiare 19, 20, 74, 89,
91, 119; affittare 155
rental noleggio m 20, 74
repair riparazione f 125
repair, to riparare 29, 118, 119,
121, 123, 125, 145
repeat, to ripetere 11
report, to denunciare 156
reservation prenotazione f 19, 23,
65, 69

reservations office ufficio prenotazioni m 19, 67
reserve, to prenotare 19, 23, 87;
riservare 36
restaurant ristorante m 19, 32, 33,
35, 67
return (ticket) andata e ritorno 69
return, to (give back) rendere 103
reverse the charges, to telefonare a
carico del destinatario 135
rheumatism reumatismo m 141
rib costola f 48, 138
ribbon nastro m 105
rice riso m 45
right destro(a) 63, 69, 77; (correct)
giusto 13, 70
ring (on finger) anello m 121
ring, to suonare 155
river fiume m 85, 90
road strada f 76, 77, 85
road assistance assistenza stradale f
78
road map carta stradale f 105
road sign segnale stradale m 79
roast arrosto 48, 50
roast beef rosbif m 48
rock masso m 79
roll (bread) panino m 38, 64
roller skates pattini a rotelle m/pl 128
roll film bobina f 124
roll-neck a collo alto 117
room camera f 19, 23, 24, 25, 28;
(space) posto m 32
room number numero della stanza m
26
room service servizio nella stanza m
23
rope corda f 107
rosary rosario m 122
rosé rosatello 57
rosemary rosmarino m 53
rouge fard m 110
round rotondo(a) 101
round-neck a girocollo 117
roundtrip (ticket) andata e ritorno 69
rowing-boat barca a remi f 91
royal reale 82
rubber gomma f 105, 118
ruby rubino m 122
rucksack zaino m 107
ruin rovina f 82
ruler (for measuring) riga f 105
rum rum m 60
running water acqua corrente f 23

s

safe *(not dangerous)* sicuro(a), senza pericolo 90
safe cassaforte f 26
safety pin spillo di sicurezza m 111
saffron zafferano m 53
sage salvia f 53
sailing-boat barca a vela f 91
salad insalata f 52, 64
salami salame m 41, 63, 64
sale vendita f 131; *(bargains)* saldi m/pl 100, svendita f 155
sales tax I.V.A. f 24, 102
salmon salmone m 41, 46
salt sale m 37, 64
salty salato(a) 61
sand sabbia f 90
sandal sandalo m 118
sandwich panino imbottito m 63
sanitary towel/napkin assorbente igienico m 109
sardine sardina f 41, 47
satin raso m 114
Saturday sabato m 151
sauce salsa f 44
saucepan casseruola f 107
saucer piattino m 107
sausage salsiccia f 48, 64
scallop arsella f 46
scarf sciarpa f 117
scenic route strada panoramica f 85
scissors forbici f/pl 107; forbicine f/pl 110
scooter motoretta f 74
Scotland Scozia f 146
Scottish scozzese 93
scrambled eggs uova strapazzate f/pl 38
screwdriver cacciavite m 107
sculptor scultore m 83
sculpture scultura f 83
sea mare m 23, 85,
sea bass spigola f 47
sea bream orata f 46
seafood frutti di mare m/pl 46
season stagione f 40, 150
seasoning condimento m 37
seat posto m 69, 70, 87
seat belt cintura di sicurezza f 75
second secondo 149
second secondo m 153
second class seconda classe f 69
second hand lancetta dei secondi f 122

second-hand d'occasione 104
secretary segretaria f 27, 131
see, to guardare 11
sell, to vendere 162
send, to mandare 31, 78, 102, 103; spedire 132; inviare 133
send up, to portare su 26
separately separatamente 62
September settembre m 150
seriously *(wounded)* gravemente 139
service servizio m 24, 62, 98, 100; *(religion)* funzione f 84
serviette tovagliolo m 36
set *(hair)* messa in piega f 30
set menu menù (a prezzo fisso) m 36, 40
setting lotion fissatore m 30; lozione fissativa f 111
seven sette 147
seventeen diciassette 147
seventh settimo 149
seventy settanta 148
sew, to attaccare 29
shade *(colour)* tonalità f 112
shampoo shampoo m 30, 111
shape forma f 103
share *(finance)* azione f 131
sharp *(pain)* acuto(a) 140
shave, to radere 31
shaver rasoio (elettrico) m 27, 119
shaving cream crema da barba f 111
she ella, lei 161
shelf scaffale m 100, 120
ship nave f 74
shirt camicia f 117
shiver, to rabbrividire 140
shoe scarpa f 118
shoelace laccio m 118
shoemaker's calzolaio m 99
shoe polish lucido m 118
shoe shop negozio di scarpe m 99
shop negozio m 98
shopping acquisti m/pl 97
shopping area zona dei negozi f 19, 82, 100
short corto(a) 30, 115,
shorts short m 117
short-sighted miope 123
shoulder spalla f 138
shovel paletta f 49, 128
show spettacolo m 86, 87
show, to mostrare 11, 12, 100, 101, 103, 119

shower doccia f 23, 32
shrimp gamberetto m 41, 46
shrink, to restringersi 114
shut chiuso(a) 13
shutter (window) imposta f 29; (camera) otturatore m 125
sick, to be (ill) sentirsi male 140, 156
sickness (illness) malattia f 140
side lato m 30
sideboards/burns basette f/pl 31
sightseeing visita turistica f 80
sightseeing tour giro turistico m 80
sign (notice) cartello m 155; (road) segnale m 79
sign, to firmare 26, 131
signature firma f 25
signet ring anello con stemma m 122
silk seta f 114, 127
silver argentato(a) 113
silver argento m 121, 122
silver plate placcato d'argento 122
silverware argenteria f 122
simple semplice 124
since da 15, 150
sing, to cantare 88
single scapolo m, nubile f 93
single (ticket) andata 69
single room camera singola f 19, 23
sister sorella f 93
sit down, to sedersi 95
six sei 147
sixteen sedici 147
sixth sesto 149
sixty sessanta 147
size formato m 124; (clothes) taglia f, misura f 114, 115; (shoes) numero m 118
skates pattini m/pl 91
skating rink pista di pattinaggio f 91
ski sci m 91
ski, to sciare 91
ski boot scarpone da sci m 91
skier sciatore m (sciatrice f) 91
skiing sci m 89, 91
ski lift sciovia m 91
skin pelle f 138
skirt gonna f 117
ski run pista di sci f 91
sky cielo m 94
sled slitta f 91
sleep, to dormire 144
sleeping bag sacco a pelo m 107
sleeping-car vagone letto m 66, 68, 69, 70

sleeping pill sonnifero m 109, 143, 144
sleeve manica f 117
slice fetta f 55, 63, 120
slide (photo) diapositiva f 124
slip sottoveste f 117
slipper pantofola f 118
slow lento(a) 13
slow down, to rallentare 79
slowly lentamente 11, 21, 135
small piccolo(a) 13, 25, 101, 118
smoke, to fumare 95
smoked affumicato(a) 41, 47
smoker (compartment) fumatori m/pl 70
snack spuntino m 63
snack bar snack bar m 67
snail lumaca f 46
snap fastener bottone a pressione m 117
sneakers scarpe da tennis f/pl 118
snorkel maschera da subacqueo f 128
snow neve f 94
snow, to nevicare 94
soap saponetta f 27, 111
soccer calcio m 89
sock calzino m 117
socket (outlet) presa f 27
soft morbido(a) 123
soft drink bibita f 64
soft-boiled (egg) molle 38
sold out (theatre) esaurito 87
sole suola f 118; (fish) sogliola f 47
soloist solista m/f 88
some del, della (pl delle, delle) 14
someone qualcuno 95
something qualcosa 36, 55, 108, 112, 113, 139
son figlio m 93
song canzone f 128
soon presto 15
sore (painful) infiammato(a) 145
sore throat mal di gola m 141
sorry (I'm) mi dispiace 11, 16
sort genere m 26
sound-and-light show spettacolo suoni e luci m 86
soup minestra f, zuppa f 43
south sud m 77
South Africa Sudafrica m 146
South America America del Sud f 146
souvenir oggetto ricordo m 127
souvenir shop negozio di ricordi m 99
Soviet Union Unione Sovietica f 146

DICTIONARY

spade paletta f 128
Spain Spagna f 146
spare tyre ruota di scorta f 75
spark(ing) plug candela f 76
sparkling (wine) spumante 57
speak, to parlare 11, 135
speaker (loudspeaker) altoparlante f
specialist specialista m/f 142
speciality specialità f 40, 60
specimen (medical) campione m
  142
spectacle case astuccio per occhiali
  m 123
spell, to sillabare 11
spend, to spendere 101
spice spezia f 53
spinach spinacio m 52
spine spina dorsale f 138
spiny lobster aragosta f 46
spit-roasted allo spiedo 50
spoon cucchiaio m 36, 61, 107
sport sport m 89
sporting goods shop negozio di articoli sportivi m 99
sprain, to distorcere 140
spring (season) primavera f 150;
  (water) sorgente f 85
square piazza f 82
squid calamaro m 46
stadium stadio m 82
staff personale m 26
stain macchia f 29
stainless steel acciaio inossidabile m
  107, 122
stalls (theatre) poltrona f 87
stamp (postage) francobollo m 28,
  126, 132
staple graffetta f 105
star stella f 94
start, to iniziare 80, 88; (car) partire
  78
starter antipasto m 41
station stazione f 19, 21, 67, 70, 73
stationer's cartoleria f 99, 104
statue statua f 82
stay soggiorno m 31, 92
stay, to restare 16, 24; trattenersi
  26; soggiornare 93
steak bistecca f 48
steal, to rubare 156
steamed cotto(a) a vapore 47
stew spezzatino m 49
stewed in umido 50
stiff neck torcicollo m 141

still (mineral water) naturale 60
sting puntura f 139
sting, to pungere 139
stitch, to (clothes) cucire 29; (shoes)
  attaccare 118
stock exchange borsa valori f 82
stocking calza da donna f 117
stomach stomaco m 138
stomach ache mal di stomaco m
  141
stools feci f/pl 142
stop (bus) fermata f 72, 73
stop! fermatevi! 156
stop, to fermarsi 21, 68, 70, 72
stop thief! al ladro! 156
store negozio m 98
straight (drink) liscio 56, 59
straight ahead diritto 21, 77
strange strano 84
strawberry fragola f 54, 55
street strada f 25
streetcar tram m 72
street map pianta della città f 19, 105
strike sciopero m 155
string spago m 105
strong forte 143
student studente(essa) m 82, 93
stuffed farcito(a) 50
subway (railway) metropolitana f 73
suede renna f 114; camoscio m 118
sugar zucchero m 37, 64
suit (man) completo m 117;
  (woman) tailleur m 117
suitcase valigia f 18
summer estate f 150
sun sole m 94
sunburn scottatura solare f 108
Sunday domenica f 151
sunglasses occhiali da sole m/pl 123
sunshade (beach) ombrellone m 91
sunstroke colpo di sole m 141
sun-tan cream crema solare f 111
sun-tan oil olio solare m 111
super (petrol) super 75
superb superbo 84
supermarket supermercato m 99
suppository supposta f 109
surfboard sandolino m 91
surgery (consulting room) ambulatorio m 137
surname cognome m 25
suspenders (Am.) bretelle f/pl 117
swallow, to inghiottire 143
sweater maglione m 117

Dizionario

sweatshirt blusa f 117
Sweden Svezia f 146
sweet dolce 57, 61
sweet caramella f 126
sweetener dolcificante m 37
swell, to gonfiare 139
swelling gonfiore m 139
swim, to nuotare 90
swimming nuoto m 89; balneazione f 91
swimming pool piscina f 32, 90
swimming trunks costume da bagno m 117
swimsuit costume da bagno m 117
Swiss svizzero(a) 18
switch interruttore m 29
switchboard operator centralinista m/f 26
switch on, to (light) accendere 79
Switzerland Svizzera f 146
swollen gonfio(a) 139
swordfish pesce spada m 46
synagogue sinagoga f 84
synthetic sintetico 114
system sistema m 138

T

table tavolo m 36; tavola f 107
tablet pastiglia f 109
tailor's sartoria f 99
take, to prendere 18, 25, 73, 102; durare 72; portare 114
take away, to (carry) portare via 63, 102
talcum powder talco m 111
tampon tampone igienico m 109
tangerine mandarino m 54
tap (water) rubinetto m 28
tape recorder registratore m 119
tax tassa f 32; I.V.A. f 24, 102
taxi taxi m 19, 21, 31
tea tè m 38, 60, 64
tear, to lacerare 140
tearoom sala da tè f 34
teaspoon cucchiaino m 107, 143
telegram telegramma m 133
telegraph office ufficio telegrafico m 133
telephone telefono m 28, 78, 79, 134
telephone, to telefonare 134
telephone booth cabina telefonica f 134
telephone call telefonata f 135, 136

telephone directory elenco telefonico m 134
telephone number numero di telefono m 96, 135, 136
telephoto lens teleobiettivo m 125
television (set) televisore m 23, 28, 119
telex telex m 133
telex, to mandare un telex 130
tell, to dire 12, 73, 76, 136, 153
temperature temperatura f 90; (fever) febbre f 140, 142
temporary provvisoriamente 145
ten dieci 147
tendon tendine m 138
tennis tennis m 89
tennis court campo da tennis m 89
tennis racket racchetta da tennis f 89
tent tenda f 32, 107
tenth decimo 149
tent peg picchetto per tenda m 107
tent pole palo per tenda m 107
term (word) termine m 131
terrace terrazza f 36
terrifying terrificante 84
terrycloth tessuto di spugna m 114
tetanus tetano m 140
than di 14
thank you grazie 9
that quello, quella 10, 100, 161
the il, lo, la (pl i, gli, le) 159
theatre teatro m 82, 86
theft furto m 156
their il, la loro (pl i, le loro) 161
then poi, in seguito 15
there là 13; ecco 13
thermometer termometro m 109, 144
these questi, queste 63, 160
they essi, loro 161
thief ladro m 156
thin fine 113
think, to pensare 62, 94
third terzo 149
third terzo m 149
thirsty, to be aver sete 12
thirteen tredici 147
thirty trenta 147
this questo, questa 10, 100, 160
those quegli, quei, quelle 160; quelli, quelle 63, 120
thousand mille 148
thread filo m 27

three tre 147
throat gola f 138, 141
throat lozenge pasticca per la gola f 109
through train treno diretto m 68, 69
thumbtack puntina f 105
thunder tuono m 94
thunderstorm temporale m 94
Thursday giovedì m 151
thyme timo m 53
ticket biglietto m 65, 69, 72, 87, 89
ticket office biglietteria f 67
tide marea f 90
tie cravatta f 117
tie clip fermacravatte m 122
tie pin spillo per cravatta m 122
tight (clothes) stretto(a) 115
tights collant m 117
time tempo m 80; (clock) ora f 137, 153; (occasion) volta f 143
timetable orario ferroviario m 68
tin (can) scatola f 120
tinfoil foglio d'alluminio m 107
tin opener apriscatole m 107
tint sfumatura f 111
tinted colorato(a) 123
tip mancia f 62
tire ruota f 75; gomma f 76
tired stanco(a) 12
tissue (handkerchief) fazzoletto di carta m 111
to a 14, 163
toast pane tostato m 38
tobacco tabacco m 126
tobacconist's tabaccheria f 99, 126
today oggi 29, 151
toe dito del piede m 138
toilet paper carta igienica f 111
toiletry articoli da toilette m/pl 110
toilets gabinetti m/pl 27, 32, 37, 67
token (telephone) gettone m 134
toll pedaggio m 75
tomato pomodoro m 52
tomato juice succo di pomodoro m 60
tomb tomba f 82
tomorrow domani 29, 151
tongue lingua f 48, 138
tonic water acqua tonica f 60
tonight stasera 29, 96; questa sera 86, 87
tonsil tonsilla f 138
too troppo(a) 14; (also) anche 15
tooth dente m 145
toothache mal di denti m 145

toothbrush spazzolino da denti m 111, 119
toothpaste dentifricio m 111
top cima f 30; alto m 145
topaz topazio m 122
torch (flashlight) lampadina tascabile f 107
torn lacerato(a) 140
touch, to toccare 155
tough duro(a) 61
tourist office ufficio turistico m, azienda di promozione turistica f 22, 80
tourist tax tassa di soggiorno f 32
towards verso 14
towel asciugamano m 27
towelling tessuto di spugna m 114
town città f 19, 76
town hall municipio m 82
tow truck carro attrezzi m 78
toy giocattolo m 128
toy shop negozio di giocattoli m 99
tracksuit tuta sportiva f 117
traffic traffico m 76
traffic light semaforo m 77
trailer roulotte f 32
train treno m 66, 68, 69, 70, 73
tram tram m 72
tranquillizer tranquillante m 109, 143
transfer (bank) trasferimento m 131
transformer trasformatore m 119
translate, to tradurre 11
transport trasporto m 74
travel, to viaggiare 92
travel agency agenzia di viaggi f 99
travel guide guida turistica f 105
traveller's cheque traveller's cheque m 18, 62, 102, 130
travel sickness mal d'auto m 108
treatment cura f 143
tree albero m 85
tremendous fantastico(a) 84
trim, to (beard) spuntare 31
trip viaggio m 93, 152; percorso m 72
tripe trippe f/pl 49
trousers pantaloni m/pl 117
trout trota f 47
truffle tartufo m 52
try, to provare 115; (sample) assaggiare 60
T-shirt maglietta di cotone f 117
tube tubetto m 120
Tuesday martedì m 151
tuna tonno m 41, 47

Tunisia Tunisia *f* 146
tunnel galleria *f* 79
tunny tonno *m* 41, 47
turbot rombo *m* 46
Turkey Turchia *f* 146
turkey tacchino *m* 51
turn, to *(change direction)* girare 21, 77
turquoise turchese 113
turquoise turchese *m* 122
turtleneck a collo alto 117
tweezers pinzette *f/pl* 111
twelve dodici 147
twenty venti 147
twice due volte 149
twin bed due letti *m/pl* 23
two due 147
typewriter macchina per scrivere *f* 27, 105
typewriter ribbon nastro per macchina da scrivere *m* 105
typing paper carta per macchina da scrivere *f* 105
tyre ruota *f* 75; gomma *f* 76

U

ugly brutto(a) 13, 84
umbrella ombrello *m* 117; *(beach)* ombrellone *m* 91
uncle zio *m* 93
unconscious svenuto(a) 139
under sotto 15
underdone *(meat)* al sangue 50; poco cotto(a) 61
underground *(railway)* metropolitana *f* 73
underpants mutande *f/pl*, slip *m* 117
undershirt canottiera *f* 117
understand, to capire 11, 16
undress, to spogliare 142
United States Stati Uniti *m/pl* 146
university università *f* 82
unleaded senza piombo 75
until fino a 14
up su, in alto 15
upper superiore 69
upset stomach mal di stomaco *m* 108
upstairs di sopra 15
urgent urgente 12, 145
urine urina *f* 142
use uso *m* 17
use, to usare 78, 134
useful utile 15
usual abituale 143

V

vacancy camera libera *f* 23
vacant libero 13, 155
vacation vacanze *f/pl* 151
vaccinate, to vaccinare 140
vacuum flask thermos *m* 107
vaginal vaginale 141
valley valle *f* 85
value valore *m* 131
value-added tax I.V.A. *f* 24, 102, 154
vanilla vaniglia *f* 55
VAT *(sales tax)* I.V.A. *f* 24, 102, 154
veal vitello *m* 48
vegetable verdura *f* 52
vegetable store negozio di frutta e verdura *m* 99
vegetarian vegetariano *m* 37
vein vena *f* 138
velvet velluto *m* 114
velveteen velluto di cotone *m* 114
venereal disease malattia venerea *f* 142
venison selvaggina *f* 51
vermouth vermouth *m* 59
very molto 15
vest canottiera *f* 117; *(Am.)* panciotto *m* 117
video cassette video cassetta *f* 119, 124, 127
video recorder video registratore *m* 119
view vista *f* 23, 25
village villaggio *m* 76, 85; paese *m* 85
vinegar aceto *m* 37
vineyard vigna *f* 85
visit, to visitare 84
visiting hours orari di visita *m/pl* 144
vitamin pills vitamine *f/pl* 109
V-neck con scollatura a punta 117
volleyball pallavolo *f* 89
voltage voltaggio *m* 27, 119
vomit, to vomitare 140

W

waistcoat panciotto *m* 117
wait, to aspettare 21, 95
waiter cameriere *m* 26, 36
waiting-room sala d'aspetto *f* 67
waitress cameriera *f* 26, 36
wake, to svegliare 26
Wales Galles *m* 146
walk, to camminare 74; andare a piedi 85
wall muro *m* 85

wallet portafogli m 156
walnut noce f 54
want, to volere 18, 35, 163; (wish)
desiderare 12
warm caldo(a) 94
wash, to lavare 29, 114
wash-basin lavabo m 28
washing powder detersivo m 107
watch orologio m 122, 127
watchmaker's orologiaio m 99; oro-
logeria f 121
watchstrap cinturino per orologio m
122
water acqua f 23, 28, 32, 38, 75, 90
waterfall cascata f 85
water flask borraccia f 107
watermelon anguria f 54, cocomero
m 54
water-ski sci nautico m 91
way strada f 76
we noi 161
weather tempo m 93
weather forecast previsioni del
tempo f/pl 94
wedding ring fede nuziale f 122
Wednesday mercoledì m 151
week settimana f 16, 24, 80, 151
weekend fine settimana m 151
well pozzo 85; (healthy) bene 9, 140
well-done (meat) ben cotto(a) 50
west ovest m 77
what che cosa 10, 12; quanto 20;
quale 20, 21
wheel ruota f 78
when quando, a che ora 10
where dove 10
which quale 10
whipped cream panna montata f 55
whisky whisky m 17, 59
white bianco(a) 57, 113
whiting merlano m 46
who chi 10
why perchè 10
wick stoppino m 126
wide largo(a) 118
wide-angle lens grandangolare m 125
wife moglie f 93
wild boar cinghiale m 51
wind vento m 94
window finestra f 28, 36; (train)
finestrino m 69; (shop) vetrina f
100, 112
windscreen/shield parabrezza m 76
wine vino m 56, 57, 61

wine list lista dei vini f 57
wine merchant vinaio m 99
winter inverno m 150
winter sports sport invernali m/pl 91
wipers tergicristalli m/pl 76
wish augurio m 152
with con 14, 163
withdraw, to (bank) prelevare 131
without senza 14
woman donna f 115
wonderful magnifico(a) 96
wood bosco m 85
wood alcohol alcool metilico m 107
woodwork lavoro in legno m 127
woodcock beccaccia f 51
wool lana f 114
word parola f 11, 15, 133
work lavoro m 79
work, to (function) funzionare 28,
119
working day giorno feriale m 151
worse peggiore 13
wound ferita f 139
wrinkle resistant ingualcibile 114
wristwatch orologio braccialetto m
122
write, to scrivere 11, 101
writing pad blocco per appunti m 105
writing-paper carta da lettere f 27
wrong sbagliato(a) 13, 135

X
X-ray (photo) radiografia f 140

Y
year anno m 149
yellow giallo 113
yes sì 9
yesterday ieri 151
yet ancora 15
yoghurt yogurt m 64
you tu, voi 161
young giovane 13
your tuo(a) (pl tuoi, tue) 161;
vostro(a) (pl vostri(e)) 161
youth hostel ostello della gioventù m
22, 32
Yugoslavia Iugoslavia f 146

Z
zero zero m 147
zip(per) cerniera f 117
zoo zoo m 82
zoology zoologia f 83

Indice italiano

Say BERLITZ®

... and most people think of outstanding language schools. But Berlitz has also become the world's leading publisher of books for travellers – Travel Guides, Phrase Books, Dictionaries – plus Cassettes and Self-teaching courses.

Informative, accurate, up-to-date, Books from Berlitz are written with freshness and style. They also slip easily into pocket or purse – no need for bulky, old-fashioned volumes.

Join the millions who know how to travel. Whether for fun or business, put Berlitz in your pocket.

BERLITZ®

Leader in
Books and Cassettes
for Travellers

A Macmillan Company

BERLITZ® Books for travellers

TRAVEL GUIDES

They fit your pocket in both size and price. Modern, up-to-date, Berlitz gets all the information you need into 128 lively pages with colour maps and photos throughout. What to see and do, where to shop, what to eat and drink, how to save.

ASIA, MIDDLE EAST	China (256 pages)
	Hong Kong
	India (256 pages)
	Japan (256 pages)
	Nepal*
	Singapore
	Sri Lanka
	Thailand
	Egypt
	Jerusalem and the Holy Land
	Saudi Arabia
AUSTRAL-ASIA	Australia (256 pages)
	New Zealand
BRITISH ISLES	Channel Islands
	London
	Ireland
	Oxford and Stratford
	Scotland
BELGIUM	Brussels

AFRICA	Kenya
	Morocco
	South Africa
	Tunisia

*in preparation

PHRASE BOOKS

World's bestselling phrase books feature all the expressions and vocabulary you'll need, and pronunciation throughout. 192 pages, 2 colours.

Arabic	Hebrew	Russian
Chinese	Hungarian	Serbo-Croatian
Danish	Italian	Spanish (Castilian)
Dutch	Japanese	Spanish (Lat. Am.)
Finnish	Korean	Swahili
French	Norwegian	Swedish
German	Polish	Turkish
Greek	Portuguese	European Phrase Book
		European Menu Reader

FRANCE	Brittany France (256 pages) French Riviera Loire Valley Normandy Paris		Costa Brava Costa del Sol and Andalusia Ibiza and Formentera Madrid Majorca and Minorca
GERMANY	Berlin Munich The Rhine Valley	**EASTERN EUROPE**	Budapest Dubrovnik and Southern Dalmatia Hungary (192 pages) Istria and Croatian Coast Moscow & Leningrad Split and Dalmatia Yugoslavia (256 pages)
AUSTRIA and SWITZER- LAND	Tyrol Vienna Switzerland (192 pages)		
GREECE, CYPRUS & TURKEY	Athens Corfu Crete Rhodes Greek Islands of the Aegean Peloponnese Salonica and Northern Greece Cyprus Istanbul/Aegean Coast Turkey (192 pages)	**NORTH AMERICA**	U.S.A. (256 pages) California Florida Hawaii Miami New York Canada (256 pages) Toronto Montreal
ITALY and MALTA	Florence Italian Adriatic Italian Riviera Italy (256 pages) Rome Sicily Venice Malta	**CARIBBEAN, LATIN AMERICA**	Puerto Rico Virgin Islands Bahamas Bermuda French West Indies Jamaica Southern Caribbean Mexico City Brazil (Highlights of) Rio de Janeiro

**NETHER-
LANDS and
SCANDI-
NAVIA**
	Amsterdam
	Copenhagen
	Helsinki
	Oslo and Bergen
	Stockholm
		EUROPE	Business Travel Guide –
			  Europe (368 pages)
			Pocket guide to Europe
			  (480 pages)
			Cities of Europe (504 pages)

PORTUGAL	Algarve Lisbon Madeira	**CRUISE GUIDES**	Caribbean cruise guide (368 pages) Alaska cruise guide (168 p.) Handbook to Cruising (240 p.)
SPAIN	Barcelona and Costa Dorada Canary Islands Costa Blanca		

**Most titles with British and U.S. destinations are available in
French, German, Spanish and as many as 7 other languages.**

DICTIONARIES

*Bilingual with 12,500 concepts each way. Highly practical for travellers,
with pronunciation shown plus menu reader, basic expressions and useful
information. Over 330 pages.*

Danish	Finnish	German	Norwegian	Spanish
Dutch	French	Italian	Portuguese	Swedish

**Berlitz Books, a world of information in your pocket!
At all leading bookshops and airport newsstands.**

Treat yourself to an hour with BERLITZ®

Just listen and repeat

It's fun, not work. And you'll surprise your friends and yourself: it's so easy to pick up some basic expressions in the foreign language of your choice. These cassettes are recorded in hi-fi with four voices. Bringing native speakers into your home, they permit you to improve your accent and learn the basic phrases before you depart.

With each cassette is a helpful 32-page script, containing pronunciation tips, plus complete text of the dual-language recording.

An ideal companion for your Berlitz phrase book, pocket dictionary or travel guide.